Women Poets
of the
Italian Renaissance

❧ *Courtly Ladies and Courtesans* ❧

Women Poets
of the
Italian Renaissance

❀ *Courtly Ladies and Courtesans* ❀

Edited by Laura Anna Stortoni
Translated by
Laura Anna Stortoni and Mary Prentice Lillie

Italica Press
New York
1997

ITALICA PRESS, INC.
595 MAIN STREET
NEW YORK, NEW YORK 10044
WWW.ITALICAPRESS.COM

LIBRARY OF CONGRESS CATALOGING-IN-PUBLICATION DATA
Women poets of the Italian Renaissance : courtly ladies and courtesans /
    edited by Laura Anna Stortoni ; translated by Laura Anna Stortoni
    and Mary Prentice Lillie.
      p. cm.
    English and Italian.
    Includes bibliographical references and index.
    ISBN 978-0-934977-43-2 (alk. paper)
    1. Italian poetry--Women authors--Translations into English.
2. Italian poetry--15th century--Translations into English.
3. Italian poetry--16th century--Translations into English.
I. Stortoni, Laura Anna, 1942-   . II. Lillie, Mary Prentice.
PQ4225.E8S838 1997
851'.30809287--dc21 97-6455
                                                                    CIP

Printed in USA and EU
5 4 3 2

Cover Art: Titian, *Woman in Fur,* Kunsthistorisches Museum, Vienna.

Contents

INTRODUCTION

Never in the history of the Western world has any literary period, except for the modern one, so abounded in poetry written by women as the Italian Renaissance. This period — spanning over two centuries — originated in fifteenth century Italy and then spread to other European countries. It is notable for an astounding number of learned, talented and powerful women, who rivaled men both in art and in political life.

Underlying Renaissance culture was a humanistic philosophy that emphasized the individual; learning, as a tool to explore human potential, became of the utmost importance. Humanism was a literary and philosophical phenomenon that blossomed in the fifteenth century, and came to permeate all aspects of life: its name derives from the Latin word "homo," meaning not man, but human being. Hence, it extends to women. It was characterized by an enthusiastic return to the world of classical antiquity, and based knowledge on the direct observation of data, rather than on the unquestioned authority of the theologians and Aristotle. It was essentially a pagan philosophy, returning to the ideal of classical beauty and balance, and shifting emphasis from heaven to earth.

The civilization of the Renaissance in Italy was essentially secular, emphasizing art, literature, beauty, amusements, dance, music, pomp, ceremony, and conversations. This refined world, described by Baldassar Castiglione in his *The Book of the Courtier* (1528), and codified by Monsignor della Casa's *Galateo* (1551-1554) — the first book of etiquette — gave more freedom of opportunity to women. The humanistic philosophy brought about a social and cultural revolution in women's lives, and the tradition of misogynist literature prevailing in the Middle Ages almost disappeared among educated people. As early as the fourteenth century, Boccaccio, a humanist *ante litteram,* wrote *De Mulieribus Claris,* a gallery of known and illustrious women, from Eve to Giovanna, Queen of Naples, whose examples were meant to educate women. In the fifteenth century, many humanists wrote in favor of women and of their education. In 1467, Antonio Cornazzano wrote *De Mulieribus admirandis* (On admirable women), and in 1480 Vespasiano da Bisticci wrote *Il libro della lode e commendazione delle donne* (The book of the praise and commendation of women). Both writers praised women mainly for what are usually regarded as feminine virtues, rather than for their role in public life. Giovanni Sabadino degli Arienti's *Gynevra de le clare donne* (1483)

(Ginevra of the illustrious women) represents an important development in the genre, since it redefines female virtues by praising women for excelling in spheres typically reserved for males. Sabatino degli Arienti's ideas were picked up later in Bartolomeo Goggio's *De laudibus mulierum* (In praise of women, 1483) and in Agostino Strozzi's *Defensio mulierum* (In defense of women, c.1601).

A common goal of humanistic writing was to make philosophical debate accessible to the lay population, including women. The humanists who wrote in favor of women wanted to enlarge the sphere of knowledge to include the female sex, or to gain a new, larger public, as well as the generous patronage of the powerful courtly ladies. Throughout the sixteenth century, the question of the role of women was pervasively discussed. In the early and High Renaissance, the misogynistic feelings that had permeated the Middle Ages, were, for the most part, substituted with a favorable attitude towards women and their endeavors. Among the poets and *literati* who wrote in favor of women and of their participation to the intellectual and social life of the country were: Ludovico Ariosto,[1] Sperone Speroni, Agnolo Firenzuola, Alessandro Piccolomini, Ortensio Landi, Ludovico Dolce, and many others. At the end of the century, women started to write important works *in their own defense.*

In his *Civilization of the Renaissance in Italy,* Jakob Burckhardt was the first historian to acknowledge the special status enjoyed by women in this era in Italy. Emphasizing the role of learning and schooling in the formation of the so-called *virago* of the sixteenth century, he stressed the forceful, or "masculine" aspects of Italian Renaissance women writers. In the refined climate of fifteenth and sixteenth-century Italy, upper class women were given a classical and philosophical education equal to men. Great heads of state and pontiffs invited scholars and artists to their courts, and had their children educated by them. At court, sons and daughters received essentially the same education, except for the training in the art of war that the boys received. Renaissance women of very high status shared more fully in the lives of their consorts and joined freely in men's pursuits, literary or political, and played the roles of scholars, artists, statesmen, and patronesses of the arts. The education they received would enable them to conduct their husbands' courts in their absence, and, if the necessity arose, to run the state as well — as happened in the cases of the widows Veronica Gàmbara and Vittoria Colonna.

The ideal Renaissance woman was described by Castiglione in his *The Book of the Courtier,* depicting life at the Court of Urbino. According to Castiglione, the qualities desirable in a courtly lady were knowledge, wit, and beauty, accompanied by spirit and character. Such qualities were essential, since the duties of a noblewoman extended from rearing and educating the children to overseeing the court. Castiglione's work reflects the humanists' conviction of the inherent equality of the sexes, and faith in the intellectual capacities of women. In reality, however, Renaissance women never achieved equality with men in the modern sense of the word: differences in life-style, in actual power, and in the division of tasks existed, but for the most part, women's intellectual and literary freedom was accepted.

The great artistic and intellectual blossoming of Italian women's talent that took place in the sixteenth century did not happen suddenly and in a vacuum. It was prepared by centuries of work, and by the examples of many women who lived in earlier times. Therefore, we have included in our anthology some of the precursors who paved the way for the women writers of the High Renaissance.

The Origins: The Precursors.
Precursors: 13th and 14th Century Writers

In this anthology, we start with women writing after 1450. Those women, however, did not start writing in a vacuum, but were following in a tradition of women's writing that had started as early as 1290, with the undocumented Nina Siciliana, and continued with the first substantially documented Italian woman poet, Compiuta Donzella, who wrote in the period of transition between the Sicilian School and the *Dolce Stil Nuovo*.

Later, in the 14th century, we find the writings of St. Catherine of Siena, a prolific writer as well as a social and religious reformer who was reputed the most important woman in Europe of her century. Other women writers emerge in the 14th century, mostly in the Petrarchan tradition. We do not have much information about them, hence their existence has been doubted by some critics. We do however, have poems attributed to Leonora della Genga, Ortensia di Guglielmo, Livia del Chiavello and Giustina Levi Perotti. In the 14th century, we also find the work of Blessed Angela of Foligno, an important mystic and theologian.

The Fifteenth Century: The Women Humanists

Although Petrarch and Boccaccio can both be considered humanists, it is in this century that we have the great blossoming of the Humanistic philosophy promoting the cultural and spiritual formation of men through the study of letters. In 1453, the fall of Constantinople to the Turks caused an exodus of Greek scholars and philosophers to the West, mostly Italy. The Greek scholars brought with them both their knowledge and their ancient texts.

In this century, we see in many Italian cities the appearance of Academies, literary clubs created according to the Greek and Platonic models in order to promote knowledge and literature.[2] The patronage of princes and rulers fostered a blossoming of artistic and literary endeavors. Since Humanism emphasized human potential, hence also women's potential, many women responded enthusiastically to it, becoming learned scholars in their own right. In this century, we find a very large group of women humanists who were schooled at court, or were taught by their fathers or family members. Their lives were amply documented, and their academic writings in the classical languages were treasured and preserved. They taught at the university level, composed orations, treatises, and poetry, and corresponded on an equal footing with male humanists.

We do not present any of the women humanists in this anthology, since, for the most part, they did not write in the Tuscan vernacular, nor did they write poetry. We must, however, stress their importance as role models for later generations of women. It was indeed the confidence in their own intellects won by women through the *studia humanitatis* that lent them faith in their own capacity for literary and poetic endeavors. In addition to increased confidence, the refinement of the Italian Renaissance courts and the prosperity of the cities enabled women to have more freedom to produce literary work.

Since Humanism was a movement comprising all aspects of learning and art forms, the humanistic education that noble Renaissance women received was quite complex: it was indispensable for a young lady of the court to be schooled in Greek and Latin (and sometimes even in Hebrew), as well as in literary and scientific subjects. A musical education was in most cases included, and the vernacular classics of the fourteenth century, with a special emphasis on Dante and Petrarch, were studied in depth. At first, women scholars were daughters of rulers or members of patrician families, able to avail themselves of the education imparted by illustrious tutors living at the court, or coming into contact with the *literati* supported or patronized by their families. Other women scholars were actually the daughters of the *literati* themselves, who would absorb their fathers' learning at home or in their cultural circles. Novella d'Andrea, daughter of Giovanni d'Andrea, professor of canon law, regularly substituted for her father at the University of Bologna.

Out of the large number of Italian women humanists, we shall single out a few for mention. Battista Malatesta (1384-ca.1458) was renowned for her orations, poems and letters in excellent classical Latin. One of the most important woman humanists, Laura Cereta (1469-1499), has received great critical attention recently for her works and her ideas. She learned Latin and Greek from her father and was in correspondence with many humanists of her time. In her writings, she provided an impassioned *apologia* of herself and of women in general, exhorting women to place more importance on their education than on their beauty, and emphasizing education and freedom. The Nogarolas, a family of famous scholars, produced two talented sisters, Ginevra Nogarola (1419-1465) and Isotta Nogarola (1418-1466), who composed prose and poetry in the classical languages. Isotta wrote Latin epistles and a famous *disputatio* (debate) on the question whether Adam or Eve was the greater sinner — taking, naturally, the defense of Eve, who, in the earlier misogynous medieval tradition, had been blamed for women's "weaker intellect." Isotta moreover engaged in learned correspondences with famous scholars of her times, such as Guarino da Verona, Ermolao Barbaro and Ludovico Foscarini. Cassandra Fedele (ca.1465-1558) was well-versed in the classical languages, composed poetry in Greek and Latin and discussed philosophy with male humanists.

Women scholars of the time also used their knowledge for social and political purposes: a noble *literata,* Costanza Varano of the lords of Camerino (1426-1447) succeeded, through the eloquence of her Latin letters, in having her family estates restored. Around 1453, Cardinal Bessarion, the Papal Legate in Bologna, was eloquently addressed in Latin by the learned Niccolosa Castellani Sanuti, who advocated the repeal of the sumptuary laws that prohibited elaborate clothing in that city; she successfully argued that sumptuous dressing was required by decorum rather than vain pomp.

During this century, several lay women also wrote in the Tuscan vernacular, and wrote poetry as well as letters: Alessandra Macinghi Strozzi (author of remarkably interesting letters to her exiled sons), Lucrezia Tornabuoni de' Medici (mother of Lorenzo il Magnifico), and the dramatist Antonia Giannotti Pulci. Tornabuoni de' Medici wrote mostly religious lauds in the popular style made famous by Savonarola and by other male writers of lauds. Giannotti Pulci, instead, wrote for the theater in a more literary style, but also about religious subjects. The letters that these women wrote are important documents of the spoken vernacular of their times.

Several writing women in this century attained sainthood: Saint Caterina Vigri of Bologna (1413-1463), a former courtier at the Este court,
became a Clarissa nun and wrote sacred compositions, lauds, and the
religious treatise *Sette armi spirituali* (Seven religious weapons, 1474). Caterina Fieschi Adorno (1447-1510), who wrote ascetic works and spiritual
treatises, was canonized under the name of Saint Catherine of Genoa. We
could not include their work for reasons of space.

The Early Sixteenth Century: The Great Blossoming

The so-called High Renaissance — from the beginning of the sixteenth
century to the closing of the Council of Trent in 1563 — was a period of
incredible cultural expansion for Italian women, who enjoyed an unprec-
edented status in society and played important roles in the literary life of
their times. Women writers wrote in prose and in poetry, and in a variety
of genres. Most of the women poets we present in this anthology lived
during this period.

The wives of Italian rulers played a leading role in the intellectual life
of the peninsula. The model and the activities of the courtly ladies affected
Italian women from all strata of society, who dedicated themselves to literary
pursuits with an enthusiasm that had never been seen before. While life in
the Middle Ages had been comparatively simple, the Renaissance, and especially the High Renaissance, was not only a time of artistic endeavors, but
also of lavishness and great elegance. Many Italian rulers held refined courts,
where they encouraged and protected artists and writers. In Florence, the
Medici dynasty, especially at the time of Lorenzo il Magnifico, supported
arts and letters, greatly fostering the development of Tuscan vernacular
literature. In Milan, Francesco Sforza, and later Ludovico il Moro, also
held sophisticated courts — Ludovico being the Duke who hosted Leon-
ardo da Vinci for many years. In the little state of Mantua, the Gonzagas
held an exquisitely elegant court. Isabella d'Este (1474-1539), daughter of
Eleonora and Ercole, wife of Duke Giovanni Francesco II, was regarded
as the most refined woman of her times. A great patroness of the arts, she
governed Mantua during her husband's long absences when he went to
war. In Ferrara, the Este dynasty patronized poets like Boiardo and Ariosto.
At the little court of Urbino, Elisabetta Gonzaga (1471-1526), wife of Duke
Guidobaldo of Montefeltro, created the ideal courtly milieu immortalized
in *The Book of the Courtier*. Giulia Gonzaga (ca.1513-1566) governed after the
death of her husband, and created a cultural center in Mantua. Two other
illustrious courtly ladies, Veronica Gàmbara (1485-1550), ruler of Correggio,

and Vittoria Colonna (1492-1547), Marchionness of Pescara, were both widowed, both rulers, and both excellent poets.

The very large number of women poets writing at this time is in itself an eloquent testimonial to the importance of Italian women in the Renaissance.[3] In addition to education, improved living conditions, and the example of the courtly ladies, the invention of print and the wide diffusion of books played a very important role in women's awareness of their own talent. The publishing capital of Italy was Venice, whose government afforded greater intellectual freedom than any other Italian state at the time. At the beginning of the sixteenth century, around the printer Aldus Manutius, a talented group of scholars prepared accurate editions of the classics of antiquity and of the classics in the Italian vernacular, editions which were to spread knowledge all over the world and make it available to all. Humanism started to become vernacular, as the Tuscan language gradually supplanted Latin and the frequency of translations made classical culture accessible.

Women often appeared in public with a small, elegant edition of Petrarch's *Rime* (called *il Petrarchino*), often hanging by a ribbon from their waistline. They often had themselves portrayed with a book in their hands, either a book they were reading, or a book they wrote. A quick walk through the Uffizi Gallery in Florence reveals some paintings of women portrayed with books: in *Girl with a Book*, by Andrea del Sarto (1486-1531), a young woman stares knowingly at the beholder, while pointing at a readable verse in the *Petrarchino* she is holding: "*Ite, caldi sospiri, al freddo core*" (Go, warm sighs, to the cold heart).[4] Two portraits by Bronzino (1503-1572) show women holding books: *Portrait of a Girl with a Book*, in which a very serious-looking young lady holds tight to her heart a small book tied with a ribbon, and the portrait of the beautiful aristocrat Lucrezia Panciatichi, seated, holding open in her right hand a book of verse. Bronzino also portrayed the poet Laura Battiferri Ammannati as a severe matron wrapped in veils, pointing to a book of verse, probably one of her own.[5] In Da Vinci's (1452-1519) *Annunciation*, an angel startles and interrupts Mary as she is absorbed in reading. Raphael's *Madonna with the Goldfinch* holds a book open with her left hand, while at the same time keeping a watchful eye on the baby Jesus and little St. John.

Women poets not only wrote in great number, but also aspired to publish their work. Rinaldina Russell states that "between 1538, the year of Colonna's first publication, and the end of the century, no fewer than two hundred books were authored by women or were anthologies of men's works that included contributions by women."[6] Russell goes on to note that the period between 1539 and 1560 was the most productive for women's literary work, with 56 editions of books authored by women.

1559 was a very important year in the history of Italian women's writing: in that year, Ludovico Domenichi published the first anthology of *solely* women's poetry, which he had collected from the works of Italian women of several regions: *Rime diverse d'alcune nobilissime et virtuosissime donne* (Lucca: Busdrago, 1559). Soon other anthologies of women's verse were to follow, such as Pietro Ribera Valenziano's *Le glorie immortali de'trionfi, ed eroiche imprese di ottocento quarantacinque donne illustri antiche e moderne* (Venice: n.p., 1609), featuring the work of eight hundred and forty five women poets; Frate Maurizio di Gregorio's *Rosario delle stampe di tutti i poeti e poetesse antichi e moderni* (Naples, n.p. 1614); Francesco Agostino della Chiesa's *Theatro delle donne letterate* (Mondovì: Ghislandi and Rossi, 1620); and Antonio Bulifon's *Rime di cinquanta illustri poetesse* (Naples: Bulifon, 1695).

Italian women poets in this time had a sense of mission and purpose, often stating in their poetry that they desired immortality and renown for their literary endeavors. As early as the fourteenth century, Giustina Levi Perotti stated that her intention in writing was to *"…after death, remain as though alive/ still shining with the illustrious life of mind."* Camilla Scarampa stated: *"Nor do I care for anything but wisdom."* Olimpia Malipiera, addressing Apollo, foresaw that her poetry would bring her luster: *"I'll sing beside a splendid beech or laurel /And rise where I have never dared before."* Gaspara Stampa, who was divided from her noble lover by a social chasm, claimed she could soar above her lowly station in life with the power of her pen. (The word feather and the word pen are the same in Italian, *penna*). Stampa, in her sonnets, often equated the two words *pena* and *penna* (pain and pen), to indicate that her sorrow is sublimated into writing that would survive. Laura Bacio Terracina exhorted women thus: *"…launch your ship of talent on the ocean,"* and urging them also *"to labor frequently with pen and paper."* Laura Battiferri Ammannati, in *When the sun stoops…*, stated that she is collecting her poetry to gain immortality: *"(I) gather up my throng of scattered thoughts/ and make them shine in heaven evermore."* She also prayed to Apollo not to let envious people hinder her *"in this high work"* of writing.

It is interesting to note that, in their writing, these women often make allusions to the feminine arts of the shuttle and needle that they have left behind, stressing the fact that the Italian words for narration and for weaving are the same, *trama*. Italian literary women simply transferred their capacity for intricate and beautiful design from the loom to the white page. Lucrezia Marinelli wrote that she was writing "with the needle of the pen." A very early, but fierce, feminist, Leonora della Genga (14th century), wrote a sonnet extolling the superiority of women's talent, starting with an imperious *"Be silent, men!"* and ending with the statement *"there never was a man/able to take from us the prize or crown."*

Women poets also felt a sense of sisterhood, taking other women writers as role models, or dedicating poems to one another, as in the case of Lucia Bertani Dell'Oro dedicating poems to Veronica Gàmbara and Vittoria Colonna, and Veronica Gambàra and Marguerite de Valois dedicating poetry to Vittoria Colonna. Laura Bacio Terracina dedicated her *Commentary on the beginning of all the cantos of Orlando Furioso* to Veronica Gàmbara.

Most of the lyric poetry in the sixteenth century was essentially Petrarchan. Petrarchism, that is, the imitation of the forms, themes and concepts of Petrarch's *Rime,* influenced most Renaissance poets, not directly, but through the works of Cardinal Pietro Bembo (1470-1547), the ultimate arbiter of the Italian vernacular and the codifier of Petrarchism. Petrarchism is, therefore, a poetry of imitation and emulation, in which a poet's originality is determined by the manner in which he or she manages to develop poems within the given conventions. For this reason, Renaissance lyric can be at times cold and traditional, in spite of its exquisite stylistic form. It is our opinion that some women poets writing at this time surpassed in originality the majority of male poets, inasmuch as they did not feel bound to follow Petrarchism so slavishly. Cardinal Bembo also upheld the use of the Tuscan vernacular as the literary language to be used by writers from all regions of Italy. In his *Prose della volgar lingua* (1525), he determined that the Tuscan language of Petrarch was to be used for poetry, and the Tuscan of Boccaccio for prose. Therefore, in our anthology, the reader will notice that the women poets we present — whether they be from the North, the center or the South of Italy — use an essentially uniform language, with the exception of a few regionalisms.

Although women painters existed in earlier times, in this century we find the first famous woman painter, Sofonisba Anguissola (1528-1626). She came from a noble family, and in her lifetime enjoyed great success, popularity and wealth. She also wrote very interesting letters, mostly about her work and commissions. In this century we also find women humanists writing in the vernacular, such as Tarquinia Molza (1542-1617), who distinguished herself by two intelligent, accurate translations of Plato's dialogues.

Women Poets of the Italian Renaissance

Veronica Gàmbara and Vittoria Colonna, the first women to attain great literary prominence in Italy, wrote primarily in the Petrarchan mode. Gaspara Stampa (1523-1554), who forms, with the first two, the triad of the most famous Italian women poets, was regarded as eccentric, both for her rather ambiguous position in life (she was a free-living *virtuosa*) and for her refusal to adhere strictly to Petrarchan canons. Different as they were, these three women have been traditionally anthologized together by Italian critics, and their names have occupied a conspicuous place in Italian literary history. Vittoria Colonna was, for a time, considered the most important of the three, owing in part to the strong moral influence she exerted over the *literati* and the artists of her time, notably Michelangelo; in part also due to her strong advocacy of religious reform in the corrupt Rome of her time; and finally to her complex poetic style, filled with bold unusual conceits and metaphors particularly admired by her contemporaries. Modern criticism, however, generally acknowledges Gaspara Stampa as the greatest and the most original of the three, as well as possibly the greatest Italian woman poet ever. Later in the century, another great woman poet, Veronica Franco (1546-1591), a lusty and outspoken Venetian courtesan, rejected Petrarchism outright, and wrote in *terza rima* and in prose.

While in the early Renaissance it was mostly the courtly ladies who excelled in poetry, towards the middle and in the first decades of the second half of the sixteenth century more women writers emerged from the ranks of the middle and upper middle classes. Among them were Chiara Matraini (1514-ca.1597), Laura Terracina (1519-1577), Laura Battiferri Ammannati (1523-1589), Lucia Bertana Dell'Oro (?-1567), and Isabella Andreini (1562-1604), who also attained fame as a *commedia dell'arte* actress. These women took writing very seriously, stating in their poetry their intention of acquiring fame, distinction and immortality with their poetic endeavors. Two women were at the forefront for their feminist feelings: Laura Bacio Terracina, a bourgeois, and Veronica Franco, a courtesan. They wrote with equal passion about the freedom of thought and action that women should have.

Many talented women in Renaissance Italy were neither from the courts nor from the emergent middle class. In the literary tradition of the West, it is a phenomenon peculiar to the Italian Renaissance that many women who wrote poetry were courtesans. The low-class courtesans, or *di candela* (of the candle, possibly because they received clients in the back of candle shops or because they were used to illuminate the inns where they stayed), or *della minor sorte* (of the lower kind), were numerous, but did not have much education or refinement. The *cortegiane honorate*, or upper class courtesans, were extremely well educated. Indeed, several of the most talented women of the Italian Renaissance practiced the profession of *cortegiana*. Often trained by their own mothers — who may have also been courtesans — for a brilliant "career," they received a classical and comprehensive education that rivaled the education of courtly women. In fact, there existed an open intellectual rivalry between the two classes of women, and courtesans held salons that equaled, and in some cases, surpassed in intellectual quality those of the ladies of the court. The "honorable" courtesans were trained in singing, music, metrics, dancing, Latin and Greek. They could paint, sing and accompany themselves on the lute or other instruments, write poetry, converse wittily, hold philosophical debates, and it is indeed in homage to their "courtly" graces that the euphemism *cortegiana*, "courtesan," was coined to distinguish them from the common prostitutes. They enjoyed a very special status and had a recognized function in the society of their time. They were, for the most part, daughters of courtesans, or brilliant and beautiful daughters of impoverished families, who were unable to aspire legally to any improvement in social class. As courtesans, however, they had the freedom and the financial means to be in contact with men of letters, and with members of the highest strata of society, even with prelates, with whom at times they formed friendships of singular depth. Thus, schooled and trained in their profession like the *hetairai* of ancient Athens, they gained access to the stimulating milieu of the male *intelligentsia* which they could not have otherwise penetrated. Noblemen, men of letters, kings and prelates were not ashamed to visit them, or even to befriend them. Veronica Franco was openly visited, so to speak, by King Henry III of France. In fact, on the occasion of the king's visit to Venice, the *Serenissima Repubblica* hired her to entertain him. She wrote two sonnets to commemorate the night she spent with him, one of which we have translated.

The high class courtesans (*honeste*) were most careful of their reputation and status, looking down on low-class courtesans, and complaining about their number and their behavior. Such honorable courtesans appeared in works of art, such as Ardelia, the noblest character in Sforza Oddi's comedy *L'Erofilomachia*, who is capable of loving Amico with a chaste and disinterested love. We see the other side of the coin in Aretino's *Dialoghi*, where courtesans are depicted as rapacious and wicked characters.

One of the most celebrated courtesans, Tullia d'Aragona (1520 ca.-1556), enjoyed in her own times a reputation as a poet even greater than

Vittoria Colonna, and represents the paradigm of the Renaissance "honest" courtesan. She never acknowledged her profession openly. Because of her respect for form and decorum, she was, without a hint of irony, called "chaste and pure" in many laudatory poems dedicated to her. She refused to wear the yellow veil which courtesans were required to wear in public in Florence, and petitioned to Duke Cosimo de' Medici, who granted her wishes because "she was a poet." In contrast, Veronica Franco talked openly about sex and money, but also wrote poignantly about the indignities and the dangers of such a life.[7]

The two major centers where courtesans flourished were Venice and Rome. While the courtesans in Rome were famous for their large numbers, accomplishments and beauty, their status was often precarious due to periodic expulsions by the popes. When expulsion came, they often moved to Venice, where the tenor of life, with its wealth, masked balls and banquets, favored their trade. In Veronica Franco's lifetime, almost 12,000 courtesans were legally registered and paid high taxes to the *Serenissima*. Veronica and her mother appear in the catalog of Venetian courtesans, with their address and fee.

Of the Roman courtesans, apart from Tullia d'Aragona, we remember Isabella di Luna, Beatrice de Bonis, Camilla la Pisana, and the famous Lucrezia Cognati, who passed into history under the glorious pseudonym of "la bella Imperia." Imperia's lifestyle seems to have been even more magnificent than Tullia d'Aragona's, and her palace in Rome, frequented by scholars and high prelates, was so luxurious that it compared favorably with the dwellings of many noblewomen.

Such fascinating women still look at us from paintings by Renaissance masters, in which they are often depicted as Mary Magdalenes, or Venuses, sensuous beauties with elaborate hairstyles interspersed with jewels and pearls, setting off the reddish blond hair so typical of Venetian women of the period and immortalized by Titian. Such hair color was obtained by painstakingly dying and exposing the hair to the sun, since, in these times, fair hair was *de rigueur*. Even the heroine of Ariosto's *Orlando Furioso*, Angelica, the princess of Cathay (China) was a blonde! The courtesans, moreover, frizzed and curled their hair in a manner clearly shown in a famous painting by Carpaccio,[8] now at the Correr Museum in Venice, regarded by Ruskin as the greatest painting of the Italian Renaissance. In this composition, two stately, seated courtesans, shown in profile, stare into the distance, absorbed in their thoughts, while playing absent-mindedly with their pets. The painter has chosen to show them, in their aloofness, more as intellectuals than as sensual beings.

The hardships and the uncertainties of the lives of women who did not come from the bourgeoisie or from the nobility — courtesans, actresses, musicians — meant that they often died at a relatively young age. Tullia d'Aragona died at 46, Gaspara Stampa at 31, Veronica Franco at 45, and Isabella Andreini at 42.

It should not be surprising that the most original poetry was produced by women who belonged to the class of the courtesans, or who, like the musician Gaspara Stampa, were on the borderline. Women of rank, kept under very close supervision as maidens, came into their own after marriage, holding court and running opulent households with the assistance of legions of servants, nurses, pages and secretaries. However, they were restricted by social mores and expectations. They were married off early, and engagements were often arranged during their childhood to noblemen whom, more often than not, they had never met. Vittoria Colonna was betrothed to the Marquis of Pescara when she was four; fortunately for her, she learned to love her husband devotedly after the marriage, and was inconsolable after his untimely death. But marriage for the nobility was usually nothing more than a means of creating powerful alliances between ruling dynasties or mergers between wealthy patrician families. Thus, for the most part, the total freedom to act and to express feelings of romantic and sensual love was the prerogative of the courtesans, to whom the social rules and restrictions did not apply. They often wrote with a freedom of expression and sincerity that was not to be attained again by Italian women writers until the twentieth century. Courtesans and musicians could transcend convention, overstep narrow circles of traditional feminine interests, and speak openly and frankly of their experiences in love, as well as their cares and sorrows. In contrast, the goal in the literary creation of nobly-born women was usually to attain a high degree of conventional elegance. To be well-versed in poetry was also a duty for a woman of high social standing, who was expected to produce a well-turned sonnet and to compose letters with eloquence, all with decorum.

In the cases of Gaspara Stampa and Veronica Franco, love was openly sensual and was expressed as a powerful erotic force. For other women, love was at times destined to be experienced outside the bonds of conjugal love, as in the tragic examples of Barbara Torelli, Isabella di Morra and Chiara Matraini. These three women experienced unusual and unsanctioned love stories outside marriage, and paid a high price for it. Morra paid with her life.

Women Poets of the Italian Renaissance

While the sixteenth century in Italy saw the apex of Italian civilization, it was politically a time of decline, during which the peninsula lost autonomy. During this time of instability and continuous wars, women were often left alone, at times in charge of family estates and of states, when their husbands, fathers and brothers went to battle. Italy became the battlefield for the fierce conflict between Francis I of France and Charles V of Spain (see *Historical Notes*). Many of the women writers we present were aware of Italy as a cultural and geographical, if not a political, entity, long before the country's late unification in 1860. They grieved over the internecine wars that tore the country apart, and lamented over the devastation caused by foreign invasions. Even as early as the 14th century, Italian women such as Livia del Chiavello and Ortensia di Guglielmo were writing patriotic poetry. In the sixteenth century, Veronica Gàmbara — being the ruler of the little state of Correggio, precariously sandwiched among other city states — was the most politically aware among the women poets we present, and wrote movingly about her *patria*, meaning both Brescia and Italy. In the sonnet *Beautiful Flora...*, Gàmbara has Italy — personified — ask her children, the Italians, to free her: *"Liberate me; make yourselves free and peaceful."* Aurelia Petrucci and Leonora Ravira Falletti also wrote to lament foreign invasions and to stir up ancient valor in the Italians. Olimpia Malipiera wrote with nostalgia about her homeland Venice when she was exiled. Vittoria Colonna, the epitome of the great courtly lady, wrote a poetic epistle (from which we have translated some excerpts) to her husband the Marquis of Pescara, in which she described in very moving tones the suffering of Italian women when their men go to war. Both Laura Bacio Terracina and Vittoria Colonna also wrote against the moral and political decline they witnessed.

It is ironic, however, that the women poets who most appeal to our modern taste are precisely the ones who, because of lack of schooling in the Petrarchan tradition, or because of their peripheral geographical situation, did not closely adhere to its canons, and thus were able to give free rein to the direct and spontaneous expressions of their feelings. Among these was the Southerner Isabella di Morra, whose lack of artifice and scarcity of verbal ornamentation make for powerful and evocative poetry. Another is the Venetian courtesan Veronica Franco, whose frank, spontaneous and sensual style was unconstrained by rules. And, in our opinion, the greatest of them was Gaspara Stampa, who had been trained as a musician, not as a poet, and overstepped all boundaries to sublimate her sorrow in powerful, spontaneous verses.

The Late Sixteenth Century: The Counter-Reformation and the Waning of the Renaissance

The Counter-Reformation was a Catholic movement designed to counter the spread of Protestantism. While it started as a religious movement, it extended to control every aspect of the political and social life of the Italian peninsula. In an attempt to repress "heresy," and to preserve the patrimony of the Catholic faith, the Church used coercive measures such as the Inquisition and the Index of forbidden books. This movement caused the decline of the artistic fervor that had permeated the High Renaissance, with its brilliant manifestations at the courts. By the closing of the Council of Trent in 1563, the situation for writers, women and male alike, had changed profoundly. Censorship led to a decline in literature and in the arts that was felt in spite of the sumptuous style fostered by the Counter-Reformation, a style known as Baroque, characterized by excessive ornamentation, bombast, artifice, and, as the poet Marino put it, emphasis on *meraviglia* (marvel).

Politically, this was an era of subservience to Spain and her religious rulers, such as Philip II. The Counter-Reformation climate of enforced piety and the censorship of books led to a swift decline in the role and activity of women writers in the Italian literary scene. All writers, however, were subjected to pre-publication censorship. As a result, they wrote and published less, and wrote more of the kinds of books whose approval was virtually guaranteed, such as books of a religious nature and on safe subjects, such as the lives of the saints, or treatises on morality. The Inquisition inquired into the religious beliefs of anyone who dared dissent, bringing suit and chastising. Freedom of thought could bring death to those whose beliefs did not conform to the stated norms. Even a noblewoman of the stature and moral character of Vittoria Colonna was questioned when her beliefs appeared to the religious authorities to be too dangerously close to those of the Protestant reformers. In 1580, Veronica Franco was brought to trial by the Inquisition for magical practices that were deemed heretical. She was finally absolved when she "confessed" and "repented," but the trauma of the trial may have been the cause of her subsequent silence as a writer.

During this period, women's lyric poetry, which had enjoyed a remarkable flourishing in the earlier part of the century, went into decline. Women writers of the late sixteenth century preferred to write either in prose or in *ottava rima*, which was a poetic form hitherto used by male writers in the epic and chivalric genres. Abandoning the lyric mode, women poets used the octave to invade, so to speak, the male domain of epic writing. Moderata Fonte (1555-1592), Lucrezia Marinelli (1571-1653), and Margherita Sarocchi Biraghi (ca.1560-1618), all wrote towards the end of the sixteenth century, emerging from the upper strata of the educated bourgeoisie. Sarocchi Biraghi wrote the epic poem *La Scanderbeide*, modeled on Tasso's *Gerusalemme Liberata,* and celebrating the exploits of the Albanian hero George Scanderbeg against the Turks. Marinelli also wrote an epic to celebrate Venice.[9]

Marinelli and Fonte on the one hand conformed to the climate of piety of the time (and they probably had no choice), but on the other hand wrote two surprisingly militant treatises defending women, and attacking the social male structure that oppressed them. Fonte, in *Il merito delle donne* (The Merit of Women), put the whole male gender on trial, denouncing men's vices and the injuries they inflicted on women. Marinelli went even further, extolling the superiority of women over men through her personal interpretation of Platonic doctrines and classical *exempla*. What had happened to make these impassioned defenses necessary? With its piety, the Counter-Reformation also brought a resurgence of the strong misogynistic feelings that had permeated the Middle Ages, and that harked back to the Church Fathers, who saw women as descendants of Eve and as evil temptresses. During the last decades of the sixteenth century, these negative feelings towards women were virulently expressed in viciously misogynist treatises, such as *I donneschi difetti* (The Faults of Women) by Giuseppe Passi, which was published in 1595, and was so successful that it had four editions in twenty years; at approximately the same time, the German philologist Valens Acidalius published *Disputatio nova contra mulieres, qua probatur eas homines non esse* (A new treatise against women, in which it is proven that they are not human beings), in which he affirmed that women have no soul. Both Fonte's and Marinelli's treatises were published in 1600 as a direct and immediate response to Passi's and Acidalius' treatises. During the Counter-Reformation, as the number of printed books and of working printers diminished, publications by women became increasingly rare. The change of direction that took place after the Council of Trent led to intellectual repression and to a decrease in the role of women in the world of letters. Paradoxically, intellectual repression and misogyny caused, by reaction, the outburst of militant feminist writing in the last decades of the sixteenth and in the first decades of the seventeenth century. In addition to Moderata Fonte and Lucrezia Marinelli, the actress-poet Isabella Andreini (1562-1604) also expressed strong feminist feelings, writing, in one of her

most famous letters, a miniature *apologia* of the female gender. In her letter on the birth of women (which we present in this anthology), Andreini
attempted to comfort a man upset by having sired a baby girl. She extolled
the gentle and patient qualities of the female gender, while at the same time
providing many *exempla* of female intelligence and fortitude from the past.
Andreini, moreover, in her dramatic play *La Mirtilla,* turned the tables on
the conventions of the pastoral play, when the heroine captures, ties up and
punishes the Satyr! The feminist feelings of the late 16th century women
poets reach their apex in the 17th century Venetian poet, Sara Copio Sul-
lam (ca. 1590-1641), who wrote in defense of her rights as a woman and
as a Jew, the actress-courtesan Margherita Costa-Ronaca (1600-1657) who
wrote openly about women's sexual freedom, and finally, Elena Tarabotti
(1604-1652), a nun against her own will, who wrote three polemic volumes
against the practice of forcing girls to enter convents for family reasons.
These three writers were not included in our anthology because they wrote
mostly after 1600.

The aim of this volume is to present the work of many Italian Renaissance women poets virtually unknown to the English speaking world. We
tried to make this volume a valuable study tool, as well as a possible point
of departure for further study. While we focused on the expression of female sensibility and on the intellectual equality of women, we also made
a point of stressing their separateness, since women's literature cannot be
studied without inevitable considerations of gender. The feminine and the
masculine worlds, especially in Mediterranean and Catholic societies, have
historically constituted separate and different realities. At times, women's
expression had to be loud and strident — as in the case of the late Renaissance feminists — in order to be heard at all.

Part of women's influence on the Italian intellectual world has been
anonymous, submerged, unrecorded: the occult yet persistent influence
of the wives, mistresses, mothers, friends, and hostesses of the salons.
This influence came in the lullabies sung by the mothers, as well as in
the treatises. Has the position of women in society changed much? In the
works of Moderata Fonte, Lucrezia Marinelli, Isabella Andreini and Elena
Tarabotti we surprisingly find the same thematic elements as in modern
women's discourse.

The flourishing of women's writing in the Italian Renaissance has been
the subject of many studies lately, shedding light on Italian women's attempt to legitimize, so to speak, the expressions of their opinions, through
the pen first, then the press, thus elevating their thoughts to the miracle of
the book: hence, the invention of the press must be considered one of the

most important events in the evolution of women's literary and social history, taking women's voices from the private world of the hearth, from the restricted, though privileged, world of the court, from the quiet mustiness of a book-lined cell, to the wide diffusion that the printed book afforded.

To conclude, I would like to address the reader with the words of the poet Luisa Bergalli Gozzi, the first Italian woman to assemble, in 1726, a large, comprehensive anthology of Italian women poets to date, *Componimenti poetici delle più illustri rimatrici d'ogni secolo*. In dedicating her book to Cardinal Pietro Ottoboni, she underlined that the quality of women's poetry is as high as that of men, and asked him to set aside any prejudice against feminine writing:

> "Nor do I believe that, because these rhymes were dictated by feminine minds, you will not deign to give them a glance.... I am sure you will be free from that almost universal prejudice that talent, sufficient to bring distinction in the fine arts to an outstanding degree, cannot flourish in a woman.... You will be sure to find in this little book style, conceits and thoughts worthy of engaging your mind, such as you might in anthologies of poetry by men, such as to add luster to Italian poetry".

–Laura Stortoni
Berkeley, Ca.
July 1995

Notes

1. Canto XXXVII of *Orlando Furioso*.
2. The *Accademie,* literary academies or intellectual coteries, were started by the humanists in Italy in the fifteenth century and flourished in the sixteenth and seventeenth centuries. These academies, with headquarters in different Italian towns, often took droll names chosen with Socratic irony: *Gli Insensati* (Those without wits), *I Rozzi* (The uncouth ones), *I Pazzi* (The crazy ones), *I Timidi* (The shy ones), etc. Upon receiving membership, members chose a fictional, often symbolic, name, that reflected their personalities and goals.
3. Joan Kelly, in her essay "Did Women Have a Renaissance?" (in *Women, History and Theory: The Essays of Joan Kelly*. Chicago: University of Chicago Press, 1984, 19-50), came to the conclusion "that there was no renaissance for women." While we agree that social restrictions on Italian women in the Renaissance were considerable, the abundance of Italian women who wrote and published poetry in the

Renaissance is staggering, and was not considered by Kelly, who appears to have known only Vittoria Colonna. We offer this list as a rebuttal to her affirmation. It speaks for itself. For the sixteenth century alone, we mention the following women poets, anthologized by Bergalli, in addition to the women poets we have translated for our anthology: Flavia Spanocchi, Laura Spinola, Maddalena Massimi, Silvia Bendinella, Margherita Malescoti, Ippolita Gonzaga, Claudia della Rovere, Livia Pia Poeti, Maria de' Ferrari, Laura Serratone, Egeria Canossa, Virginia Martini Salvi, Caterina Pellegrina, Atalanta Sanese, Livia Torniella Borromea, Alda Torella Lunata, Maria Spinola, Vittoria Corombana, Narda Fior, Cassandra Petrucci, Ermelina Aringhieri de' Ceretani, Giulia d'Aragona, Faustina Valentina, Olimpia Caraffa, Lucrezia Figliucci, Maria Langosca, Lucia Albana, Candida Gattesca, Maddalena Pallavicina, Diamante Dolfi, Francesca Sanese, Fausta Tacita, Bianca Aurora d' Este, Giulia Premarini, Fiammetta Malaspina Soderini, Dianora Sanseverina, Emilia Brembata, Laudomia di San Gallo, Cassandra Giovia Magnacavallo, Cornelia Cotta, Giulia Cavalcanti, Leonora Maltraversa, Celia Romana, Laura Gabrieli degli Alciati, Ortensia Lomelina de' Fieschi, Nicoletta Celsa, Leonora Cibo de' Vitelli, Isotta Brembata Grumella, Giannetta Tron, Rosa Levi, Ortensia Aliprandi, Beatrice Salvi, Andromeda Felice, Anna Colfarini, Ersilia Cortese, Isabella Pepoli De' Riari, Onorata Peci, Cornelia Brunozzi de' Villani, Lisabetta di Cepparello, Giulia Braccalli, Francesca Baffa, Lucrezia di Raimondo, Maria Martelli de' Panchiatichi, Selvaggia Braccalli, Silvia di Somma, Costanza d'Avalo, Laudomia Forteguerri, Liona Aldo-brandini, Ippolita Mirtilla, Pia Bichi, Virginia Papa, Gerolama Castellana, Fiorenza Piemontese, Bartolomea Costanza, Cintia della Fratta, Vittoria Telea Noci, Barbara Torelli Benedetti, Ersilia Spolverini, Catella Marchesi, Lecella di Zucco, Valeria Miani, Laura Guidoccioni Lucchesini, Lucchesia Sbarra Coderta, Ludovica Sbarra Collalto, Livia Spinola, Flavia Spanochi, Maddalena Massimi, Silvia Bandinella, Margherita Malescoti, Lucrezia Marcelli, Lucida Nalli, Orsina Bertolaia Cavalletta, Adriana Trevisana Contarini, Leonora Bellati Bernardi, Laura Beatrice Cappelli, Maddalena Campiglia, Isocratea Monte, Bartolomea Costanza, Antonia Doni, In-nocenza Carrari, Barbara Cavalletta, Ippolita Benegni Manfredi, Minerva Bartoli, Vittoria Galli, Elena Bianca Stanchi; in addition to these, who are all positively identified by Bergalli with brief biographies, we have quite a few marked "incerta," meaning women whose identity is not positively known.

In addition to the above, for the sixteenth century, De Blasi anthologized: Tommasina Battista Vernazza, Giulia Braccali Ricciardi of Pistoia, Virginia Gemma de' Zuccheri of Orvieto, Silvia di Somma of Naples, Cornelia Brunozzi Villani of Pistoia, Virginia Papa, Lisabetta di Cepparello of Florence, Baroness Isabella Capece of Naples, Dafne Piazza, Suor Dea de' Bardi of Florence, Costanza d'Avalos of Naples, Livia Tornielli Borromeo of Lombardy, Cornelia Cotta, Catella Marchesi of Udine, Ermellina Arenghieri de' Cerretani of Siena, Cassandra Petrucci of Siena, Diamante Dolfi of Bologna, Virginia Martini Salvi of Siena, Ersilia del Monte of Rome, Maria Spinola Porrara of Genoa, Santa Caterina de' Ricci of Florence, Antonia Doni, Suor Girolama Castellani of Bologna, Fiammetta Malaspina Soderini of Florence, Santa Maria Maddalena de' Pazzi, Vittoria Accoramboni Peretti Orsini (known also as Vittoria Corombana) duchess of Bracciano, Orsola Cavalletti Bertolai of Ferrara, Barbara Cavalletti Losti of Ferrara, Lucia Albani Avogadro of Bergamo,

Tarquinia Molza Porrini of Modena, Maddalena Salvetti Acciaioli of Florence, Lucchesia Sbarra Coderta Rota of Conegliano, and Livia Spinola.

For the fourteenth century, Bergalli anthologized Lisabetta Trebbiani and Bartolomea da Martigliano; for the fifteenth century, Battista da Montefeltro Malatesta, and Saint Caterina Vigri.

Of the early poets, we find in Jolanda de Blasi's anthology: Selvaggia Vergolesi (XIII-XIV century), Giovanna Branchetti Bonsignori (XIV), Battista Malatesta (XV), Beata Battista Varano (1458-1526).

4. Petrarch, *Rime,* sonnet 153.

5. The painting is now in the Palazzo Vecchio in Florence.

6. *Italian Women Writers: A Bibliographical Sourcebook.* Ed. Rinaldina Russell. Westport, CT & London: Greenwood Press, 1994, p. xix.

7. See *Letter to a mother who wanted her daughter to become a courtesan.*

8. Prof. Rosenthal comments: "There is presently a lot of controversy about this painting. The Getty Museum owns the top panel of it, and it seems that it depicts a hunting scene suggesting that it was intended as furniture decoration. Also, some say that the women are bored noblewomen, and not courtesans as previously depicted."

9. Marinelli and Biraghi were omitted for reasons of space and date.

Editor's Note

I became interested in Italian Renaissance women poets in Prof. Louise G. Clubb's continuing seminar in lyric poetry at the University of California, Berkeley, and, at that time, I started to translate some poetry by Gaspara Stampa and Veronica Franco. In 1980, I was fortunate enough to meet Mary Prentice Lillie, an excellent poet and poetry translator, who shared my interest in Italian literature and my enthusiasm for translating it. We decided to team up to make a volume to include not only Stampa and Franco, but as many other Italian women poets of the Renaissance as we could find. We worked at a pleasant and leisurely pace for years, collecting and translating material, and taking two trips to Italy to visit some libraries. Sadly, after a few years, Mary Prentice Lillie, who is considerably older then myself, could no longer work on the project. Both the present anthology and the Gaspara Stampa volume that we had been working on (which has since appeared with Italica Press, 1994) were shelved for many years, until they were rescued from the closet by the kind interest of Prof. Nancy Vine Durling, who encouraged me to complete them and send them around to publishers.

The bulk of the poetry in this volume was translated in collaboration with Mary Prentice Lillie. All of the critical apparatus (biographies, bibliographies, general bibliography, etc.) is new and done solely by myself. Between the time that Mary Prentice Lillie and I stopped working together and the present day, a great deal of new material was published, and the work of many Renaissance women became available. I continued translating on my own, including some work that was not available earlier.

I dedicate this volume to my dear friend and mentor Mary Prentice Lillie, whose light is veiled but still shines, and whose influence on me and my poetry has been incalculable.

Laura Anna Stortoni
Berkeley, California
July 1995

This volume is intended for scholars of Italian as well as for the general public, and its aim is to introduce the English reader to this largely unknown body of distinguished Italian women poets. We present the selected works of 19 women poets, of which the Italian originals are provided. Each poet is presented in chronological order (approximate when we did not have exact dates) and introduced by a brief biography placing her in historical context.

Initially, we undertook this project not as scholars but as poets, putting together a book of poetry in translation. We selected poems primarily because they appealed to us and because we felt they could successfully be translated into English. It soon became apparent that a biographical and bibliographical apparatus was essential in order for the reader to properly understand our translations. Footnotes were also necessary for the sake of clarity, given the abundance of mythological, classical or political allusions. We attempted to provide the reader with sufficient historical background in the context of the complex and bloody period of Italian history during which these women lived. Moreover, we included an essential bibliography for each poet, giving the source of the poems presented and other important bibliographical data, as well as a comprehensive general bibliography. In the individual bibliographies, we have listed the actual works by the author in chronological order of publication. The rest of the works about the authors have been listed, instead, in alphabetical order.

Whenever possible, we took the original text from critical editions, such as in the case of Gaspara Stampa, Veronica Franco and Vittoria Colonna, or from modern reprints. For the rest, we drew from Renaissance editions and earlier anthologies, and especially from Luisa Bergalli's comprehensive anthology of the best women poets before her, *Componimenti poetici delle più illustri rimatrici d'ogni secolo.*

In making these verse translations from Renaissance Italian, we felt it of prime importance to keep within the feeling of the period, since the poetry of distant times requires a translation of style and tone as well as of words. To this end, we made a careful study not only of the age itself, but also of each individual writer. We purposely avoided what to the modern ear may have sounded like artificially old-fashioned diction, and attempted to strike a balance between modern English and the Italian usage in the poet's time, since it did not seem right to present the poems in too striking a modern form. In the Italian versions, we preserved the spelling and the diacritical marks of the originals; in the English versions we used standard modern English punctuation for the sake of clarity.

Each of the poets we translated has, of course, her individual style, and we tried to bring out such differences in the style of the English as well. The *gentildonna* and religious reformer Vittoria Colonna, for instance, wrote in a different style — rhetorical, metaphysical, complex and allusive — from the outspoken, bold and independent courtesan Veronica Franco, a difference of tone and manner that we have tried to maintain.

As translators, our philosophy has been to try to remain as close as possible to the literal sense of the original, while at the same time striving to create a composition that would read as a poem in the English version. We feel strongly that poetry in translation should be presented as verse rather than prose, since the sight of verse on the page raises higher expectations in the readers' minds, thus preparing them for a deeper emotional response.

As far as was possible, we preserved the formal metrics of the original Italian texts, although we did not keep the end-rhyme patterns; this process would have resulted in distortion of sense, since the Italian language, owing to its abundance of vowels, is richer in rhymes than English. The virtue of a translation is to be as transparent and fluent as possible, and the struggle to rhyme interferes with that aim; we did, however, occasionally use rhyme, near-rhyme and assonance, but only when it occurred naturally and without strain, and when the absence of such devices would have resulted in a certain flatness, as in the case of the madrigals, in which musical sound is more important than content.

Thus, we consistently translated sonnets as sonnets, madrigals as madrigals, *sestinas* as *sestinas,* and so on. The majority of the poems in this volume are sonnets, since most of the translated poets wrote during a time in which Petrarchism was *de rigueur.* The reader may remember that the Italian sonnet (a poetic composition originating in medieval Sicily and re-elaborated by the *Stil Nuovo* poets) differs from the Shakespearean sonnet, in that it comprises two quatrains (four-line stanzas) followed by two tercets (three-line stanzas). To translate sonnets into English, we used the unusual form of the unrhymed sonnet, preserving the line count and the structure of thought, while not straining for rhyme, although occasionally we used assonance. Since English verse depends on stress rather than syllable count, we used the iambic pentameter to represent the Italian hendecasyllable (eleven-syllable line). Thus, some English lines have ten, and others eleven, as in Shakespeare or other poets using blank verse (that is, unrhymed iambic pentameter). This proved to be a very viable form, since in blank verse the structure of thought survives the absence of rhyme.

The madrigals — short monostrophic compositions intended to be sung — may sound deceptively simple, since their effect does not lie in the lyric text, but rather in the variations and repetitions of the melodic line, and in the complexity of the accompanying musical counterpoint. In translating these compositions, we made a special effort to give an approximation of the vowel sounds for musical effect. For the canzone, a favorite Petrarchan poetic form with several variations, we mirrored the structure of the original poem, down to the number of stanzas and verse length. The sestina is a poetic form with six six-line stanzas, and one three-line *envoi,* in which the end-rhymes are substituted by six end-words repeated in each stanza in a well-determined rotating position. We have translated also a few *capitoli,* or *terze rime,* long narrative compositions in tercets which were very well-liked by Gaspara Stampa and Veronica Franco. In the English versions, we indicated the tercet with two hendecasyllables followed by a decasyllable line. This is similar to, but not exactly the same as, the device used by T.S. Eliot in his imitation of Dante in one of his *Four Quartets.* In the rare cases in which a poet used an original or unidentified poetic form, we simply translated it counting a corresponding number of syllables in English for each verse.

We are well aware of the fact that every translation is at best approximate; we therefore hope that, with the Italian original facing the English text, it will be possible for the reader with some knowledge of Italian to follow the original well enough to hear the beauty of its music. We intend our translations not only to read as poems in English, but also to serve as arrows pointing in the direction of the original text. While it was unfortunately impossible to render in English the musicality of the Italian language, it *was* possible to render the eloquent messages that these indomitable women, from a distance of many centuries, still send to us in a clear, loud voice.

It is our hope that this book may serve as a useful introduction to the remarkable richness of this pioneer body of women's poetry, unique even in the Europe of the Renaissance and virtually unknown to readers of English today, as well as an inspiration to modern women, who will be glad to know that the roots of their aspirations go so deep into history.

Acknowledgments

This book owes much to previous anthologists of Italian women poets, especially Luisa Bergalli, the first Italian woman poet to author a comprehensive anthology of Italian women poets. I also acknowledge my debt to the work of Jolanda de Blasi and of Maria Bandini Buti.

I acknowledge a large, more recent, debt to the work of Natalia Costa-Zalessow, author of the anthology *Scrittrici italiane dal XIII at XX secolo* and of many articles on the subject of Italian women writers. She is a pioneer in this field, and her work has been a constant source of inspiration for me. Of invaluable help for some sections of this anthology was also Rinaldina Russell's *Italian Women Writers, A Bio-Bibliographical Sourcebook.* I also want to acknowledge the excellent work by scholars in the field of Renaissance and Women's Studies, some of whom I have had the pleasure of meeting, such as Margaret Rosenthal, Natalie Zemon Davis and Ann Rosalind Jones. Thanks also should be given to Colomba Ghigliotti of the Frank De Bellis Collection at San Francisco State University, and to Mary Jane Parrine, Curator of the Romance Languages Library at Stanford University. My gratitude also goes to all my friends who gave me moral support and took great interest in the completion of this volume, and especially my friend Juliet Viola and fellow-translator Patrick Diehl, for their keen eyes in helping me to correct the final proofs of this volume. Last, but not least, I want to thank my research assistant, Louisa Mackenzie for her untiring work on this time-consuming project.

Women Poets
of the
Italian Renaissance

❧ *Courtly Ladies and Courtesans* ❧

LUCREZIA TORNABUONI DE' MEDICI
(1425-1482)

Lucrezia Tornabuoni was one of the most influential women in fifteenth century Italy for her literary production, for her role in the social and political world of Florence and the whole Italian peninsula, and for her generosity and taste as a patroness of the arts. She belonged to the powerful Florentine family of Tornabuoni. Born in 1425, she inherited from her family a love of domestic virtues, a great respect for learning and an inclination towards the fine arts. In 1444, she married Piero de' Medici, son of Cosimo, the old banker-prince. Her first son Lorenzo (who was to be named the Magnificent) was born in January 1447, and Giuliano a few years later. During her marriage, Lucrezia devoted herself to her family, the education of her children, and to works of charity. She endowed many convents and bestowed dowries on orphaned girls so they could be married honorably.

In 1458, while she was spending the summer at the Villa of Cafaggiolo (near Fiesole), her husband Piero was summoned by his father to join in a political coup which gave the Medici family complete control over Florence. Her life was embittered by two tragic events: in 1466, a plot against her husband Piero; in 1478, the Pazzi plot in which Lorenzo was wounded and Giuliano was killed. After the Pazzi plot, Lorenzo escaped and lived to consolidate the political power of the Medici. After the death of her husband, Lucrezia retired to the villa at Careggi, from which she still managed to take care of her large family.

She was so talented politically that the Medici men greatly valued her advice, and even the independent Lorenzo trusted her insights when he became lord of Florence. In 1467, her husband sent her to Rome on a diplomatic mission to the Pope. On this occasion, Lucrezia sent him a letter in which she described very perceptively Clarice Orsini, a prospective bride for Lorenzo. Although Lorenzo was in love with Lucrezia Donati (a beautiful Florentine maiden of the same family as Dante's wife), his marriage to a Florentine would have created internecine conflicts in the precarious political equilibrium of the city. Thus he married Clarice, of the princely Roman family Orsini, on June 4, 1469.

Lucrezia played an active part in the Medici's humanistic agenda, which reassessed, translated and promoted the corpus of literary and philosophical knowledge of the time as well as promoting and ennobling the Italian vernacular, in which both Lucrezia and Lorenzo chose to write. Deeply religious, she was to become the grandmother of two Medici Popes, Leo X and Clement VII. Her faith, combined with her musical and literary talent, prompted her to compose hymns and poems, the primary motivation of which was to educate and amuse her own children, her family and her court. Lorenzo's own exceptional poetic taste and love of the arts were undoubtedly inspired by his mother's. Lucrezia was a patroness of the arts, and thanks to her encouragement the poet Luigi Pulci wrote *Morgante Maggiore,* one of the greatest works of fifteenth century Italy, which led to Ariosto's and Tasso's poems in the next century.

We have forty-nine private letters written by Lucrezia between 1446-1476 that are still extant, mostly written to family members from the different Tuscan villa where she resided during the summer. These letters are extremely interesting in that they reveal the inner workings of the Medici family. Particular attention has been given to the letter written to her husband on March 28, 1467, describing Clarice Orsini, showing how young women of marriageable age were assessed as prospective brides in those days.

Of her religious writing, only the nine Lauds and three out of the five sacred poems, or *storie,* have been published. The poems are in *ottava* or *terza rima.* While the Lauds in their subject matter are within a well-established fifteenth century genre, Tornabuoni's treatment upgrades and elevates the traditional religious matter. Written in stanzas of *settenari* and *ottonari* (seven- and eight- syllable verses), and although religious in subject, they were performed and sung to profane melodies and even dance-songs. Four of them are set to the same accompaniment as Poliziano's song *Ben venga il maggio.* The most successful of the Lauds, *Behold the Mighty*

3

King..., which we present here, is a celebration of Christ's descent into Limbo and the liberation of the patriarchs and prophets. She also wrote Lauds on Christmas and on the life of Christ.

Tornabuoni's epic poems, or *storie,* are versified adaptations of biblical stories, of which the most noticeable is the story of Judith. In all of her religious and dramatic poetry, she not only conveys religious faith but also shows a great capacity for dramatic development. Her use of vernacular Italian is strong and immediate, and fostered its adoption and acceptance in intellectual milieus of the time.

After Lucrezia's death, her brother, Giovanni Tornabuoni, commissioned Ghirlandaio to paint the magnificent fresco in the church of Santa Maria Novella, in which scenes of contemporary Florentine life are depicted and in which Lucrezia herself appears in a group of Florentine ladies.

The text of the *Laude* we present is from the Bergalli anthology, and the letter is from de Blasi's.

BIBLIOGRAPHY

Works by Lucrezia Tornabuoni de' Medici:
Tre lettere di Lucrezia Tornabuoni a Pietro de' Medici. Ed. Cesare Guasti. Florence: Le Monnier, 1859.
Le laudi di Lucrezia de' Medici. Ed. Gaetano Volpi. Pistoia: Flori, 1900.
I poemetti sacri di Lucrezia Tornabuoni. Ed. F. Pezzarossa. Florence: Olschki, 1978.
Lettere. Ed. Patrizia Salvadori. Florence: Olschki, 1993.

Anthologies containing works by Lucrezia Tornabuoni de' Medici:
Bergalli, *op. cit.*
Costa-Zalessow, *op. cit.*
de Blasi, *op. cit.*

Studies and other works:
Berrigan, Joseph. "Lucrezia Tornabuoni." In *An Encyclopedia of Continental Women Writers.* Vol. 2. Ed. Katharina M. Wilson. New York: Garland, 1991, 1245.

Bosanquet, Mary. *Mother of the Magnificent*. London: Faber & Faber, 1960.

Coppola, D. *La poesia religiosa del secolo XV.* Florence: Olschki, 1963, 63-69.

Dizionario enciclopedico, op. cit. V, 305.

Enciclopedia biografica e bibliografica, op. cit.

Felice, Berta. "Donne medicee avanti il Principato." *Rassegna Nazionale* 146 (1905): 631-60.

Levantini Pieroni, G. "Lucrezia Tornabuoni, donna di Cosimo de' Medici." In *Studi storici e letterari*. Florence: Le Monnier, 1853, 1-83.

Maffei, G. *Storia della letteratura italiana*. Florence: Le Monnier, 1853.

Maguire, Yvonne. "Lucrezia Tornabuoni." In *The Women of the Medici*. London: Routledge, 1927, 60-126.

Poesia del Quattrocento e del Cinquecento (Parnaso italiano IV). Ed. C. Muscetta and D. Ponchiroli. Turin: Einaudi, 1959, 52-55.

Rinaldina Russell. "Lucrezia Tornabuoni." In *Italian Women Writers, op. cit.*, 431-440.

Ecco il Re forte,
   Ecco il Re forte!
   Aprite quelle porte
   O Prencipe infernale;
   Non fate resistenza: 5
   Egli è il Re celestiale,
   Che vien con gran putenza;
   Fategli riverenza!
   Levate via le porte!
Chi è questo potente,   10
   Che vien con tal vittoria?
   Egli è Signor di gloria:
   Avuto ha la vittoria;
   Egli ha vinto la morte.
Egli ha vinto la guerra   15
   Durata già molt'anni;
   E fa tremar la terra,
   Per cavarci d'affanni,
   Riempir vuole gli scanni,
   Per ristorar sua corte.   20
E vuole il Padre antico,
   e la sua compagnia;
   Abel vero suo amico,
   Noè si metta in via:
   Moisè quì non stia,   25
   Venite alla gran corte.

BEHOLD THE MIGHTY KING!

Behold the mighty King![1]
  Behold the mighty King!
  Now open up the gates
  O thou infernal prince![2]
  Do not resist His will.   5
  He is the heavenly King
  who comes with mighty power.
  Treat Him with reverence!
  O lift you up ye gates!
Who is this Holy One   10
  who comes, victorious?
  He is the King of Glory,
  His is the victory,
  for He has conquered death.
And He has won the war   15
  that raged so many years.
  He made the whole earth quake
  to save us from our ills,
  to fill the heavenly seats,
  to re-instate His court.   20
He calls our ancient sire[3]
  and all His company:
  Abel, His loyal friend,
  sets Noah on the way;
  Moses stays not behind: 25
  "Come all to the great Court!"

1. Christ. This *Lauda* is based on Psalm 24 and on the medieval tradition of the Harrowing of Hell. See the Apostle's Creed: "He descended into hell...." See also Dante, *Inferno* IV, 52-63. 2. Satan. 3. Adam.

O Abraam Patriarca,
   Seguite il gran Signore,
   La promessa non varca,
   Venuto è il Redentore: 30
   Vengane il Gran cantore
   A far degna la corte.
O Giovanni Battista,
   Orsù senza dimoro
   Non perdete di vista;   35
   Su nell'eterno coro,
   E Simion con loro
   Dietro a se fa la scorta.
O parvoli innocenti,
   Innanzi a tutti gite;   40
   Or siete voi contenti
   Delle aute ferite!
   O gemme, or margarite,
   Adorate la corte.
Venuto siate al regno   45
   Tanto desiderato,
   Poichè nel Santo legno
   I' fu morto e straziato;
   Ed ha ricomperato
   Tutta l'umana sorte.   50

Patriarch Abraham,
    follow your mighty Lord
    whose promise will not fail.
    Now the Redeemer comes!   30
    Come, David, lord of song,
    To dignify the Court.
O Baptist, holy John,
    arise without delay.
    Do not lose sight of Him   35
    in the eternal choir;
    and Simeon along
    leads an escorting throng.
O Holy Innocents![1]
    Run out ahead of all.   40
    Are you contented now
    with sword-thrusts you have borne?
    O pearls and other gems,
    adorn[2] the heavenly Court!
To the kingdom you have come   45
    that was so long desired.
    Since on the Holy Tree[3]
    He suffered and He died,
    ransoming with His death
    all of human kind.   50

1. The children massacred by Herod. 2. Reading "adornate" for Bergalli's "adorate." 3. The Cross.

ANTONIA GIANNOTTI PULCI
(1452? - ?)

We have little data on the life of this remarkable dramatic woman poet. She was presumably born in Florence, and in 1470 she married Bernardo Pulci, a brother of the great poet Luigi Pulci, author of the celebrated *Morgante*. Bernardo was himself a poet of some renown. She did not have children, and dedicated herself instead to literature, religion and the composition of sacred dramas. After her husband's death in 1488, she retired to a convent. We do not have much information about her life after that, and we do not know when she died.

Like most of the women writers of the fourteenth century, she deals with religious themes. Three religious dramatic works can be definitely attributed to Pulci: *Santa Domitilla, San Francesco,* and *Santa Guglielma*; a fourth play, *La rapresentatione del figliol prodigo,* whose first extant edition is dated 1450, is also credited to Pulci, but with no definite evidence.

Santa Guglielma, from which we present an excerpt here, is a mystery play written in *ottava rima*; it tells the story of the daughter of the King of England, who married the King of Hungary. After her husband's departure for the Holy Land, Guglielma is wrongfully accused of adultery by her wicked brother-in-law. Condemned to death at the stake, her life is saved by a sympathetic executioner. But her misfortunes are not over. She is abandoned to die in a desert, where she is saved by the intervention of the Holy Virgin, who also bestows upon her the gift of healing repentant sinners. With this gift, Guglielma cures her brother-in-law of leprosy after his public confession. The end of the play celebrates her virtue as well as the redeeming quality of the Christian faith.

Like her contemporary, Lucrezia Tornabuoni de' Medici, also a writer of dramatic religious works, Pulci has a powerful and simple style combined with a powerful sense of dramatic structure. In the fifteenth century, we have on the one hand a copious flowering of women humanists writing in the classical languages, and on the other hand women who wrote poetry in the vernacular, for the most part religious dramatic poetry in *ottava rima*. The critic Alessandro D'Ancona was the first modern critic to recognize Pulci's importance, when he included *Santa Guglielma* in his 1872 edition of mystery plays. Other modern critics, such as de Blasi and more recently Luigi Banfi, notice how, in Pulci's work, the profane element and a preoccupation with contemporary social issues began to supplant the sacred.

The lines we have translated from *Santa Guglielma* are a strong condemnation of the custom of obedience of the times, which often forced maidens to marry against their will, a theme we have already represented with the earlier poet Compiuta Donzella.

We have taken the Italian text from the de Blasi anthology.

BIBLIOGRAPHY

Works by Antonia Giannotti Pulci :
Guglielma in Sacre rappresentazioni fiorentine del Quattrocento. Ed. Giovanni Ponte. Milan: Marzorati, 1974.
La rappresentatione di Santa Domitilla. Florence: Miscomini or Bonaccorsi, 1490-95.
La rappresentatione di Santa Guglielma. In *Sacre rappresentazioni del '400.* Ed. L. Banfi. Turin: UTET, 1963, 533-77.
S. Francesco in l'antico dramma sacro italiano. Florence: Libreria Editrice Fiorentina, 1927. Vol. 2.

Anthologies containing works by Antonia Giannotti Pulci:
Costa-Zalessow, op. cit.
de Blasi, op. cit.

Studies and other works:
Banfi, Luigi. *Sacre rappresentazioni del '400.* Turin: UTET, 1963.
D'Ancona, Alessandro. *Le origini del teatro italiano.* 2 vols. Turin: Loescher, 1891.
Enciclopedia biografica e bibliografica, op. cit.
Newbigin, Nerida. *Nuovo 'corpus' di sacre rappresentazioni fiorentine del Quattrocento.* Bologna: Commissione per i testi di lingua, 1983.
Russell, Rinaldina. "Antonia Pulci." In *An Encyclopedia of Continental Woman Writers,* 2, op. cit., 1018-1019.
———. *Italian Women Writers: A Bio-Bibliographical Sourcebook.* Westport, CT: Greenwood Press, 1994, 344-352.
Torraca, Francesco. *Il teatro italiano dei secoli XIII, XIV, XV.* Florence: Sansoni, 1885.
Toscani, Bernard. "Antonia Pulci." In *Italian Women Writers, op. cit.,* 344-352.

LAMENTO DI GUGLIELMA

O sventurata me, per qual peccato
debb'io senza cagion patir tormento?
O dolce padre, dove hai tu mandato
la tua cara Guglielma in perdimento?
Ahi, crudo sposo, come hai sentenziato   5
colei ch'a te non fe' mai fallimento?
Per premio sarò data a tal supplicio,
come fu Isàc al Santo Sacrificio.
    O Padre mio, sol per tuoi preghi presi
marito contra tutte le mie voglie: 10
di viver pura e casta sempre intesi.
A noia m'eran le mondane spoglie
per le qual'or sostegno gravi pesi.
Finisco la mia vita in pianti e in doglie,
misera me, perchè volli seguire   15
il mondo lasso pien d'ogni martìre.
    Son queste le delizie e somme feste
che mi son dal mio sposo riservate!...

Stortoni & Lillie

GUGLIELMA'S LAMENT

Alas for my misfortune! For what sin
must I, without all cause, suffer such torment?
O my dear father! Where have you dispatched me,
your child Guglielma, into what perdition?
Ah, cruel husband! Why have you condemned me,   5
who never gave you cause, nor sinned against you?
I shall be offered, an unhappy victim,
like Isaac, in the holy sacrifice.

Oh, father! only at your supplication
did I accept a husband, though unwilling.   10
I wished to live a chaste and holy life.
The prizes of the world disgusted me.
For them I bear a weight of heavy sorrow.
I must wear out my life in painful weeping.
Alas for me! Why did I wish to follow   15
this wicked world, so full of woe and evil?

Are these the pleasures and the high enjoyment
reserved for me, alas, by my own husband?...

CAMILLA SCARAMPA
(15th Century)

Camilla Guidoboni Scarampa (or Scarampi) was an important literary figure of the fifteenth century. Matteo Bandello, who held her in great esteem, dedicated to her the thirteenth of his *Novelle*. According to some historians, she was born in Mantua, while others (Tiraboschi among them) believe that she was born in Milan of the Senator Scarampo Scarampi.

We know very few details about her life. She was married at eighteen to Ambrogio Guidoboni. She was also directly involved in literary society: from 1454 to 1500 she held her own academy of poetry and music. She was regarded so highly for her artistic talent that after her death the poet Luca Valenziano of Tortona published the poem *Camilleo* in her honor.

Luisa Bergalli liked her poetry so much that she anthologized several of her sonnets, from which we present *Let those who wish to blame me...*, in which Scarampa voices, like other Renaissance women before and after her, the firm determination to follow the path of wisdom and learning, in spite of the criticism of "the blind crowd".

BIBLIOGRAPHY

Anthologies containing works by Camilla Scarampa:
Bergalli, *op. cit.*
de Blasi, *op. cit.*
Parnaso italiano. Ed. A. Ronna. Paris: Baudry, 1847.

Studies and other works:
Bandello, Matteo. *Novelle.* Ed. G. Brugnolino. Bari: Laterza, 1928.
Comba, Eugenio. *Donne illustri italiane proposte ad esempio alle giovinette.* Turin: Paravia, 1920.
Della Chiesa, Francesco Agostino. *Theatro delle donne letterate.* Mondovi: G. Ghislandi & G.T. Rossi, 1620.
Enciclopedia biografica bibliografica italiana, op. cit.

Biasimi pur chi vuol la mia durezza,
    Che seguir voglio il mio casto pensiero,
    Il qual mi scorge per il buon sentiero,
    Che fa gli spirti miei vaghi d'altezza.

Fugga pur gioventù, venga vecchiezza,   5
    Che sol nella virtù mi fido, e spero,
    E per lei il mio cor sdegno, ed altero
    Disprezza quanto il cieco vulgo apprezza.

Né d'altro, che di questa più mi cale,
    Ed ho di lei sì la mia mente accesa,   10
    Che ogn'altra mi par opra vana, e frale.

E però vo seguir l'alta mia impresa;
    Poichè beltà senza virtù non vale.
    Non fia chi faccia al mio voler contesa.

Stortoni & Lillie

Let those who wish to blame me for my hardness
blame me, since I must follow my chaste mind,
which urges me to travel the right path,
making my spirit eager for the heights.[1]

Let my youth flee, let old age come upon me,   5
I put my faith and hope only in virtue,
and for her sake my proud disdainful heart
despises what the blind crowd values most.

Nor do I care for anything but wisdom,
and for her sake my mind is so enkindled,   10
that every other thing seems weak and frail.

Therefore I'll follow my exalted aim,
for beauty lacking virtue has no worth:
let here be none to hinder my desire.

1. Heights of poetic inspiration or wisdom.

BARBARA BENTIVOGLIO STROZZI TORELLI
(c.1475-1533)

Born in Guastalla in approximately 1475, daughter of Marsiglio
Count of Montechiarugolo, this noblewoman was married to Ercole
Bentivoglio in 1491. Several years later, she fell in love with Ercole
Strozzi (a poet and writer of refined Latin elegies), and separated
from her first husband in order to marry Strozzi in 1508. Shortly
after the wedding Strozzi was murdered under mysterious circum-
stances. Torelli spent the last years of her life in Reggio Emilia, and
died in Bologna in 1533. Around the tragic vicissitudes of her life,
Romantic critics created an alluring legend, as, later, in the case of
Gaspara Stampa.

The poem we present, which has been hailed as one of the best
ever written in the Italian language, contains open and direct references to Strozzi's death. Torelli wrote other *Rime* in the Petrarchan
mode, but this sonnet stands out for its perfect form and powerful
expression.

It has often been anthologized under Torelli's name, and we are
convinced of her authorship. It should be mentioned, however,
that some critics have questioned her authorship on the grounds
that this poem surpasses by far the quality of her other literary
production. But, as the last line of this sonnet says, this is what
"Love can do."

We are taking the text of the poem we present from the de
Blasi anthology.

BIBLIOGRAPHY

Anthologies containing works by Barbara Torelli:
Bergalli, *op. cit.*
de Blasi, *op. cit.*
Lirici del '500. Ed. Carlo Bo. Milan: Garzanti, 1941.
Lirici del Cinquecento. Ed. Daniele Ponchiroli. Turin: U.T.E.T., 1968, 421-423.
Poesia del Quattrocento e del Cinquecento (Parnaso italiano, IV), op. cit,. 1257.
Rime scelte de' poeti ferraresi antichi e moderni. Ed. G. Baruffaldi. Ferrara: n.p., 1713.

Studies and other works:
Catalano, M. "La tragica morte di Ercole Strozzi e il sonetto di Barbara Torelli." *Archivio romanico* (1926): 221-253.
Enciclopedia biografica e bibliografica italiana, op. cit.
Falchi, L. "Per un sonetto attribuito a Barbara Torelli." *Rassegna bibliografica della letteratura italiana* (1929): 105-106.
Mortara, A.M. "La morte di Ercole Strozzi, poeta ferrarese." *Rassegna bibliografica della letteratura italiana* (1928): 237-249.

Spenta è d'Amor la face, il dardo è rotto
e l'arco e ogni faretra e ogni sua possa,
poi che Morte crudel la pianta ha scossa,
a la cui ombra cheta io dormìa sotto.

    Deh perchè non poss'io la breve fossa   5
seco entrar dove l'ha il destìn condotto,
colui che appena cinque giorni ed otto
Amor legò pria de la gran percossa?

    Vorrei col foco mio quel freddo ghiaccio
intepidire e rimpastar col pianto   10
la polve e ravvivarla a nuova vita;

    e vorrei poscia baldanzosa e ardita
mostrarlo a lui che ruppe il caro laccio,
e dirgli: "Amor, mostro crudel, può tanto."

Quenched is the torch of love, his dart is broken,
As are his quiver, bow and all his power,
Since cruel death has stricken down the tree
Beneath whose shade I used to sleep in peace.
Ah, why can I not enter in with him   5
The early grave where Destiny had laid him
To whom but barely thirteen days ago
Love grafted me, before the monstrous blow?[1]
I wish that with my ardor I could melt
That icy cold, and moisten with my tears   10
His dust, and so remold him to new life[2];
And then, with courage and with boldness, show
This miracle to him[3] who snapped our bond,
And say, "See, heartless beast, what Love can do!"

1. The murder of Ercole Strozzi, thirteen days after the wedding. 2. She wishes she could resuscitate him with her tears. 3. The mysterious murderer.

Veronica Gàmbara
(1485-1550)

Together with Vittoria Colonna and Gaspara Stampa, Veronica Gàmbara belongs to the traditional trio of the best-known Italian women poets. She was born in Pratoalboino, near Brescia, of a noble and powerful family. She boasted two illustrious female ancestors: her paternal grandmother was Ginevra Nogarola, a Humanist and the sister of the famous Isotta Nogarola; her maternal aunt was Emilia Pio, the graceful and witty interlocutor of Castiglione's *Il Cortegiano*. In 1509 she married by proxy Gilberto X, lord of the small state of Correggio, from which the famous painter Antonio Allegri took his nickname. This state was well-known as an elegant and refined court and a center for learning and the arts. Because of its small size and difficult geographical position, the rulers of Correggio had to do a delicate balancing act in the precarious political equilibrium of the time.

Gàmbara had two children from this marriage, but was left a widow in 1518. From then on, she managed the family as well as the state, performing her duties with great skill. Her tasks included forming strategic military alliances, since the Correggios were *condottieri* who hired themselves out to the more powerful lords. She had loved her husband dearly, and after his death her sorrow was so great that she ordered her whole court to wear black, from courtiers to horses. On the entrance door to her palace she had inscribed Vergil's verses in which Queen Dido laments the death of her Sichaeus:

> *Ille meos primus, qui me sibi iunxit, amores*
> *abstulit, ille habeat secum, servetque, sepulchro.*
>
> (Aeneid, IV, 28-9)

> He, who first linked me to himself, has taken away my heart:
> may he keep it with him, and guard it in the grave.
>
> (Loeb's translation)

Unlike Dido, who went on to fall in love with Aeneas, Gàmbara never remarried, and her widowhood allowed her great freedom of action and of expression. Her most noteable political and diplomatic activity, and most of her literary output, occur after her husband's death.

She was an energetic and combative ruler: in 1538, she resisted a fierce attack on Correggio by Galeotto Pico della Mirandola, thus becoming a symbol of the Renaissance *virago*. She composed numerous poems, filled her court with scholars of renown, and kept a regular correspondence with others. She was a friend of Bernardo Tasso, father of the great poet Torquato; she was also friends with Matteo Bandello and the writer-adventurer Pietro Aretino; she held in special esteem Cardinal Bembo, the codifier of Petrarchan lyric to whom she submitted her own work for literary advice. During her rule, artists as important as Ariosto and Titian were her honored guests and even the Emperor Charles V, to whom she was bound by family loyalty and military alliance, stopped at her court twice. She spent some time in Bologna in 1529-1530, on the occasion of the coronation of Charles V. She died in 1550.

She is considered the first great woman poet of Italian literature, and she was highly regarded by Vittoria Colonna, for whom she served as a role model both for her style of life and for her literary work. (See Colonna's sonnet dedicated to her.) Although she wrote within the tenets of Petrarchism, her poetry is very personal when expressing the sense of bereavement and the sadness of widowhood, a theme which she held in common with other women poets of the Renaissance. Fiercely political, she also shared with other Renaissance women a keen sense of patriotism and a concept of Italy as an entity centuries before unification, apparent in some of the sonnets we present.

Characteristic also of her poetry is the intertwining of pagan themes — showing her thorough knowledge of classical texts — and personal statements. Though not as bold in her similes and metaphors as the later Vittoria Colonna or Chiara Matraini, she was remarkable for the musicality of her sound (some of her love sonnets were eventually set to music), and for her sense of nature. In her literary personality, the *virago* and the delicate poet coexisted in harmony. We have 150 of Gàmbara's letters extant, written in varied and vivacious prose; since they were never intended for publication, they reveal the more personal side of this woman. From these letters we present a letter to Ludovico Rosso in which she admits to feeling tired of her responsibilities, and to wishing for a simpler life. About 80 of her poems are extant, most of which date from the period of her widowhood. The great poet Ariosto had a special appreciation for her. He described her as standing out from a crowd of beautiful and wise women as especially "pleasing to Apollo and the Muses." (*Orlando Furioso,* Canto XLVI, 3). Laura Bacio Terracina, who wrote several years after her, dedicated *Il discorso sopra il principio di tutti i canti di Orlando Furioso* to her. (See Laura Bacio Terracina in this anthology.)

From Gàmbara's love poetry we have selected the madrigal *Brilliant and Lovely Eyes...,* written for her husband and set to music by Luca Marenzio; *Loosen your Golden Tresses...,* an epithalamium showing Gàmbara's classical formation; and from the period of her widowhood we have chosen *That Knot...,* in which she expresses her grief in touching verse. We have also included an encomiastic sonnet to Vittoria Colonna, who returned the compliment. We refer the reader also to the two sonnets of Lucia Bertana in this anthology addressed to Veronica Gàmbara, since these poetic exchanges attest to the respect and consideration that these women felt for one another, and to the debt that they owed each other.

Because Gàmbara was the most politically conscious of all Renaissance women poets, quite a few of the poems we have selected from her literary production refer to the difficult political situation in Renaissance Italy, which had become the battlefield for the military powers of France and Spain: *With Such a Warm Desire...,* referring to her homeland Brescia (when Gàmbara refers to her "patria" she refers to Brescia, where she was born, to Correggio, the state she ruled, and, in more general terms to Italy); *O Happy Wearer of the Glorious Mantle...,* a prayer to Pope Paul III to defend Italy from foreign invasions; *Beautiful Flora...,* exhorting the

Italians to liberate their land; and finally *Look Lord...*, a prayer for the happy outcome of the next pontifical elections. Gàmbara characterizes Italy and the Roman Church as a ship without a pilot and a flock without a shepherd.

In 1693, Bulifon published Gàmbara's *Rime,* together with those of Lucrezia Marinelli and Isabella di Morra. The first complete collection was published in Brescia in 1759 under the title *Rime e lettere di Veronica Gàmbara.* Most of the poems we present here are taken from, and follow the numbering of, Guerrini's *Rime di tre gentildonne del secolo XVI,* except for *Look Lord Upon this Weary Little Bark...,* taken from de Blasi's anthology, which we have placed at the end. We have taken the letter to Lodovico Rosso from *Lettere del Cinquecento,* edited by G. Ferrero, Turin: UTET, p. 333.

BIBLIOGRAPHY

Works by Veronica Gàmbara:
Rime. With a "Life" by B.C. Zamboni. Ed. Francesco Rizzardi. Brescia: Rizzardi, 1759.
Rime e lettere di Veronica Gàmbara. Ed. Pia Mestica Chiappetti. Florence: Barbèra, 1879.
Rime inedite e rare di Veronica Gàmbara. Ed. A. Salza. Ciriè: Cappella, 1915.

Anthologies containing works by Veronica Gàmbara:
Bergalli, *op. cit.*
Costa-Zalessow, *op. cit.*
de Blasi, *op. cit.*
Jerrold, Maud F. "A Sister Poet. Veronica Gàmbara." In *Vittoria Colonna with Some Accounts of Her Friends and Her Times.* London: Dent, 1906.
Lettere del Cinquecento. Ed. G. Ferrero. Turin: U.T.E.T., 1967, 333-341.
Lirici del Cinquecento. Ed. L. Baldacci. Florence: Salani, 1957, 271-277.
Poesia del Quattrocento e del Cinquecento, op. cit., 1263-1265.
Ponchiroli, *op. cit.*
Rime delle signore Lucrezia Marinella, Veronica Gàmbara ed Isabella Morra. Naples: Bulifon, 1693.
Rime di tre gentildonne del secolo XVI. Ed. O. Guerrini. Milan: Sonzogno, 1930, 343-375.
Rime di diversi eccellenti autori bresciani. Ed. Girolamo Ruscelli. Venice: Pietrasanta, 1583.

Studies and other works:

Bellonci, G. "Veronica Gàmbara e la poesia del Cinquecento." *Giornale emiliano,* August 3, 1950.

Bonora, Ettore. "Le donne poetesse." In *Critica e letteratura nel Cinquecento.* Turin: Giampichelli, 1964, 91-110.

Cataloghi delle lettere di Veronica Gàmbara. Ed. F. Manzotti. Verona: Nova Historia, 1951.

Croce, Benedetto. "La lirica cinquecentesca." In *Poesia popolare e poesia d'arte.* Bari: Laterza, 1930, 425-26.

De Courten, C. *Veronica Gàmbara, una gentildonna del Cinquecento.* Milan: Est, 1934-5.

Dizionario enciclopedico, op. cit., III, 30.

Enciclopedia biografica e bibliografica italiana, op. cit.

Leone, G. "Per lo studio della letteratura femminile del Cinquecento." *Convivium* (1962, 3): 293-300.

Lettere di donne italiane del secolo decimosesto. Venice: Alvisopoli, 1832, 11-29.

Poss, Richard. "Veronica Gàmbara: A Renaissance gentildonna." In *Women Writers of the Renaissance and Reformation.* Ed. Katharina M. Wilson. Athens, GA: The University of Georgia Press, 1987, 47-65.

Russell, Rinaldina. "Veronica Gàmbara." In *Italian Women Writers, op. cit.,* 145-153.

Veronica Gàmbara e la poesia del suo tempo nell'Italia settentrionale. Atti del Convegno (Brescia - Correggio), 17-19 October, 1985. Ed. C. Bozzetti, P. Gibellini, and E. Sandal. Florence: Olschki, 1989.

1

Mentre da vaghi e giovenil pensieri
　　Fui nodrita, or temendo, ora sperando,
　　Piangendo or trista, ed or lieta cantando,
　　Da desir combattuta or falsi, or veri,
Con accenti sfogai pietosi e feri　　　　　　　　5
　　I concetti del cor, che spesso amando
　　Il suo male assai più che 'l ben cercando,
　　Consumava dogliosa i giorni interi.
Or che d'altri pensieri e d'altre voglie
　　Pasco la mente, a le già care rime　　　　　10
　　Ho posto ed a lo stil silenzio eterno.
E, se allor, vaneggiando, e quelle prime
　　Sciocchezze intesi, ora il pentirmi toglie,
　　Palesando la colpa, il duolo interno.

2

O de la nostra etade unica gloria,
　　Donna saggia, leggiadra, anzi divina,
　　A la qual riverente oggi s'inchina,
　　Chiunque è degno di famosa istoria,
Ben fia eterna di voi qua giù memoria,　　　　5
　　Nè potrà 'l tempo con la sua ruina
　　Far del bel nome vostro empia rapina,
　　Ma di lui porterete ampia vittoria.
Il sesso nostro un sacro e nobil tempio
　　Dovría, come già a Palla e a Febo, alzarvi　10
　　Di ricchi marmi e di finissim'oro.
E, poichè di virtù siete l'esempio,
　　Vorrei, Donna, poter tanto lodarvi,
　　Quanto io vi riverisco, amo ed adoro.

1

When I was nourished by sweet youthful thoughts,
At times in fear, at others filled with hope,
Weeping one moment, singing next in joy,
Assailed by my desires, some true, some false,
In words now pitiful, now wild, I uttered   5
The thoughts within my heart, while often loving
Its evil more than seeking out its good,
I spent entire days in fruitless grieving.
Now that with other thoughts and other wishes
I feed my mind, I put my rhymes and pen,   10
Once loved so dearly, to eternal silence;
Whereas then, in my wondering thoughts, I knew
Only those early follies, I repent,
Disclosing here my faults, my inner sorrow.

2

O unique glory of our present age![1]
Lady of wisdom, graceful and divine,
To whom all who are worthy of remembrance
Will bow today in deepest reverence.
Your memory here below will be eternal,   5
Nor can old Time himself with ruinous hand
Wreak dire destruction of your lovely name:
Over him you will win great victory.[2]
Our sex should raise to you a noble temple
As in the past to Pallas[3] and to Phoebus,[4]   10
Built of rich marble and of finest gold.
And since you are a model of all virtue,
I wish, Lady, that I could sing your praises
As much as I revere, love, and adore you.

1. To Vittoria Colonna. 2. A pun referring to her name Vittoria. 3.
Athena, or Minerva, alternative names for the goddess of wisdom. 4.
God of poetry.

29

3

La bella Flora, che da voi sol spera,
    Famosi eroi, e libertate e pace,
    Fra speranza e timor si strugge e sface,
    E spesso dice or mansueta, or fera:
O de' miei figli saggia e prima schiera,   5
    Perchè di non seguir l'orme vi piace
    Di chi col ferro e con la mano audace
    Vi fe' al mio scampo aperta strada e vera?
Perchè sì tardi al mio soccorso andate?
    Già non produssi voi liberi e lieti,   10
    Perchè lasciaste me serva e dolente.
Quanta sia in voi virtù dunque mostrate,
    E col consiglio e con la man possente
    Fate libera me, voi salvi e queti.

10

Tu che di Pietro il glorioso manto
    Vesti felice, e del celeste regno
    Hai le chiavi in governo, onde sei degno
    Di Dio ministro, e pastor saggio e santo,
Mira la greggia a te commessa, e quanto   5
    La scema il fiero lupo; e poi sostegno
    Securo l'una dal tuo sacro ingegno
    Riceva e l'altro giusta pena e pianto.
Scaccia animoso fuor del ricco nido
    I nemici di Cristo or che i duo regi   10
    Ogni lor cura e studio hanno a te vòlto.
Se ciò farai, non fia men chiaro il grido
    De l'opre tue leggiadre e fatti egregi,
    Che sia di quello il cui gran nome hai tolto.

3

Beautiful Flora,[1] who has put her trust
In you, brave heroes, for her peace and freedom,
Is now undone between her hopes and fears,
And often speaks to you, mildly or fiercely:
"O first and wisest of my throng of children,   5
Why will you never follow in the footsteps
Of those who with audacious hand and steel
Have made an open roadway to my aid?
Why are you slow in coming to my side?
I did not bear you to be free and happy   10
For you to leave me as a grieving slave.
Now show me how much valor you can muster,
And with your wisdom and your powerful hands
Liberate me; make yourselves free and peaceful."

10[2]

O happy wearer of the glorious mantle
Of holy Peter, you who hold the keys
To heaven's kingdom, with great worthiness,
Servant of God, wise and most holy pastor:
Look on the flock[3] under your care, see how   5
The savage wolf preys on it; and make sure
That by your sacred aid one side is heartened,
While pain and just lament fall on the other.
Drive with decisive force from this rich nest
The enemies of Christ, now that both kings[4]   10
Have turned all their regard and zeal to you.
If you do this, the cry will ring out clear
Of your most gracious works and noble deeds,
Worthy of Him,[5] whose great name you have taken.

1. Flora represents Italy. 2. To Pope Paul III, urging him to protect Italy from foreign invaders. 3. The Italians. 4. Francis I of France and Charles V of the Holy Roman Empire. 5. Referring to the Apostle Paul.

MADRIGALE *1*

Occhi lucenti e belli,
    Com'esser può che in un medesmo istante
    Nascan da voi sì nove forme e tante?
Lieti, mesti, superbi, umili, alteri
    Vi mostrate in un punto, onde di speme   5
    E di timor m'empiete,
    E tanti effetti dolci, acerbi e fieri
    Nel core arso per voi vengono insieme
    Ad ognor che volete.
    Or poi che voi mia vita e morte sete,   10
    Occhi felici, occhi beati e cari,
    Siate sempre sereni, allegri e chiari.

17

Quel nodo, in cui la mia beata sorte
    Per ordine del ciel legommi e strinse,
    Con grave mio dolor sciolse e discinse
    Quella crudel che 'l mondo chiama morte.
E fu l'affanno sí gravoso e forte,   5
    Che tutti i miei piaceri a un tratto estinse;
    E, se non che ragione alfin pur vinse,
    Fatto avrei mie giornate e brevi e corte.
Ma téma sol di non andare in parte
    Troppa lontana a quella, ove il bel viso   10
    Risplende sovra ogni lucente stella,
Mitigato ha 'l dolor, che ingegno od arte
    Far nol potea; sperando in paradiso
    L'alma vedere oltra le belle bella.

Stortoni & Lillie

Brilliant and lovely eyes
How can it be that in one single instant
You give birth to so many varied moods?
Happy and sad, exalted, humble, proud —
You shine forth in a flash, in which, with hope   5
And fear you fill me full,
And many sweet effects — bitter and wild —
All come together in a heart on fire
With you, when you desire.
Now that you are both life and death to me,   10
O joyful eyes, O blessèd eyes and dear,
Be evermore serene, happy and clear.

17

That knot, in which my one-time blissful fate,
By heaven's order, tied and so constrained me,
Was loosened and unbound, to my great grief,
By that most cruel thing the world calls Death.[2]
My sorrow was so heavy and so grave   5
That it destroyed all pleasure at one blow.
If Reason had not conquered in the end
I would have made my days here brief and short.[3]
Only the fear of not reaching a place
So far above the brightest of the stars[4]   10
Has eased the bitter pain no human heart
Could mitigate, granting me hope one day
To see that soul,[5] fairest among the fair.

1. Set to music by Luca Marenzio. See A. Einstein, *The Italian Madrigal.* 2. Her husband had just died. 3. Suicide. 4. Paradise. 5. Her dead husband's soul.

STANZE *I*

Con quel caldo desio che nascer suole
Nel petto di chi torna, amando, assente
Gli occhi vaghi a vedere, e le parole
Dolci ad udir del suo bel foco ardente,
Con quel proprio voi, piagge al mondo sole,   5
Fresch'acque, ameni colli, e te, possente
Più d'altra che 'l sol miri andando intorno,
Bella e lieta cittade, a veder torno.

Salve, mia cara patria, e tu, felice,
Tanto amato dal ciel, ricco paese,   10
Che a guisa di leggiadra alma fenice,
Mostri l'alto valor chiaro e palese;
Natura, a te sol madre e pia nutrice,
Ha fatto a gli altri mille gravi offese,
Spogliandoli di quanto avean di buono   15
Per farne a te cortese e largo dono.

Non tigri, non lioni e non serpenti
Nascono in te, nemici a l'uman seme,
Non erbe venenose, a dar possenti
L'acerba morte, allor che men si teme;   20
Ma mansuete greggie e lieti armenti
Scherzar si veggon per li campi insieme,
Pieni d'erbe gentili e vaghi fiori,
Spargendo graziosi e cari odori.

Ma, perchè a dir di voi, lochi beati,   25
Ogn'alto stil sarebbe roco e basso,
Il carco d'onorarvi a più pregiati,
Sublimi ingegni e gloriosi lasso.
Da me sarete col pensier lodati
E con l'anima sempre, e ad ogni passo   30
Con la memoria vostra in mezzo il core,
Quanto sia il mio poter, farovvi onore.

Stortoni & Lillie

With such a warm desire as must arise
In absent lover's heart, who yearns to see
The lovely and belovèd eyes, and hear
Sweet words from her, who is his dearest flame,
I see you once again, o land unique   5
On earth, with your fresh waters, pleasant hills,
Loveliest of lands seen by the wandering sun,
And, most of all, my fair and happy city.

Hail, my belovèd fatherland, most happy
Prosperous country, dearly loved by heaven,   10
Which, as a gracious spirit, phoenix-like
Displays its valor clearly in the open.
Nature, your only mother, loving nurse,
Has plundered many thousand other lands,
Stealing whatever good they may possess   15
To make a rich and courteous gift to you.

No tigers and no lions and no serpents
Are born in you, enemies to mankind,
No poisonous herbs, having the power to deal
Death to the very one who fears them least;   20
But gentle flocks, contented, happy herds,
One sees frolicking in the fields together,
Fields full of tender grass and dainty flowers
Scattering fragrant and delicious odors.

But since to speak of you, most blessèd place,   25
Even the highest style seems rough and rude,
The task of honoring you I now must leave
To nobler geniuses, sublime in fame.
By me you will be lauded, in my thoughts
Always, and in my soul; with every step   30
Your memory is cherished in my bosom.
As much as in my power, I honor you.

21

Sciogli le trecce d'oro, e d'ogn'intorno
   Cigni le tempia de' tuoi mirti e allori,
   Venere bella, e teco i santi amori
   Faccian concordi un dolce, almo soggiorno.
E tu, sacro Imeneo, cantando intorno,   5
   Di vaghe rose e di pupurei fiori
   Col plettro d'oro in versi alti e sonori
   Rendi onorato questo altero giorno.
E voi tutti, o gran dei, che de' mortali
   Siete al governo, a man piena spargete   10
   Gioia, pace, dolcezza, amore e fede;
Acciò che i casti baci e l'ore liete,
   Spese tra due, sieno felici e tali
   Che dar non possa il cielo altra mercede.

21[1]

Loosen your golden tresses, lovely Venus,
And crown your head with myrtle and with laurel,
So may these loves, hallowed by holy vows,
Make harmony with you in peaceful sojourn.
And you, o sacred Hymen[2] with your singing,   5
With roses and with other purple flowers,
Honor this gracious day, with golden plectrum[3]
Singing your lofty and sonorous verses.
And all of you, great gods, the governors
Of mortal men, scatter with generous hand   10
Joy, peace and sweetness, love and faithfulness,
So that chaste kisses and the pleasant hours
Spent by these two, will bring such happiness
That heaven itself can give no greater joy.

1. An epithalamium or wedding song. 2. The god of marriage. 3. Instrument for plucking the lyre.

37

Mira, Signor, la stanca navicella
di Pietro che nel mar, da fieri venti
spinta, va errando; e par che si lamenti
di questa fluttüosa e rìa procella.

Mira che sola in questa parte e in quella   5
smarrita corre, e con dogliosi accenti
ti domanda soccorso. E tu consenti
che finor posi in lei nemica stella.

Nave senza nocchier, senza pastore
non può star gregge, chè dall'onde l'una,   10
l'altro è da lupi travagliato e morto.

Signor, dunqne provvedi; e il tuo favore
spira a chi sappia in la maggior fortuna
questa barca condur felice in porto.

37

Look, Lord, upon this weary little bark
Of Peter[1] which goes wandering on the sea,
Driven by violent winds; she seems to mourn
Because of this tempestuous, evil storm!
See how she wanders from this side to that,   5
Bewildered, and with pitiful laments
She begs for succor. And will You allow
This evil star forever to pursue her?
A ship without a pilot,[2] with no guide,
A flock without a shepherd, cannot last.   10
One is pursued by waves, the other, wolves.
O Lord, provide for her, send down Your favor
On him who knows, against the worst ill fortune,
To lead this bark into a happy harbor.

1. Traditional expression for the Church; the poet, writing at a time of troubles in the Catholic Church, is praying for the election of a good pontiff. 2. Note the influence of Dante, *Purgatorio,* VI, 77; but Dante is speaking of Italy, not of the Church.

AURELIA PETRUCCI
(1511-1542)

Aurelia Petrucci was born in Siena in 1511, and died at the age of thirty-one on November 1st, 1542, according to the epitaph on her tomb in the church of Saint Augustine.

In the sonnet we are presenting, taken from the de Blasi anthology, the Italian people are urged to unite and to make "a single body of the scattered limbs" at the time of the invasions of Italy by Spain and France. The author shows a remarkable vision of Italian political unity long before it became a reality.

BIBLIOGRAPHY

Anthologies containing works by Aurelia Petrucci:
Bergalli, *op. cit.*
de Blasi, *op. cit.*
Rime di cinquanta illustri poetesse. Naples: Bulifon, 1695.
Rime diverse d'alcune nobilissime et virtuosissime donne. Ed. L. Domenichi.
    Lucca: Busdrago, 1559.

Studies and other works:
Enciclopedia biografica bibliografica italiana, op. cit.

Dove sta il tuo valor, Patria mia cara,
poichè il giogo servil misera scordi
e solo nutri in sen pensier discordi,
prodiga del tuo mal, del bene avara?

All'altrui spese, poco accorta, impara   5
che fa la civil gara, e in te rimordi
gli animi falsi e rei, fatti concordi
a tuo sol danno e a servitute amara.

Fa' delle membra sparse un corpo solo,
ed un giusto voler sia legge a tutti,   10
che allor io ti dirò di valor degna.

Così tem'io, anzi vegg'io, che in duolo
vivrai, misera, ognor piena di lutti:
che così avvien dove discordia regna.

Where is your valor, my belovèd country,
Since you ignore your wretched servile yoke
And nourish in your breast discordant thoughts,
Prodigal of your ill, sparing of good?
At others' hands[1] unthinkingly you learn   5
What civil war can do, and should reject
The false and evil souls who band together
To bring you harm and bitter servitude.
Make of your scattered limbs one single body,[2]
And may one upright will be law for all,   10
Then I will call you worthy of all valor.
And yet I fear, indeed I see, that sorrow
Will be your life, filled with eternal mourning,
Which is the case wherever discord reigns.

1. The author is writing at the time of the invasions of Italy by Spain and France. 2. At a time in which Italy was divided into many independent and often hostile states, this author was prophetically aware of the necessity for Italian unification, which finally happened in 1860. Of course, this follows a poetic tradition that stems from Dante through Petrarch, etc.

LEONORA RAVOIRA (OR RAVIRA) FALLETTI
(Sixteenth Century)

Leonora Ravoira (or Ravira) Falletti, Princess of Melazzo in Monferrato, flourished during the sixteenth century. Biographers disagree as to whether she lived in the early or late part of the century. Some critics, including Luisa Bergalli, believed her to be from Savona, in Liguria; others believed she was from Casale Monferrato. She married Giorgio Falletti.

The critic Alberti believed Leonora Falletti and Leonora Rivoira to be two different people, without offering justification for his hypothesis. According to Luisa Bergalli, her *Rime* were published in 1519, whereas according to Della Chiesa, the date was around 1565. Maria Bandini Buti reports that she was highly praised by the *literati* Luca Contile and by Giuseppe Betussi. The latter dedicated to her his book *L'immagine della virtù* (The image of virtue). Leonora gratefully addressed him a sonnet.

She published her rhymes late in life under the title *Conversione a Dio* (Conversion to God). The sonnet we present here is an eloquent and impassionate denunciation of the foreign invasions of Charles V and Francis I, and of the disastrous effects of such wars on the Italian land.

We have taken our Italian text from the de Blasi anthology.

BIBLIOGRAPHY

Anthologies containing works by Leonora Ravira Falletti:
Antologia di poetesse italiane del secolo decimosesto. Ed. A. De Gubernatis. Florence: Arte della Stampa, 1883.
Bergalli, *op. cit.*
de Blasi, *op. cit.*
Rime di cinquanta illustri poetesse. Naples: Bulifon, 1695.
Rime diverse. Ed. L. Domenichi. Lucca: Busdrago, 1559.

Studies and other works:
Enciclopedia biografica bibliografica italiana, op. cit.

Che colpa han nostri sfortunati tetti,
gli antichi abitatori e il fertil piano,
de l'ostinato e rio desir insano
chiuso, per altro, in due sì chiari petti?

Fûr da' nostri avi questi nidi eletti,   5
senza onorar più Cesare che Giano,
ed or convien ch'al Franco ed all'Ispano
siamo, miseri noi, servi e soggetti.

Si terminasse almen la dura impresa
che passa il quarto lustro e più rinforza,   10
acciò un sol giogo ci tenesse avvinti.

Che così temo, e 'l mio timor non erra,
ch'i patrii lari abbandonar fia forza,
o che sarem da lunga fame vinti.

What fault is there in our unhappy homes,
Their old inhabitants, or the rich plain[1]
That such self-willed, evil, mad desires
Are closed within those two illustrious breasts?[2]
Here in days past our fathers chose these hearths —   5
Without revering Caesar more than Janus[3] —
Now we, most miserable, must be slaves
Either of the French or of the Spaniards.
At least if this hard enterprise[4] were ended,
Which has endured for more than twenty years,   10
While it grows ever fiercer all this time,
We should be subject to one yoke alone.
This makes me fear — my fear is not mistaken —
That we must leave behind our household gods,[5]
And in the end we shall be slain by hunger.   15

1. The fertile Po Valley in Northern Italy. 2. Francis I of France and Charles
V of the Holy Roman Empire, at this time fighting for supremacy in Italy.
3. The meaning is somewhat obscure — perhaps war or peace? — Caesar,
the great general, and Janus, the god of entrances and exits, whose temple
was closed in time of peace. 4. The long war between France and Spain,
culminating in the battle of Pavia, 1525. 5. Literally, "Lares," the household
gods of the Romans.

VITTORIA COLONNA
(1492-1547)

Vittoria Colonna is the epitome of the great lady poet of the Renaissance, combining nobility, grace, learning, and lofty intellect. She was born in Marino in 1492 (although this date is not certain), on the Alban hills near Rome, of the illustrious family of the Colonna princes.

In 1509, she was married to Ferrante Francesco d'Avalos, Marquis of Pescara, to whom she had been betrothed since the age of three. This desirable political match solidified the family's ties with the Neapolitan rulers. Brief periods of happiness with her husband were spent at their castle on the island of Ischia, times which she would later remember fondly in her poetry. Since Ferrante was in the service of the Emperor Charles V, then at war with Francis I of France, he did not remain long at her side. In 1512, the Marquis was taken prisoner after the battle of Ravenna (see *My highest Lord, I am writing this letter...*). He was one of Charles V's most important military leaders and died of wounds received in the battle of Pavia in 1525, during which Francis I was taken prisoner. After his death, Vittoria led a semi-monastic life in the remembrance of past happiness. The marriage was childless, and Colonna raised her husband's orphaned cousin, Alfonso del Vasto, as their heir.

Although her family urged her to remarry, she devoted herself instead to scholarship, religious reform and pious works. Profoundly religious by nature, she became even more so in widowhood. On some moral issues, she held views similar to those of the Counter-Reformation religious reformers Ochino and Valdès, and took an active part in the evangelic movement designed to purify and renew Catholicism. Her friendship with Ochino led the Inquisition to investigate her beliefs, saddening her final years.

As witnessed by her voluminous correspondence, she had close literary friendships with many prominent writers and scholars of her age, among whom were Bembo, Aretino, Castiglione, Molza, Ariosto and others. She played a great role in the intellectual, social and political life of her time, inspiring many artists. Galeazzo di Tarsia, one of the greatest lyric poets of the Renaissance, deeply respected her and dedicated to her his *Canzoniere.* Her life as a widow was enriched by a deep Platonic friendship (starting around 1530) with Michelangelo, who felt great love and admiration for her. For her, especially after her death, the sculptor wrote some of his most powerful verses, acknowledging her as his literary and spiritual guide. It is interesting to note that Michelangelo often referred to her in the masculine gender (as in *Morte m'ha tolto un grande amico*), possibly intending to compliment her on her intellect and "masculine" fortitude.

In *The Lives of the Painters,* Vasari wrote: "Michelangelo sent a vast number of poems by his own hand, receiving answers in rhyme and in prose, to the most illustrious Marchionness of Pescara, of whose virtues he was enamored and she likewise of his; and she went many times to visit him, and Michelangelo designed for her a dead Christ in the lap of Our Lady, with two little angels, all most admirable, and a Christ fixed on the cross, who, with the head uplifted, is recommending his spirit to the Father, a divine work..." The historian Condivi also wrote about their relationship in his *Life of Michelangelo,* describing at great length Vittoria's death in the convent of the Benedettine di Sant' Anna in Rome, in which she expired, attended by the grieving artist. She had been suffering from a debilitating illness from 1543 until her death in 1547.

Ariosto, in the *Orlando Furioso,* hailed her as the most illustrious woman of her time:

> She is Vittoria and justly crowned
> As one to victory and triumph born.
> Where e'er she walks, the laurel leaves abound
> And diadems of fame her brow adorn.
> Like Artemisia, lauded and renowned,
> Who her Mausolus never ceased to mourn,
> She is a yet more pious, loving wife:
> She gives her spouse not burial, but life.
>
> (*Orlando Furioso,* XXXVII, translated by Barbara Reynolds)

Vittoria Colonna's features appear to us in a portrait of her by Girolamo Muziano, painted after her death, now in the Colonna Palace in Rome. Some critics also believe that Veronese depicted her as the Virgin in his *Marriage at Cana,* now in the Louvre. Moreover she may have been depicted by Michelangelo in the Final Judgement in the Sistine Chapel, as one of the women next to Mary.

Before her husband's death, Vittoria wrote very little, and only the Epistle in *terza rima* written in 1512 to her husband survives from this period. This extraordinary poetic letter, of which we present only excerpts, is Colonna's most personal statement, in which she expresses the pain and anguish of the separation caused by war, speaking for herself as well as for all Italian women. These feelings were later expressed in sonnet XXIX, addressed to the Emperor Charles V and King Francis I of France, exhorting them to settle the wars that were tearing Italy apart.

Colonna's lyric poetry is essentially Petrarchist, and her style is complex, intellectual and replete with many unusual conceits and rhetorical figures for which she was greatly admired. Her poetry (and especially her religious poetry) is imbued with Neoplatonism, a philosophy giving a Christian interpretation to Plato's doctrines. In her times, and for several centuries afterwards, she was regarded as Italy's greatest woman poet. To the modern reader, however, she may sound too logical and distant, though one cannot fail to admire her intelligence as well as her moral courage and religious zeal.

Colonna was a modest woman who did not seek recognition for her writing. Admirers read her work in manuscript form as she did not permit publication for many years. Her poetry was printed for the first time in 1538, without her involvement; in fact, she never personally edited any of the editions of her work. Her poetry was greatly admired, to the extent that twenty editions came out in the sixteenth century alone. Among these editions, one of the best is the 1558 *Rime* edited by Rinaldo Corso. In 1760 Giambattista Rota published her complete *Rime* in one volume for the first time. In 1830, P.E. Visconti published an edition which was considered the best before the excellent 1982 Bullock critical edition. We have followed the Bullock edition for the original text and the numbering of the poems that we present here.

Bullock divides the entire corpus of Colonna's poetry (approximately four hundred poems) into *Rime Amorose* (love lyrics), written for her dead husband; *Rime Spirituali* (spiritual lyrics); and *Rime Epistolari* (poetic letters to friends and occasional poetry). In her love lyrics, of which we have translated a few, Colonna presents an idealized portrait of the Marquis of Pescara, recollecting the happy times spent together. In her spiritual poems, regarded as her best, Colonna expresses her deep faith and her concerns about the corruption of the Church (See *If it rained gold and silver...*), voicing the need for reform in terms that make her sound at times very close to the ideas of Protestant reformers.

BIBLIOGRAPHY

Works by Vittoria Colonna:
Rime della diva Vittoria Colonna da Pescara. Venice: per Bartolomeo detto l'Imperador, 1544.
Rime. Ed. Lodovico Dolce.Venice: Giolito, 1552.
Rime. Ed. G.E. Saltini. Florence: Barbèra, 1860.
Carteggio. Ed. Ermanno Ferrero, Domenico Tondi and Giuseppe Muller. Turin: Loescher, 1892.
Rime. Ed. Alan Bullock. Rome and Bari: Laterza, 1982.

Anthologies containing works by Vittoria Colonna:
Costa-Zalessow, *op. cit.*
de Blasi, *op. cit.*
De' Lucchi, Lorna. *An Anthology of Italian Poems. 13th-19th Century.* New York: Biblio & Tannen, 1922, 1967.
Le più belle pagine di Gaspara Stampa, Vittoria Colonna, Veronica Gambara, Isabella di Morra. Ed. Giuseppe Toffanin. Milan: Treves, 1935.
Lettere del Cinquecento, op. cit., 343-353.
Lirici del Cinquecento, op.cit., 381-392.
Poesia del Quattrocento e del Cinquecento, op. cit., 1301-1309.
Rime di tre gentildonne del secolo XVI. Ed. Olindo Guerrini. Milan: Sonzogno, 1882, 17-175.

Studies and other works:

Bainton, Roland H. "Vittoria Colonna." In *Women of the Reformation in Germany and Italy.* Minneapolis: Augsburg, 1971, 201-18.

Bassanese, Fiora A. "Vittoria Colonna." In *Italian Woman Writers, op. cit.,* 84-94.

Bellonci, G. "La religione di Vittoria Colonna." In *Pagine e idee.* Rome: Sapientia, 1929.

Dizionario enciclopedico, op.cit., 88-89.

Gibaldi, Joseph. "Vittoria Colonna: Child, Woman and Poet." In *Women Writers of the Renaissance and Reformation.* Ed. Katharina M. Wilson. Athens, GA: University of Georgia Press, 1987, 22-46.

Greco, A. "Vittoria Colonna." In *Letteratura italiana - I minori,* II. Milan: Marzorati, 1961.

Jung, E.M. "Vittoria Colonna: Between Reformation and Counter-Reformation." *Review of Religion* 15 (1950-1951): 144-59.

Macchia, G. "Quattro Poetesse del Cinquecento." *Rivista rosminiana* XXXI (1937): 2.

Mollaretti Nobbio, Raffaela. *Vittoria Colonna e Michelangelo: nel V centenario della sua nascita: 1490-1990.* Florence: Firenze Libri, 1990.

Reumont, A. *Vittoria Colonna marchesa di Pescara. Vita, fede, e poesia nel secolo XVI.* Turin: Loescher, 1883.

Russell, Rinaldina. "The mind's Pursuit of the Divine. A Survey of Secular and Religious Themes in Vittoria Colonna's Sonnets." *Forum Italicum* 26,1 (1992): 14-27.

Tordi, D. *Il codice delle rime di Vittoria Colonna appartenenti a Margherita d'Angoulême.* Flori: Pistoia, 1900.

Tusiani, Joseph. *Italian Poets of the Renaissance.* Long Island City, N.Y.: Baroque Press, 1971.

RIME AMOROSE 1

Scrivo sol per sfogar l'interna doglia
ch'al cor mandar le luci al mondo sole,
e non per giunger lume al mio bel Sole,
al chiaro spirto e a l'onorata spoglia.

Giusta cagion a lamentar m'invoglia;   5
ch'io scemi la sua gloria assai mi dole;
per altra tromba e più sagge parole
convien ch'a morte il gran nome si toglia.

La pura fe', l'ardor, l'intensa pena
mi scusi appo ciascun; ché 'l grave pianto   10
è tal che tempo né ragion l'affrena.

Amaro lacrimar, non dolce canto,
foschi sospiri e non voce serena,
di stil no ma di duol mi danno vanto.

3

Nudriva il cor d'una speranza viva
fondata e colta in sì nobil terreno
che 'l frutto promettea giocondo e ameno;
morte la svelse alor ch'ella fioriva.

Giunser insieme i bei pensier a riva,   5
mutossi in notte oscura il dì sereno
e 'l nettar dolce in aspero veleno;
sol la memoria nel dolor s'aviva.

Ond'io d'interno ardor sovente avampo;
parmi udir l'alto suon de le parole   10
giunger concento a l'armonia celeste,

e veggio il fulgorar del chiaro lampo
che dentro il mio pensiero avanza il sole.
Che fia vederlo fuor d'umana veste?

Stortoni & Lillie

1

I write only to ease the inner sorrow
  On which my heart feeds, wishing nothing more —
  Not to add light to my belovèd sun[1]
  Who left behind on earth such honored spoils.
Reason enough have I for these laments —   5
  Although I greatly fear to scant his glory.
  Some better pen, perhaps, with wiser words
  May come to raise his great name from the grave.
Pure faith, warm ardor, and consuming pain
  Be my excuse to all the world, to write,   10
  For neither time nor reason can withhold me.
Thus, bitter weeping, not delightful song,
  Dark sighs, and no serene melodious voice —
  Not style, but grief alone, give me the praise.

3

I nourished in my heart a lively hope
Gathered in a happy, noble land,
Which promised crops of sweet and pleasant fruit.[2]
But Death uprooted it while still in bloom.
The well-loved shore has vanished from my thoughts,   5
The tranquil day is changed to darkest night,
Sweet nectar was transformed to bitter poison:
Thus, I become deprived of all my joy.
The blow[3] which tore apart the sacred bond —
Twisting together both our lives in one —   10
Destroyed action in him, feeling in me.
That lovely light[4] now welcomed in high heaven
Was, first and last, beacon of my desire,
And here on earth outshone all other lights.

1. Her late husband, the Marquis of Pescara. In these poems the image "sun"
refers to the writer's husband (or lover) when not capitalized. Capitalized,
it refers to God. 2. Colonna is referring to her husband's untimely death,
which left her widowed and without children. 3. Death. 4. Again, her
dead husband.

9

Oh che tranquillo mar, che placide onde
solcavo un tempo in ben spalmata barca!
Di bei presidi e d'util merce carca
l'aer sereno avea, l'aure seconde;
   il ciel, ch'or suoi benigni lumi asconde,   5
dava luce di nubi e d'ombre scarca;
non de' creder alcun che sicur varca
mentre al principio il fin non corrisponde.
   L'aversa stella mia, l'empia fortuna
scoverser poi l'irate inique fronti   10
dal cui furor cruda procella insorge;
   venti piogge, saette il ciel aduna,
mostri d'intorno a divorarmi pronti,
ma l'alma ancor sua tramontana scorge.

19

Quanti dolci pensieri, alti desiri,
nudriva in me quel Sol che d'ogn'intorno
sgombrò le nubi e fe' qui chiaro giorno
mentre appagò sua vista i mie' martiri!
   Soave il lacrimar, grati i sospiri   5
mi rendea il sereno sguardo adorno,
mio vago lume e mio sì bel soggiorno
ch'or scorgo tenebroso ovunque io miri.
   Veggio spento il valor, morte o smarrite
l'alme virtuti, e le più nobil menti   10
per il danno commun meste e confuse.
   Al suo sparir dal mondo son fuggite
di quell'antico onor le voglie ardenti,
e le mie d'ogni ben per sempre excluse.

9

O, what a tranquil sea, what shining waves
My polished bark used formerly to plough,
Adorned and laden with so rich a cargo
In the pure air and with a favoring breeze![1]
Heaven, which now conceals his[2] loving eyes,   5
Then offered light, serene and free from shadows.
Alas, how much should carefree travellers fear!
The end may not reflect a fair beginning.
Behold, how cruel and inconstant Fortune
Bared her iniquitous and angry brow   10
Out of whose rage a mighty tempest rose.
She gathered winds and rains and lightning flashes
And evil monsters eager to devour me.
But my soul still perceives her faithful star.[3]

19

How many loving thoughts, what high desires
My heart was fed by that most noble sun[4]
Who scattered all the clouds till daylight shone.
Now all is dark wherever I may turn.
Sweet were the tears and pleasing were the sights   5
Inspired in me by this brief sojourn:
Wise words were his: and when on me he turned
His eyes, they calmed, in part, my martyr's fires.[5]
Now I see valor quenched, virtue destroyed,
Which once was loved, and many noble minds   10
Bewildered, grieving over this great loss.
Since his departure every soul is void
Of antique love for honor; in my mind
Banished forever all its former joys.

1. The sea around the island of Ischia, where she lived for some time
with her husband. 2. Referring to her dead husband. 3. Again, her dead
husband. 4. Her dead husband. 5. Her suffering when he was about to
leave for war.

45

   Amor, tu sai che già mai torsi il piede
dal carcer tuo soave, né disciolsi
dal dolce giogo il collo, né ti tolsi
quanto dal primo dì l'alma ti diede;
   tempo non cangiò mai l'antica fede;   5
il nodo è stretto ancor com'io l'avolsi;
né per il frutto amar ch'ognor ne colsi
l'alta cagion men cara al cor mi riede.
   Vist'hai quanto in un petto fido e ardente
può oprar quel caro tuo più acuto dardo,   10
contra del cui poter Morte non valse.
   Fa' omai da te che 'l nodo si rallente,
ch'a me di libertà già mai non calse;
anzi, di ricovrarla or mi par tardo.

53

   Provo tra duri scogli e fiero vento
l'onde di questa vita in fragil legno;
l'alto presidio e 'l mio fido sostegno
tolse l'acerba morte in un momento.
   Veggio il mio male e 'l mio rimedio spento,   5
il mar turbato e l'aer d'ira pregno,
d'atra tempesta un infallibil segno,
e 'l valor proprio al mio soccorso lento.
   Non ch'io sommerga in le commosse arene
temo, né rompa in perigliose sponde,   10
ma duolmi il navigar priva di spene.
   Almen se morte il ver porto m'asconde,
mostrimi il falso suo, ché chiare e amene
ne parran le sue irate e turbide onde.

45

O Love, you know I never moved my foot
From your dear prison, nor have I unbound
My neck from your sweet yoke, nor taken back
Anything that my soul first gave to you.
Time has not changed my faithfulness of old, 5
The knot I tied is just as firm as ever;
Nor, from the bitter fruit I since have plucked,
Is my high cause¹ less precious to my heart.
You see what fire the sharpest of your darts
Can light within a faithful, ardent breast, 10
A flame death never can avail to quench.
Now loosen, if you can, the knot you tied,
For liberty was never my concern.
The time for its retying seems too slow.

53

Between harsh rocks and violent wind I feel
The waves of life striking my fragile bark
Which I have neither wit nor art to steer;
All help will come too late to save me now.
In one brief moment bitter death extinguished 5
The lodestar of my life, my constant guide;
I have no help against the turbulent sea
And threatening clouds. Now ever more I fear,
Not the sweet singing of the cruel sirens,
Nor shipwreck here between these lofty cliffs, 10
Nor sinking helplessly in shifting sands,
But to sail on forever in rough waters,
Cutting my furrow with no gleam of hope;
For death conceals from me my sheltering port.

1. Her love for her dead husband.

73

Quant'io di vivo avea nei sensi acerba
morte in un giorno col mio Sol mi tolse,
ma lui d'affanno e me d'error disciolse;
non vivo io qui, lui miglior parte or serba.
   Per me i frutti del mondo sempre in erba   5
veggio, né fronde pur unqua ne colse
l'alma, da l'or ch'i suo' pensier raccolse
in sé e se stessa in lor chiusa riserba
    per colui che si fe' morendo vivo,
e me fa viver morta; ch'ei dal Cielo   10
fuor di me tienmi, e solo in lui m'appago,
    e mentre il viver mio raccolto e schivo
scorge ei, col fren in man del mortal velo,
sent'io lo spirto suo del mio amor vago.

89

   Mentre la nave mia, lungi dal porto,
priva del suo nocchier che vive in Cielo,
fugge l'onde turbate in questo scoglio,
per dar al lungo mal breve conforto
vorrei narrar con puro acceso zelo   5
parte de la cagion ond'io mi doglio,
e di quelle il martir che da l'orgoglio
di nimica Fortuna e d'Amor empio
ebber più chiaro nome e maggior danno
col mio più grave affanno   10
paragonar, acciò che 'l duro scempio
conosca il mondo non aver exempio.
   Penelope e Laodamia un casto ardente
pensier mi rappresenta, e veggio l'una

73

Whatever life I once had in my senses
Bitter death[1] seized on one day, with my sun,
Delivering him of care and me of error;
I live no more; his better part heaven holds.
For me, I feel the fruits of earth as grass —   5
My soul could never gather even leaves —
And when she recollects his former thoughts
She keeps herself enclosed within their bounds.
Because he made himself alive[2] by dying,
He made me dead, alive, and still from heaven   10
Keeps me from self, content only with him.
And, while he sees my life withdrawn and fearful,
Holding a bridle on my mortal flesh,
I feel his spirit still desires my love.

89

To give my long distress some fleeting comfort
    While my sad ship, alas, far from its port,
    Without its pilot,[3] who now lives in heaven,
    Flees from the turbulent waves of this great rock,
    I wish to tell, with pure and burning zeal,   5
    Part of the reason why I so lament,
    And see whether the weight of those whose value,
    Raised to so high a pitch by pride of Fortune,
    Equals my mortal and acute distress
    And see if greater sorrow   10
    Steals from these others their delight and freedom,
    Or if I am unique on earth in torment.
Penelope and Laodamia,[3] a chaste
    And ardent thought brings to my mind. I see

1. Her husband, the Marquis of Pescara, who died an untimely death.
2. His death and his deeds have made him immortal. 3. Vittoria's dead
husband. 3. Penelope, wife of Ulysses, eventually with him; Laodamia,

aspettar molto in dolorose tempre,   15
e l'altra aver, con le speranze spente,
il desir vivo, e d'ogni ben digiuna
convenirle di mal nudrirsi sempre;
ma par la speme a quella il duol contempre,
quest'il fin lieto fa beata, ond'io   20
non veggio il danno lor mostrarsi eterno,
e 'l mio tormento interno
sperar non fa minor, né toglie oblio,
ma col tempo il duol cresce, arde il desio.

    Aräanna e Medea, dogliose erranti,   25
odo di molto ardir, di poca fede
dolersi, invan biasmando il proprio errore;
ma se d'un tal servir da tali amanti
fu il guiderdone d'aspra e ria mercede
disdegno e crudeltà tolse il dolore;   30
e 'l mio bel Sol ognor pena ed ardore
manda dal Ciel coi rai nel miser petto,
di fiamma oggi e di fede albergo vero;
né sdegno unqua il pensero,
né speranza o timor, pena o diletto   35
volse dal primo mio divino obietto.

    Porzia sovra d'ogn'altra me rivolse
tant'al suo danno che sovente inseme
piansi l'acerbo martir nostro equale;
ma parmi il tempo che costei si dolse   40
quasi un breve sospir; con poca speme
d'altra vita miglior le diede altr'ale;
e nel mio cor dolor vivo e mortale
siede mai sempre, e de l'alma serena
vita immortal questa speranza toglie   45

-----

wife of Protesilaus, who was slain at Troy, whom the gods allowed to see
her husband alive for three hours after his death, and then go with him
to Hades.

The one who waits so long in bitter straits,   15
The other who, with all her hopes destroyed,
Desire still living, starved of every good,
Must feed forever on nothing but evil.
But since hope tempers sorrow to the one,
The other finds a happy end to bless her,   20
I do not find their misery eternal.
Whereas my inner torment
Hope does not soften, nor oblivion end;
With passing time my grief and longing grow.
Ariadne and Medea,[1] mournful wanderers,   25
    I hear lamenting both their lovers' courage
    And want of faith, blaming themselves in vain.
    But if the fickle Fates and faithless lovers
    Gave them harsh recompense for their true service,
    Disdain and cruelty removed their grief,   30
    While my fair sun sends down on me from heaven
    Continual pain and ardor to my bosom,
    True shelter of my flaming love and faith.
    My thoughts hold no disdain;
    Never have hope or fear, delight or pain   35
    Moved me away from my first holy love.
Portia[2] above all others turned my mind
    So much to her distress, that with her, often,
    I mourned our sufferings, so great, so equal.
    But, if perhaps she mourned so short a time   40
    While I forever mourn, her lack of hope
    For any better life, gave her new wings,
    But my great load of grief, live and immortal,
    Stays in my heart, because my living faith
    In a serene, eternal life, removes   45

1. Both women were deserted by their lovers, whom they aided in their adventures — Ariadne could "disdain" Theseus, since she was loved by Dionysus after being deserted; while Medea took cruel vengeance on Jason and their children when he deserted her. 2. Wife of Marcus Junius

forza a l'ardite voglie;
né pur sol il timor d'eterna pena,
ma 'l gir lungi al mio Sol la man raffrena.

    Exempi poi di veri e falsi amori
ir ne veggio mill'altri in varia schiera,   50
ch'al miglior tempo lor fuggì la spene;
ma basti vincer quest'alti e maggiori,
ché pareggiar a quei mia fiamma altera
forse sdegna quel Sol che la sostiene,
ché quante io leggo indegne o giuste pene,   55
da mobil fede o impetüosa morte
tutte spente le scorgo in tempo breve;
animo fiero o leve
aperse al sdegno od al furor le porte,
e fe' le vite a lor dogliose e corte.   60

    Onde a che volger più l'antiche carti
de' mali altrui, né far de l'infelice
schiera moderna paragon ancora,
se 'nferïor ne l'altre chiare parti,
e 'n questa del dolor quasi fenice   65
mi veggio rinovar nel foco ognora?
Perché 'l mio vivo Sol dentro innamora
l'anima accesa, e la copre e rinforza
d'un schermo tal che minor luce sdegna,
e su dal Ciel l'insegna   70
d'amar e sofferir, ond'ella a forza
in sì gran mal sostien quest'umil scorza.

    Canzon, fra' vivi qui fuor di speranza
va' sola, e di' ch'avanza
mia pena ogn'altra, e la cagion può tanto   75
che m' è nettar il foco, ambrosia il pianto.

Brutus, committed suicide when she heard of his death, for she had no
fear of eternal punishment.

Force from a daring will,
Nor does the fear of endless pain restrain me
I only fear to lose my heaven's sun.[1]
Then I see, with true love or false aflame,
A thousand more pass by in varied throngs   50
Who have lost hope for any happy life.
Enough for me to conquer these great souls!
For, to compare them with my higher flame,
The sun[2] who feeds it might regard with scorn.
What I have read of pains, just or unjust,   55
Of wavering faith or else impetuous death,
I see extinguished in but little time.
Proud souls or lighter ones
Opened the gate to fury or disgrace,
Cutting their life-spans short, just as they willed.   60
Why should I, then, turn over these old pages
Of others' ills, making comparisons
Of these unhappy ones with modern cases?
If I am less than they in brilliant fame,
Or in the pitch of grief, now like the Phoenix   65
I feel myself ever renewed in ardor
Because my living sun keeps love alive
Within my burning heart, and covers it
With such a shield that it scorns lesser light,
And from the sky instructs me   70
To love and to endure, giving me strength
To bear my humble life in such great sorrow.
Song, go alone to greet all hopeless souls,
And say my pain surpasses
All others, but its cause is so tremendous   75
It makes fire nectar, tears ambrosia.

1. Vittoria on the other hand, believing in life after death, could not do as Portia did, for fear of not rejoining her husband if she were condemned to hell for suicide; hence her lack of Portia's daring. 2. Colonna's husband, her "sun," the marquis of Pescara.

RIME AMOROSE DISPERSE
LETTERA A FERRANTE FRANCESCO D'AVALOS, SUO CONSORTE,
DOPO LA BATTAGLIA DI RAVENNA

Excelso mio Signor, questa ti scrivo
per te narrar fra quante dubbie voglie,
fra quanti aspri martir dogliosa io vivo....
    Altri chiedevan guerra; io sempre pace,
dicendo: assai mi fia se 'l mio Marchese   5
meco quïeto nel suo stato giace.
    Non noce a voi seguir le dubbie imprese,
m'a noi, dogliose, afflitte, ch'aspettando
semo da dubbio e da timore offese;
    voi, spinti dal furor, non ripensando   10
ad altro ch'ad onor, contr'il periglio
solete con gran furia andar gridando.
    Noi timide nel cor, meste nel ciglio
semo per voi; e la sorella il fratre,
la sposa il sposo vuol, la madre il figlio;   15
    ma io, misera! cerco e sposo e patre
e frate e figlio; sono in questo loco
sposa, figlia, sorella e vecchia matre....
    Tu vivi lieto, e non hai doglia alcuna,
ché, pensando di fama il novo acquisto,   20
non curi farmi del tuo amor digiuna;
    ma io, con volto disdegnoso e tristo,
serbo il tuo letto abbandonato e solo,
tenendo con la speme il dolor misto,
    e col vostro gioir tempr'il mio duolo.   25

LETTER TO FERRANTE FRANCESCO D'AVALOS, COLONNA'S
HUSBAND, AFTER THE BATTLE OF RAVENNA (EXCERPTS)

My highest Lord, I am writing this letter
to tell you in what sadness I exist,
torn among doubt and loneliness and pain....
    When others asked for war, I called for peace,
sufficing me that my belovèd Marquis   5
should dwell with me content and satisfied.
    Risky endeavors of war do not harm men;
but we women — afflicted and forsaken —
are hurt by fear and anxious care alike.
    Compelled by your belligerence, you think   10
only of honor, and with loud war cries
you rush straight into the perils of battle.
    But left behind, we, fearful and sad,
worry for you: the sister wants the brother,
the bride the bridegroom, and the mother her son.   15
    Wretchedly lonely, I long for my husband,
for my father and son: I am at once
spouse, daughter, sister and aging mother....
    Independent you live, devoid of cares
and thinking only to gain fame and acclaim —   20
you do not care if I yearn for your love.
    My face darkened by sadness and disdain,
I lie alone in a forsaken bed,
feeling hope intertwined with bitter pain,
    and tempering my sorrows with your joy.   25

RIME SPIRITUALI 4

S'in man prender non soglio unqua la lima
del buon giudicio, e, ricercando intorno
con occhio disdegnoso, io non adorno
né tergo la mia rozza incolta rima,
    nasce perché non è mia cura prima   5
procacciar di ciò lode, o fuggir scorno,
né che, dopo il mio lieto al Ciel ritorno,
viva ella al mondo in più onorata stima;
    ma dal foco divin, che 'l mio intelletto,
sua mercé, infiamma, convien ch'escan fore   10
mal mio grado talor queste faville;
    e s'alcuna di lor un gentil core
avien che scaldi mille volte e mille
ringraziar debbo il mio felice errore.

33

Vedremmo, se piovesse argento ed oro,
ir, con le mani pronte e i grembi aperti,
color che son de l'altra vita incerti
a raccor lieti il vil breve tesoro,
    e sì cieco guadagno e van lavoro   5
esser più caro a quei che son più esperti,
ché le ricchezze danno e non i merti
oggi le chiare palme e 'l verde alloro.
    Ma non si corre a Dio, che dal Ciel porta
dentro la piaga del Suo dextro lato   10
d'infinito tesor perpetua pioggia,
    e se spirito alcun Gli apre la porta
dicon che inganna il mondo, o ch' è ingannato
dal suo pensier, che troppo in alto poggia.

4

If I too seldom take in hand the file
Of sober judgment, and searching around
With haughty eye, do not put forth the pains
To beautify and polish my rough rhymes,
This is because my prime concern is not   5
To seek for praise or to escape from scorn,
Nor that, when I have fled, joyful to heaven,
My verse should live on earth with high regard.
If from the holy fire, that lights my mind
By grace of God, there should come forth such sparks   10
Almost despite myself, that later may
Perchance bring warmth to gentle loving hearts,
Who turn to reading them one day — a thousand
And thousand times I'll thank my happy error.

33[1]

If it rained gold and silver, we would see
Those who lack faith in any future life
Going around with eager hands, and laps
Open to gather in the vile, brief treasure,
And see that empty gain and worthless labor   5
Are much more dear to the most learnèd, even;
For riches, and not merit, nowadays,
Confer the shining palm and the green laurel.
Men do not run to God, Who from the heavens
Carries within the wound on His right side   10
Infinite bounty of perpetual treasure.
If anyone opens the door to Him,
People today will say he cheats the world,
Or is deceived, setting his thoughts too high.

1. This sonnet is against the corruption of the Rome of her days.

46

Qual digiuno augellin, che vede ed ode
batter l'ali a la madre intorno quando
li reca il nudrimento, ond'egli amando
il cibo e quella si rallegra e gode,
    e dentro al nido suo si strugge e rode   5
per desio di seguirla anch'ei volando,
e la ringrazia, in tal modo cantando
che par ch'oltra il poter la lingua snode;
    tal io, qualor il caldo raggio e vivo
del divin Sole onde nudrisco il core   10
più de l'usato lucido lampeggia,
    movo la penna, mossa da l'amore
interno, e senza ch'io stessa m'aveggia
di quel ch'io dico le Sue lodi scrivo.

64

In forma di musaico un alto muro
d'animate scintille alate e preste,
con catene d'amor sì ben conteste
che l'una porge a l'altra il lume puro,
    senza ombra che vi formi il chiaro e scuro   5
ma pur vivo splendor del Sol celeste
che le adorna, incolora, ordina e veste,
d'intorno a Dio col mio pensier figuro;
    e Quella, poi, che in velo uman per gloria
seconda onora il Ciel, più presso al vero   10
lume del Figlio ed a la Luce prima,
    la cui beltà non mai vivo pensero
ombrar poteo, non che ritrar memoria
in carte, e men lodarla ingegno in rima.

46

As a starved little bird, who sees and hears
His mother's wings fluttering round about him
To bring him food, whose heart is filled with love
Both for her and the food, who then, rejoicing
— Though in the nest he pines and is consumed   5
With eagerness to follow her and fly —
Will thank her by his singing, far beyond
His usual power of song, with tongue set free,
So I, whenever the warm living rays
Of the divine Sun,[1] nourishing my heart,   10
Will shine on me with unaccustomed brightness,
Take up my pen, impelled by inner love;
Without quite knowing what it is I say,
As best I can, I write His praises down.

64

Like a mosaic on a lofty wall,
I see in my mind's eye, surrounding God,
A mass of living sparks, wingèd and swift,
So strongly interwoven with love's chains
That each shines on the other with pure light   5
Without a shade to set off bright from dark,
But live reflections of the heavenly Sun[2]
Who colors, clothes, adorns, and orders them;
And her[3] I see, whom still in human veil[4]
Heaven honors with a glory second only   10
To the true gleam of the Son, and the First Light,
Whose beauty never can a living mind
Aspire to sketch, nor memory recall
On paper, much less fairly praise in rhyme.

1. God. 2. God. 3. The Virgin Mary. 4. Colonna believed that while still
alive Mary was raised up bodily to heaven.

RIME SPIRITUALI DISPERSE 8

Qual edera a cui sono e rotti ed arsi
gli usati suoi sostegni, onde ritira
il vigor dentro e intorno si raggira,
né cosa trova u' possa in alto alzarsi;
    tal l'alma ch'ha i pensier qui in terra sparsi   5
sempre s'avolge fuor, dentro s'adira,
perch'al bel segno, u' per natura aspira,
sono gli appoggi umani e bassi e scarsi
    mentre non corre al glorïoso legno
de la nostra salute, ove erga e annodi   10
le sue radici infin a l'alta cima;
    avolta, unita a quel sacro sostegno,
vuol rivederla il Padre, ove Egli in prima
l'avea legata con sì dolci nodi.

RIME EPISTOLARI 13

Di novo il Cielo de l'antica gloria
orna la nostra etate, e sua ruina
prescrive, poscia che fra noi destina
spirto ch'ha di beltà doppia vittoria.
    Di voi, ben degna d'immortal istoria,   5
bella donna, ragiono, a cui s'inchina
chi più di bello ottiene, e la divina
interna parte vince ogni memoria.
    Faranvi i chiari spirti eterno tempio,
la carta il marmo fia, l'inchiostro l'oro,   10
ché 'l ver constringe lor sempre a lodarvi.
    Morte col primo, o col secondo ed empio
morso il tempo, non ponno omai levarvi
d'immortal fama il bel ricco tesoro.

8

Like ivy, whose supports are burned and broken,
From which it used to draw its inner strength,
Now turning on itself in futile circles —
For it finds nothing which can raise it up —
Likewise the soul whose thoughts are bound to earth,   5
Involved in earthly goods, raging within;
Because, towards that fair sign[1] to which our nature
Aspires, human supports are low and scarce,
Until it runs to find the glorious tree[2]
Of our salvation, where it should be bound   10
From its dark roots up to the highest peak,
Twisted, united to that sacred frame;
It[3] longs to see the Father, where He first
Had bound it to Himself with loving knots.

13[4]

The heavens once again with ancient glory
Adorn our age, and for a time defy[5]
Ruin, since they have destined for our age
A soul who twice wins beauty's victory.[6]
Of you, deserving of eternal story,   5
Most lovely lady, now I speak, to whom
All bow who know true beauty, and the godlike
Spirit within, surpassing memory.
Bright souls build for themselves eternal temples;
Paper is turned to marble, ink to gold,   10
For truth compels them still to praise your name.
Death, time's first thievish blow — oblivion
His second, still more cruel — cannot steal
From you your treasure of immortal fame.

1. God, or heaven. 2. The Cross. 3. The soul. 4. To Veronica Gàmbara, answering her sonnet "O unique glory." 5. Reading "proscrive" for Guerrini's "pre scrive." 6. Reflecting Gàmbara's use of the name Vittoria, that is, "victory."

29

Vinca gli sdegni e l'odio vostro antico,
Carlo e Francesco, il nome sacro e santo
di Cristo, e di Sua fe' vi caglia tanto
quanto a voi più d'ogn'altro è stato amico.

    L'armi vostre a domar l'empio nimico   5
di Lui sian pronte, e non tenete in pianto
non pur l'Italia, ma l'Europa, e quanto
bagna il Mar Indo valle o colle aprico.

    Il gran Pastor, a cui le chiavi date
furon del Cielo, a voi si volge e prega   10
che de le greggi sue pietà vi prenda;

    possa più in voi che 'l sdegno la pietate,
coppia real; un sol desio vi accenda:
di vendicar chi Gesù sprezza o nega.

29

O may the hallowed, sacred name of Christ
Conquer your ancient scorn and mutual hate,
Francis and Charles,[1] and calm you with His Faith
As He has favored you above all others.
And let your arms be swift to dominate   5
His impious enemies,[2] and not draw tears
From Italy, from Europe, and all lands
Bathed by the ocean, bound in by warm hills.
May the great shepherd[3] who received from God
The keys of heaven, turn to you and pray   10
That pity for his flocks will capture you.
May mercy more than wrath kindle your zeal,
O royal pair, one single wish inspire you:
To punish those who scorn Christ and deny Him.

1. To Emperor Charles V and King Francis I of France. This poem has been
wrongly attributed to Veronica Gàmbara and appears under her name in
Guerrini, *Rime di tre gentildonne.* 2. The Turks. 3. Pope Clement VII (de'
Medici).

OLIMPIA MALIPIERA
(?-1559?)

We know very little about Olimpia, except that she belonged to the noble Venetian family of the Malipieri. We do not know the reasons keeping her away from the beloved Venice that she remembers with nostalgia in her poems.

Maria Bandini Buti quotes Giovanni Palazzi describing her as "a person of great integrity, of lucid intellect and lofty talent," adding that she was particularly adept at Latin letters, and that she excelled in "the vernacular" (Italian). The same Palazzi left her portrait in an unusual deck of cards, now at the Correr Museum in Venice.

Olimpia's poems first appeared in *Rime d'alcune nobilissime e virtuosissime donne,* edited by Ludovico Domenichi, and were later included in several other anthologies. We present here two of her poems, *Almost two years of life have passed me by...,* (from the de Blasi anthology), in which the exiled poet expresses her yearning for her Venice; and *As far as my weak talent lets me sail...,* (taken from the Bergalli anthology), which is interesting in that the poet refers to the voyages of discovery taking place in her times, while espressing the hope that literary inspiration may set her life on a sure and stable course.

BIBLIOGRAPHY

Anthologies containing works by Olimpia Malipiera:
Bergalli, *op. cit.*
de Blasi, *op. cit.*
Rime d'alcune nobilissime e virtuosissime donne, op. cit.
Rime in morte di Irene delle Signore di Spilimbergo. Ed. D. Attanasio. Venice: n.p., 1561.
Parnaso italiano. Ed. A. Ronna. Paris: Baudry, 1847.

Studies and other works:
Enciclopedia biografica bibliografica italiana, op. cit.

D'un lustro un terzo è già passato intero,
che da te lungi e mesta ognor soggiorno,
Vinegia mia, nè mai visto ho più giorno
da indi in qua se non malvagio e fero.

 Come affannato in mar stanco nocchiero,   5
cui stringa oscura notte d'ogni intorno,
brama di pigliar porto e far ritorno
al desiato suo dolce emispero;

 tal io vorrei l'altrui lito lasciare,
e 'l dubbio navigar delle trist'onde,   10
ed in te, amata patria, il cor posare;

 onde mai sempre liete aure seconde
prego mi scorghin fide al dolce mare,
che felice ti cinge ambe le sponde.

❦

Quanto lontan mio basso ingegno varca
 Dal mar profondo in quel sapere vero,
 Che l'uom quantunque chiuso in picciol'arca
 Tien vivo in questo, e in quell'altro emisfero;
Tanto alla fragil mia spalmata barca,   5
 Nettun si mostrò più sdegnato, e fero;
 Onde di gioia priva, e di duol carca,
 Il porto rivedere ormai dispero.
Ma se tu, sacro Apollo, un vivo raggio
 Mi porgi, spero col tuo chiaro lume   10
 Volger in dritto il torto mio viaggio.
E fuor del pigro usato mio costume,
 Cantando, a pie d'un bel lauro, o d'un faggio,
 Ergermi lieta or'alma or non presume.

78

Almost two years[1] of life have passed me by
While I, sadly, must linger far from you,
O Venice, my dear city, and have seen
No days but evil ones, perverse and hard.
Like an afflicted, weary mariner,   5
Whom dark of night hems in all round about,
Who yearns to reach his port, and to return
To his own hemisphere, so long desired,
So I would wish to leave these foreign shores
And helpless sailing on unhappy seas,   10
And rest my heart in you, dear fatherland;
And so I pray that gentle favoring winds
May shepherd me to that delightful sea[2]
Which happily surrounds you on both sides.

❧

As far as my weak talent lets me sail
From ocean depths to find that heavenly truth
Which man, enclosed within a little boat,
Pursues in this and in the other hemisphere[3];
Neptune unleashed his wrath and violence   5
Upon my fragile little polished bark,
Until, deprived of joy, laden with grief,
I have lost hope of ever finding port.[4]
But if you, great Apollo, send to me
One living ray, I hope with your clear light   10
To turn from my wrong course to the right way.[5]
And turning from my earlier lazy customs
I'll sing beside a splendid beech or laurel,
And rise where I had never dared before.

1. Literally "one third of a *lustrum,*" a period of five years in the Roman calendar, marking time for ritual purification. 2. The Adriatic Sea. 3. This poem was written at the time of the voyages of exploration to the New World. 4. Note the strong influence of Dante. 5. She prays to Apollo to inspire her, so that her literary work may set straight the course of her life and ensure her reputation.

TULLIA D' ARAGONA
(c.1510-1556)

The most famous and celebrated of the *cortegiane honeste* of the Italian Renaissance, Tullia was born around 1510 in Rome of the courtesan Giulia Campana, from Ferrara. Although her paternity is questioned, she adopted the name of Cardinal Luigi d'Aragona. Her appearance can still be seen in a famous painting by Moretto da Brescia, now at the City Museum of that town, depicting her as Salome. She looks serious, with piercing, intelligent eyes, and wears a royal headdress of pearls entwined in her hair, while she rests her arm on a stone bearing the Latin inscription "quae caput saltando obtinuit" [she who obtained the head (of the Baptist) with her dancing], probably to commemorate her excellence in the art of Terpsichore.

She was soon to follow in her mother's footsteps in her "career," after receiving a thorough literary and musical education, which she exploited for her advancement in the world. She lived in Siena, Ferrara, Rome, Venice and in other major Italian cities, and was very active in the cultural and intellectual life of her time. She was in Ferrara at the same time as Vittoria Colonna, at a time in which her own fame obscured that of the Marchioness. The anthologist de Blasi quotes that it was said in Ferrara, when both Tullia d'Aragona and Vittoria Colonna were present, "Dio fece quaggiù Vittoria una luna e Tullia un sole" (Here God made Vittoria the moon and Tullia the sun). De Blasi also quotes Ercole Bentivoglio describing her, in spite of her profession, as chaste, noble and capable of overcoming lust with celestial love: "Ogni basso desir spento in noi giacque // e un bel desir, un dolce amor celeste..." (Because of you, every low thought has been extinguished in us, and a lively desire, a sweet celestial love has inflamed us). While in Ferarra she befriended Girolamo Muzio; there she also addressed a sonnet to the Capuchin Bernardo Ochino (which we have included in our selection) in which she criticizes his excessive strictness.

While living in Florence, she held a literary salon frequented by renowned men of letters, such as Bernardo Tasso and Benedetto Varchi, with whom she exchanged poems. The famous scholar Sperone Speroni cast her as one of the main characters in his *Dialogue on Love,* published in 1542. In Siena, some time after 1543, she married a certain Silvestro Guicciardini, to whom she bore a child, but she did not remain with him for long.

In 1547, her *Rime della Signora Tullia d'Aragona et di diversi a lei* were published with a dedication to Eleonora di Toledo, wife of Duke Cosimo, who had saved her from the humiliation of wearing the yellow veil which courtesans in Florence were obliged by law to wear, as we see in Savoldo's famous painting "Woman with a Yellow Veil." This extraordinary privilege was granted to her, as the ducal edict said, in view of the fact that "she was a poet," and because many influential friends, such as Varchi, had intervened on her behalf to save her social image. She was more famous for her intellectual gifts than for her amatory exploits, over which she cast a Neo-Platonic veil. It must be noted, however, that Piero Aretino, who bitterly opposed her, may have taken her as an example for the pretentious and rapacious courtesan in his *Ragionamenti.* When Aragona returned to Rome in 1548, the Church was increasing restrictions on the members of her profession. In 1556, like many other courtesans, she died in poverty and obscurity at an early age.

Her *Rime* were extremely successful, as evidenced by the three reprints in 1549, 1557 and 1560. It is a collection comprising one hundred and thirty poems, of which only fifty six were authored by Aragona. The rest are the works of well-known *literati* who addressed poetic compositions to her. Aragona writes in full compliance with the canons of Petrarchism, and is quite skilled in versification, trying her hand at sonnets, madrigals, *canzoni, sestine,* and other forms. The *Rime* opens with thirteen encomiastic sonnets addressed to Duke Cosimo de' Medici and Eleonora di Toledo. Several critics have remarked that the preoccupation with literary exchange with prominent and famous figures was an attempt on Aragona's behalf to increase her own status and respectability in spite of her profession. Only ten of her sonnets are about love, the rest are encomiastic or epistolary compositions directed to famous figures: her special friend Varchi, Muzio, Bembo, Grazzini, Manelli, and others.

Aragona also wrote an *ottava rima* rendering of a popular Spanish romance, *Il Meschino altrimenti detto il Guerrino,* which appeared in 1560 in Venice, the original of which, however, was the prose *romanzo* by Andrea da Barberino. In the preface of *Guerrino,* Aragona shows a moralistic streak, reproaching Boccaccio for his sexual license. She was one of the few women in the early sixteenth century who attempted a narrative chivalric poem in addition to lyric poetry.

She is also remembered for her prose work *Dialogo dell'infinità d'amore* (On the Infinity of Love), 1547, a debate between herself and Benedetto Varchi, which supposedly took place in Aragona's salon. In this witty dialogue, fully in the spirit of the Neo-Platonic dialogues of the Renaissance, Aragona argues favorably that love is infinite, rejecting lower forms of love, such as erotic love: an amazing conclusion in view of her profession. Unlike the later courtesan Veronica Franco, Aragona never acknowledged her condition as a courtesan, and all her writing fits perfectly the mold of the Neo-Platonic doctrines permeating the literary circles of her times. It has been speculated that her humanist friends Varchi and Muzio wrote the dialogue for her, but anyone who has read the stilted prose of the two *literati* in question, and then compared it to the fresh, lively and pert style of the work, would discount that hypothesis.

Tullia d'Aragona has recently received much critical attention, especially from Rinaldina Russell and Ann Rosalind Jones. The latter, in "The Poetics of Group Identity" in *The Currency of Eros,* presents an interesting study of Aragona's dilemma on how to express herself at a time when the dominant modes of discourse belonged to men. According to Jones, Aragona wrote herself into literary history not by opposing the male reader, but rather by presenting herself as the worthy literary correspondent of distinguished male figures. Thus, according to Jones, her work is "collective".

Aragona offers praise, and praise is returned to her. She includes the replies to her addresses in her *Rime,* and enhances her stature since the fame of her male coterie reflects favorably on her.

All recent critical work, including ours, is based on the 1891 edition of the *Rime,* which has been recently reprinted (Bologna: Formi, 1968). We present four sonnets addressed to famous men, Ochino, Bembo, Manelli and Muzio, followed by two sonnets of a more personal nature, in which Aragona shows some genuine feeling. We also present a brief excerpt from the *Dialogue on the Infinity of Love,* a work that deserves to be translated in full, as well as a beautiful anonymous madrigal addressed to Tullia d'Aragona.

For more information on this complex and interesting writer, we refer the reader to the work of Rinaldina Russell in *Italian Women Writers*, cit., and the work of Ann Rosalind Jones mentioned above.

Bibliography

Works by Tullia d'Aragona:
Rime della Signora Tullia d'Aragona e di diversi a lei. Venice: Giolito, 1547.
Le Rime di Tullia d'Aragona. Ed. E. Celani. Bologna: Romagnoli, 1891. Repr. Bologna: Forni, 1968.
Dialogo dell' Infinità di Amore. In *Trattati d'amore del Cinquecento.* Ed. M. Pozzi. Rome & Bari: Laterza, 1975.
Il Meschino detto il Guerrino. Venice: G. Antonelli, 1839-40.
Biagi, Guido. "Un'etera romana. Tullia d'Aragona." In *Nuova Antologia,* ser. 3,4,16, (1886): 655-711 (contains eight letters to Varchi).

Anthologies containing works by Tullia d'Aragona:
Ponchiroli, *op. cit.,* 391-396.
Poesia del Quattrocento e del Cinquecento, op. cit., 1293-1296.
Costa-Zalessow, *op. cit.*

Studies and other works:
Bassanese, Fiora. "Private Lives and Public Lies: Texts by Courtesans of the Italian Renaissance." *Texas Studies in Literature and Language* 30 (1988): 295-319.

Bassnett, Susan. "Tullia d'Aragona." In *An Encylopedia of Continental Women Writers,* 1, *op. cit.*

Bausi, Francesco. "'Con agra zampogna.' Tullia d'Aragona a Firenze (1545-48)." *Schede umanistiche* m.s. 2 (1993): 61-91.

Bongi, Salvatore. "Il velo giallo di Tullia d'Aragona." *Rivista critica della letteratura italiana* 3,4 (1886): 86-95.

——. "Rime della Signora Tullia d'Aragona." In *Annali di Gabriel Giolito de'Ferrari,* 1. Rome: Presso i principali librai, 1890, 150-99.

Camerini, E. "Tullia d'Aragona o la cortigiana illustre." In *Precursori del Goldoni.* Milan: Sonzogno, 1972.

Dizionario enciclopedico, op. cit., I, 163-165.

Filippi, L. "Un poema poco noto 'Il Meschino altrimenti detto il Guerrino.'" In *Le orme del pensiero.* Ferrara: Taddei, 1919.

Jones, Ann Rosalind. "The Poetics of Group Identity. Self-Commemoration through Dialogue in Pernette du Guillet and Tullia d'Aragona." In *The Currency of Eros: Women's Love Lyric in Europe, 1540-1620.* Bloomington: Indiana University Press, 1990.

——. "New Songs for the Swallow: Ovid's Philomela in Tullia d'Aragona and Gaspara Stampa." *Refiguring Women: Perspectives and Identity and the Italian Renaissance.* Ed. M. Migiel and J. Schiesari. Ithaca: Cornell University Press, 1991, 263-77.

Lawner, Lynn. *Lives of the Courtesans.* New York: Rizzoli, 1987.

Masson, Georgina. "Tullia d'Aragona, the Intellectual Courtesan." In *Courtesans of the Italian Renaissance.* London: Secker & Warburg, 1975, 91-131.

Rizzi, F. *L'anima del Cinquecento e la lirica volgare.* Milan: Treves, 1928.

Rosati, S. *Tullia d'Aragona.* Milan: Treves, 1936.

Russell, Rinaldina. "Tullia d'Aragona." In *Italian Women Writers, op. cit.,* 26-34.

Savino, L. "Di alcuni trattati e trattatisti d'amore italiani nella prima metà del secolo XVI." *Studi di letteratura italiana* IX (1909): 233-435.

A Ochino

Bernardo, ben potea bastarvi averne
    Co'l dolce dir, ch'a voi natura infonde,
    Qui dove 'l re de' fiumi ha più chiare onde,
    Acceso i cori a le sante opre eterne;
Ché se pur sono in voi pure l'interne   5
    Voglie, e la vita al destin corrisponde,
    Non uom di frale carne e d'ossa immonde,
    Ma sète un voi de le schiere superne.
Or le finte apparenze, e 'l ballo, e 'l suono,
    Chiesti dal tempo e da l'antica usanza,   10
    A che così da voi vietate sono?
Non fôra santità, fôra arroganza
    Tôrre il libero arbitrio, il maggior dono
    Che Dio ne diè ne la primera stanza.

A Bembo

Bembo, io, che fino a qui da grave sonno
    Oppressa vissi, anzi dormii la vita,
    Or dalla lucevostra alma infinita,
    O sol d'ogni super maestro, e donno.
Desta apro gl'occhi, sì che aperti ponno   5
    Scorger la strada di virtù smarrita;
    Ond'io lasciato ove il pensier m'invita,
    della parte miglior per voi m' indonno.
E quanto posso il più mi sforzo anch'io
    Scaldarmi al lume di sì chiaro foco   10
    Per lasciar del mio nome eterno segno.
Ed oh, non pur da voi si prenda a sdegno
    Mio folle ardir; che se il saper è poco,
    Non è poco, Signor, l'alto desio.

Stortoni & Lillie

To Ochino

Bernardo,[1] it should be enough for you,
With that sweet speech infused in you by Nature,
To light our hearts to high eternal works,
Here[2] where the King of Rivers[3] flows most clearly.
Since your own inner wishes are sincere,   5
And your own life reflects a pure intent,
You're rather an inhabitant of heaven.
As to these masquerades, dances, and music,
Sanctioned by time and by the ancient customs —
Why do you now forbid them in your sermons?[4]   10
Holiness it is not, but arrogance
To take away free will, the highest gift
Which God bestowed on us from the beginning.

To Bembo

Bembo,[5] I who have lived oppressed by slumber —
Indeed, it seems I slept my life away —
But now, roused by the light of your great spirit,
O only lord and master of all knowledge,
I wake, open my eyes, till they, now open,   5
Perceive the way of virtue I had lost;
So I, leaving the place where my thoughts led me,
Master the best part of my mind for you.
As truly as I can, I try, myself,
To warm me by the flame of this clear fire   10
And leave eternal record of my name.
Oh, may my foolish boldness not offend you
Because my knowledge is so very little —
Yet my high aspiration is not small.

1. A religious reformer, Bernardo Ochino (1487-1564). 2. At Ferrara. 3. The Po River. 4. Ochino wanted to do away with the customs of Carnival. 5. Pietro Bembo (1470-1547), famous writer and scholar of the Renaissance.

A MUZIO

Voi ch'avete fortuna sì nemica,
    Come animo valor, e cortesia,
    Qual benigno destino oggi v'invia
    A riveder la vostra fimma antica?
Muzio gentil, un'alma così amica,   5
    E soave valore all'alma mia,
    Ben duolmi della dura, alpestre via
    Con tanta non di voi degna fatica.
Visse gran tempo l'onorato amore,
    Che al Po' già per me v'arse, e non cred'io,   10
    Che sia sì chiara fiamma in tutto spenta.
E se nel volto altrui si legge il core,
    Spero, che in riva all'Arno il nome mio
    Alto per voi suonare ancor si senta.

A MANELLI

Se forse per pietà del mio languire
    Al suon del tristo pianto in questo loco
    Ten' vieni a me, che tutta fiamma e foco
    Ardomi, e struggo colma di desire,
Vago augellino, e meco il mio martire,   5
    Che in pena volge al passato gioco,
    Piangi cantando in suon dolente e roco,
    Veggendomi del duol quasi morire;
Pregoti per l'ardor che sì m'addoglia
    Ne voli in quella amena e cruda valle   10
    Ov'è chi sol può darmi e morte e vita.
E cantando gli di' che cangi voglia
    Volgendo a Roma 'l viso e a lei le spalle,
    Se vuol l'alma trovar col corpo unita.

To Muzio

You who have Fortune for an enemy —
As in your soul dwell courtesy and valor —
What happy destiny sends you today
To see for one more time your ancient flame?
My gentle Muzio,[1] a soul so friendly   5
Is such a sweet enrichment to my heart
That I must grieve for the hard rocky way
That gives you such fatigue, quite undeserved.
That honored love which you burned for me
In the Po Valley[2] once, endured so long   10
That I can't think so clear a fire has died.
For, if in someone's face his heart is seen,
I hope that by the Arno's banks[3] my name
May still be heard to ring through your sweet songs.

To Manelli[4]

If you, perhaps for pity of my sorrow,
O lovely little bird, have come to me,
Hearing my plaintive cries here in this place,
To suffer with me, as I burn in flames,
Consumed with such a passionate desire   5
That I must turn to pain all my past joys,
And weep with me, singing your doleful songs,
Seeing me almost dead from constant grief,
I beg you, for the ardor that so pains me,
To fly into that lovely, cruel valley   10
Where he is who can give me death or life,
And, singing, tell him he should change direction,
Turning his back from here, his face toward Rome,[5]
If he should wish to find me still alive.

1. Girolamo Muzio (1496-1576), Humanist and poet, former lover of d'Aragona. 2. In northern Italy. 3. The Arno river flows through Florence. 4. Piero Manelli, a young Florentine nobleman with whom Tullia was in love at this time, inspired several of her love sonnets. 5. The poet is now in Rome.

❦

Se ben pietosa madre unico figlio
   Perde talora, e novo alto dolore
   Le preme il tristo e sospiroso core
   Spera conforto almen, spera consiglio.
Se scaltro capitano in gran periglio   5
   Mostrando alteramente il suo valore,
   Resta cinto e prigion, spera uscir fuore
   Quando che sia con baldanzoso ciglio.
S'in tempestoso mar giunto si duole
   Spaventato nocchier già presso a morte,   10
   Ha speme ancor di rivedersi in porto.
Ma io, s'avvien che perda il mio bel sole,
   O per mia colpa o per malvagia sorte,
   Non spero aver, né voglio, alcun conforto.

❦

Amor un tempo in così lento foco
   Arse mia vita, e sì colmo di doglia
   Struggeasi il cor, che qual altro si voglia
   Martir fôra ver lei dolcezza e gioco.
Poscia sdegno e pietade a poco a poco   5
   Spenser la fiamma; ond'io più ch'altra soglio
   Libera da sì lunga e fiera voglia
   Giva lieta cantando in ciascun loco.
Ma il ciel né sazio ancor, lassa, né stanco
   De' danni miei, perchè sempre sospiri,   10
   Mi riconduce a la mia antica sorte:
E con sì acuto spron mi punge il fianco,
   Ch'io temo sotto i primi empi martiri
   Cadere, e per men mal bramar la morte.

Stortoni & Lillie

❧

Even a loving[1] mother, having lost
Her only son, whose sighing heart is laden
With such a new, so high and deep a sorrow,
May yet expect some comfort and advice;
So, a sagacious captain, in great peril,   5
Showing with lofty soul his inner courage,
Though conquered and in prison, may yet hope
Some day to be set free, with fearless brow;
And in a stormy sea a frightened pilot,
Who weeps, fearing the imminence of death,   10
May yet take heart to see his port again.
But I, if I should lose my lovely sun,[2]
Through fault of mine, or through malicious Fortune,
Can neither hope, nor wish for, any solace.

❧

Love once consumed me with a slow, fierce fire,
Scorching my life; until my heart, brim-full
Of pain, was devastated, and all sorrow
Beside this were but sweetness and a game.
Then pride and suffering, by slow degrees,   5
Put out that flame; so I, at last released
From such a long and sharp desire, went singing
More joyfully than I had done before.
But heaven, not yet satisfied, nor weary
Of my distress, to make me sigh once more,   10
Leads me again to my old hopeless fate.
And with so sharp a spur it pricks my side
That I must fear to fall beneath my anguish
Of old. For lighter ills, I'd long for death.

1. "Pietosa" here can mean loving as well as piteous. 2. Her lover.

CHIARA MATRAINI
(1515-1604?)

Chiara Matraini is the first great woman poet of the sixteenth century to have emerged from the middle class. Her family slowly rose from the weaving trade and was involved in the 1531 uprising in Lucca which sought to extend the right to public office to the lesser nobility. She was born in Lucca, Tuscany, in 1515, and was married at the age of sixteen to Vincenzo Contarini, with a dowry of three hundred *scudi,* a sum later contested by her son, after she was widowed.

We have few sure data about her life, parts of which are still shrouded in mystery. We know that she was widowed by 1542. Chronicles of the time tell us that, by 1547, she had become the object of local gossip because of her relationship with Bartolomeo Graziani, a man who was possibly much younger than she, and who appears, from some references in her poems, to have died or been murdered.

By 1550, Matraini had already devoted herself to her literary interests; she was well versed in the study of philosophy and history, and kept in contact with many prominent scholars, such as Varchi, Domenichi, Giraldi Cinthio, Annibal Caro, and others. In 1555, her complete poems up to that date were included in Domenichi's anthology *Rime dei signori napoletani ed altri*; her poetry later appeared in other anthologies of the time.

Around 1560, she began a lasting relationship with Cesare Coccopani, a judge practicing in Lucca. She also engaged in a law suit with her own son, Federico, who refused to return her dowry money, attesting to the fact that she was seeking a financial independence that would have allowed her greater intellectual freedom.

In 1576, Matraini returned to Lucca, and set to work planning the image she wished to leave to posterity. She commissioned a portrait of herself as a Sibyl for the chapel of Santa Maria Forisportam. At this time she started writing spiritual works, which reflect a preoccupation with approaching death, as well as

Counter-Reformation spirituality: in 1581, *Meditazioni spirituali* (Spiritual Meditations); in 1587, *Considerazioni sui sette salmi penitenziali* (Reflections on the Seven Penitential Psalms); and, in 1590, the *Vita della vergine* (The Life of the Virgin).

In her later years she enjoyed a good reputation as a *literata* and published her collected works in 1595 and 1597. Her last work, *Dialoghi spirituali* (Spiritual Dialogues) appeared in 1602. In addition to her lyric poetry, and to her religious works, she wrote many letters, collected in *Lettere con la prima e seconda parte delle rime* (Venice: Moretti, 1597), as well as the philosophical and religious works mentioned above. She wrote the introduction to the third edition of the Rime which appeared that year, and probably died in 1604.

Chiara Matraini showed great originality and spirit for a woman of her time: she did not let her middle-class origins deter her from her literary aspirations, she kept her maiden name throughout her life, she had two relationships outside marriage, and, as evident in chronicles of the time, she had enough spirit to fight for her own dowry that represented financial independence.

Although Matraini was well-known in her time, her poetry fell into obscurity after her death until it was rediscovered by the critic Luigi Baldacci, who, in 1953, hailed her as one of the most original poets of her time. Together with Vittoria Colonna, who clearly influenced her, she was one of the great poetic stylists of the Renaissance. Her poetry is not only stylistically interesting, but also suffused with a delicate sensibility. The selection we present shows her capacity for bold metaphors and conceits that remind us of the English metaphysical poets. Particularly moving are the four poems in which she laments the untimely death of her young lover: *How can I stay alive...*, *O dear and faithful beacons...*, *These fierce and contrary winds...*, and *High are these mountains....*

Lately Matraini has received critical attention thanks mainly to the work of Giovanna Rabitti, who in 1989 published a critical edition of her work. We have taken our Italian texts from *Lettere con la prima e seconda parte delle Rime* (Venice: Moretti, 1597).

BIBLIOGRAPHY

Works by Chiara Matraini:

Rime e prose di madonna Chiara Matraini. Lucca: Busdrago, 1555.

Meditazioni spirituali di madonna Chiara Contarini de' Matraini. Lucca: Busdrago, 1581.

Considerazioni sopra i sette salmi penitenziali. Lucca: Busdrago, 1586.

Breve discorso sopra la vita e laude della Beatiss. Verg. e Madre del Figliuol di Dio. Lucca: Busdrago, 1590.

Lettere con la prima e seconda parte delle Rime. Venice: Moretti, 1597.

"Inediti Vaticani di Chiara Matraini." In *Studi di filologia e critica offerti dagli allievi a Lanfranco Caretti,* 1. Rome: Salerno Editrice, 1985, 225-250.

Rime e lettere. Ed. Giovanna Rabitti. Bologna: Commissione per i testi di lingua, 1989.

Anthologies containing works by Chiara Matraini:

Bergalli, *op. cit.*

Costa-Zalessow, *op. cit.*

de Blasi, *op. cit.*

Lettere di donne italiane. Ed. Bartolomeo Gamba. Venice: Alvisopoli, 1832, 157-164.

Lirici del Cinquecento, op. cit., 497-530.

Poesia del Quattrocento e del Cinquecento, op. cit., 1297-1300.

Studies and other works:

Baldacci, L. *Chiara Matraini, poetessa lucchese del XVI secolo.* Paragone 42 (Letteratura) (1953): 53-67.

Bullock, Alan, and Gabriella Palange. "Per una edizione critica delle opere di Chiara Matraini." In *Studi in onore di Raffaele Spongano.* Bologna: Boni, 1980, 235-62.

Dizionario enciclopedico, op. cit., 551-552.

Enciclopedia biografica bibliografica italiana, op. cit.

Maclachlan, Elaine. "The Poetry of Chiara Matraini: Narrative Strategies in the Rime." Ph.D. dissertation, University of Connecticut, 1992.

Malpezzi Price, Paola. "Chiara Matraini: Petrarchist or Anti-Petrarchist? The Dilemma of a Woman Poet." In *Donna: Women in Italian Culture.* Ed. Ada Tagliaferri. Toronto: Dovehouse, 1989.

Rabitti, Giovanna. "Linee per il ritratto di Chiara Matraini." *Studi e problemi di critica testuale* 22 (1981): 141-65.

———. "La metafora e l'esistenza nella poesia di Chiara Matraini." *Studi e problemi di critica testuale* 27 (1983): 109-45.

———. "Chiara Matraini." In *Italian Women Writers, op. cit.,* 242-252.

Fera son io di questo ombroso loco,
   Che vo con la saetta in mezzo al core,
   Fuggendo, lassa, il fin del mio dolore,
   E cerco chi mi strugge a poco a poco.
E com'augel che fra le penne il foco   5
   Si sente acceso, onde volando fuore
   Dal dolce nido suo, mentre l'ardore
   Fugge, con l'ale più raccendo il foco.
Tal io fra queste fronde a l'aura estiva
   Con l'ali del desio volando in alto,   10
   Cerco il foco fuggir che meco porto.
Ma quando vado più di riva in riva
   Per fuggir 'l mio mal, con fiero assalto
   Lunga morte procaccio al viver corto.

❦

Viva mia bella e dolce calamìta
   Che partendo con sì mirabil modo
   Stringeste l'alma in quel tenace nodo
   Ch'a voi sol la terrà più sempre unita;
Non è la mente mia da voi smarrita,   5
   Se ben, lontana a voi, di voi non godo
   L'amata vista, anzi via più sempr'odo
   Da voi chiamarmi ove il desio m'invita.
Per voi sì puro laccio Amor m'avinse
   Di salda e pura fede al collo intorno   10
   Ch'ogn'altra umil catena sdegna il core.
Sciols'ogni nodo quando questo strinse,
   E ruppe l'arco con vittoria il giorno
   Ch'in me fe eterno l'ultimo suo ardore.

Stortoni & Lillie

I am a wild deer in this shady wood
With a sharp arrow driven through my heart.
I flee, alas, that which would end my pain
And seek him who destroys me bit by bit;
And like a bird that feels among her feathers   5
A lighted fire, which makes her fly away
From her belovèd nest: the heat goes with her
And all the time her wing-beats fan the flame.
So I, among these leaves in summer air,
Flying on high with wings of strong desire,   10
Attempt to quench the flame I carry with me.
But howsoever much from bank to bank
I go to flee my ill, with fierce assault
I gain a long death for my little life.

❧

My sweet and lovely magnet lives in me,
When we are parted, with miraculous power
That binds my soul in a resistless knot
And keeps me ever tied to you alone.
Not that my spirit ever strays from you,   5
Though, with you far away, I have no joy
Of your belovèd presence; yet the more
I hear your voice calling where Love invites.
Love binds about my neck so strong a cord
Of sound and perfect loyalty to you   10
That from my heart I cast all lesser chains.
All other knots were loosed when this was tied,
And that day broke the bow[1] of victory,
When Love made this last flame in me eternal.

1. Breaking the bow was a sign of victory.

❦

Quant' ho più da lontan l'aspetto vostro,
  Più lo sento ne l'alma a parte a parte
  Scolpito e vivo, e 'n chiascheduna parte
  Insignorirsi del mortal suo chiostro.
Nè poggio, sasso, o valle Amor m'ha mostro   5
  Fin dove il Serchio arriva o dove parte,
  Ch'io non vi veda con mirabil arte
  Scritto il nome ch'adorna il secol nostro.
Così potesse del mio amor far fede
  Il cor che nel partir vi lassai in pegno,   10
  Ond'ugual fosse amor sempre tra noi;
Chè sì nel petto il bel nodo mi sede
  Ch'unqua nol cangerà tempo nè sdegno,
  Ma sempre v'amerò viva e dapoi.

❦

Com'esser può che in tanta doglia i' viva,
  Rimasta senza te, dolce mia vita,
  E fra sì perigliose ombre smarrita,
  Del mar del pianger mio non giunga a riva?
O mia scorta celeste eletta e diva,   5
  Puot'esser ver che sia da te sbandita
  Su in ciel quella pietà che mi dea aita
  E 'l cor nel pianto a' dolenti occhi apriva?
Tu pur m'amasti, e di virtute ardente
  Fu qui 'l tuo amore, al mio pur sempre uguale,   10
  Il quale ancor non hai d'aver a sdegno.
Deh, se come ti calse, ancor ti cale
  Di me che vivo misera e dolente,
  Mostrami di pietate un caro segno.

Stortoni & Lillie

The farther your sweet presence is from me,
The more I feel it deeply in my soul
Engraved and living, and in every part
Reigning as lord over this mortal cloister.[1]
No hill, no rock, no valley has love shown me   5
In the entire region of the Serchio[2]
Where I do not perceive, with wondrous art,
Your name inscribed, the honor of the age.
And so I wish my love to keep its faith —
The heart I gave as pledge when you departed —   10
That equal love should reign between us two,
And in my breast the lovely knot should hold,
Keeping us safe from time and disregard,
That I should love you now, and evermore.[3]

How can I stay alive with such sharp pain,
Ever deprived of you,[4] my lovely life,
And, lost among these fearful waves of tears
How is it that I never reach the shore?[5]
O my elect, celestial, heavenly guide,   5
Can it be true that up in heaven, pity
Has left you, which on earth gave me such help,
Touching your heart to weep for my sad eyes?
You loved me once, and with its ardent power
Your love on earth was equal then to mine —   10
Such love as ours you should never disdain.
Ah, if you still care, as you used to care,
For me, who live on sadly and in pain,
Show me, in pity, one more loving sign.

1. The body, cloister of Love. 2. River that flows through Lucca. 3. In Italian, "dappoi," in the future life. 4. This sonnet is written to her dead lover. 5. Meaning here the shore of her tears, i.e., the end of her sorrow.

❧

O luci del mio cor fidate e care,
    Come da gl'occhi miei vi dipartiste
    Tacite, e nell'occaso vi copriste
    Eternamente, senza mai tornare!
Già non ponno veder più fosche amare   5
    Notti quest' occhi o sconsolate e triste
    Di queste, ahi lassa, ch'al mio core apriste,
    Turbando l'ore mie serene e chiare.
Ben conobbi 'l mio duolo e 'l vostro caso,
    O speranze qui prese a' nostri danni,   10
    Ma chi può andar contr'al mortal suo corso?
Piangete, occhi infelici, che rimaso
    Altro non v'è che lagrime et affanni,
    Privi del vostro dolce almo soccorso.

❧

Questi venti contrari e così fieri
    Che sospingon qui l'onde in questi scogli
    Sembran de' miei nemici i grandi orgogli
    Contra a gl'alti miei stabili pensieri.
E quegl'orridi nembi e così neri
    Là 've più 'l tempo rio par che si accogli,   5
    Sembran gli spessi miei gravi cordogli
    Contra ad ogni mia pace empi guerrieri;
E quella stanca e debol navicella
    A cui si vede tronco arbore e sarte,   10
    Senza nocchiero, infra l'orribil onde,
Sembra l'alma mia afflitta e di sua stella
    Priva e di tutte sue speranze sparte,
    Poi che l'alma sua luce il ciel gl'asconde.

Stortoni & Lillie

O dear and faithful beacons of my heart,
How have you silently bereft my eyes
When in your setting you concealed yourselves,
Eternally, without hope of return![1]
These eyes of mine, alas, will never see   5
More bitter nights or more disconsolate
Than these you opened to my loving heart,
Effacing all my hours of calm and peace.
I knew too well my sorrow and your fate —
O hopes, conceived only to bring us grief!   10
But who can run against his mortal course?
Weep, weep, unhappy eyes, for there remains
Nothing for you but sorrow and salt tears,
Deprived of your supporting aid forever!

These fierce, contrary winds that drive the waves
Against the rocks seem like the haughty pride
Of those who are my enemies, who strike
Against my stable and exalted thoughts.
And these threatening clouds, lowering so black,   5
Gathered most thickly where the tempest rages,
Seem like my frequent, heavy griefs of heart,
Pitiless warriors beating down my peace.
And this poor weak and weary little vessel
With broken mast and sails in rags and tatters,   10
Without a pilot in the dreadful waves,
Seems like my sorrowing heart and my ill star,
Deprived and robbed of all its fragile hopes,
For heaven hides from me my only light.[2]

1. The poet is lamenting the untimely death of her young lover. 2. Her lover.

❦

Alti son questi monti et alti sono
 Li miei pensier di cui l'alma s'ingombra:
 Questi con piante sterili gl'adombra,
 Le mie speranze senza frutto sono.
Scendon fonti da lor con alto suono,   5
 contrari venti a le lor cime et ombra
 Di nubi stanno, e'l duol da me disgombra
 Pianto e sospir di cui sempre ragiono.
Nemiche fere in essi, empie e rapaci
 S'annidan solo; e nel mio petto alberga   10
 Fiera doglia che'l cor m'ange e divora.
Godon pur questi le superne faci
 Qualor vil nebbia almo seren disperga,
 Ma i' non vedo mai 'l sol che l'alma adora.

Stortoni & Lillie

High are these mountains, and equally high
My thoughts of him by whom my soul is burdened,
Which overshadow them like barren trees:
My thousand hopes are doomed to bear no fruit.
Streams pour forth from the heights with dreary sound,   5
Winds blow against the peaks, and heavy shadows
Of clouds obscure them, while grief draws from me
Deep sighs and tears for him I think of always.
Rapacious beasts alone make here their dens,
None others; while within my breast is lodged   10
A furious grief that tears and eats my heart.
Even those beasts enjoy the light of heaven
Whenever clearing skies dispel the clouds;
I never see the sun my soul adores.[1]

1. The sonnet was written for her young lover after his death.

LAURA BACIO TERRACINA
(1519-1577?)

One of the few Southern Italian women presented in this anthology, Bacio Terracina was born in 1519, and grew up in the austere and proud environment of the pro-Spanish nobility in Naples. Most of what we know about her life is gleaned from her work. Her family was originally from Brescia, and later moved to Rome; as a reward for helping the Pope against the powerful Colonna family, it obtained the fief of Terracina. After moving to Naples, the family gave allegiance to the French d'Anjou dynasty. At the end of the fifteenth century, the family was granted sovereignty over the territory of Vatio or Bacio, from which came the double name Bacio Terracina.

She was a prolific writer, publishing nine volumes of poetry between 1548 and 1561. Early in life, she became a member of the *Accademia degli Incogniti* under the name of Febea, already attesting to her poetic vocation as a devotee of Phoebus. Her two-year (1545-47) membership in the Academy gave her valuable contacts with Neapolitan intellectuals, which in some cases she kept for the rest of her life. Among the poets and scholars she was in touch with were the lyric poets Luigi Tansillo, A.F. Doni and Lodovico Domenichi. The latter edited her volume of *Rime* (Venice: Giolito, 1548), which had great immediate success and gave her considerable renown as a wise and moral poet. This first book of poetry, a collection of lyrics still within the Petrarchan tradition, was so successful that it was reprinted five times in the sixteenth century and twice in the seventeenth.

Her second book of poetry, appropriately called *Rime seconde,* was published in Florence in 1549, and was not as successful as the first. Her third, however, *Discorso sopra tutti i primi canti di Orlando Furioso* (Commentary on all the first cantos of *Orlando Furioso*), was immensely popular, capitalizing as it did on Ariosto's fame and acclaim. This work had nine reprints before 1608, and is composed of 46 brief cantos in *ottava rima*; the peculiarity of each canto is that it is composed of seven ottavas, the final verses of which are taken from the first stanza of the corresponding verse of the *Orlando Furioso*. Thus, both the form and the content of Ariosto's corresponding *ottavas* are reversed for the opposite effect, and Ariosto's opening verses are used as a startling and effective punch line for Bacio Terracina's statements. In Canto XXXVII of the *Discorso,* the poet takes Ariosto's ottava praising women as a point of departure, using this occasion to scold women for not dedicating enough time to letters. The reader should also note that the dedicatory *ottava* is to Veronica Gàmbara, whereas Ariosto in Canto XXXVII of *Orlando Furioso* had singled out Vittoria Colonna as the greatest woman of his time.

The *Discorso* shows Bacio Terracina's remarkable ingenuity and technical skill. Such derivative work may seem artificial to the modern reader; however, we should remember that the Renaissance concept of originality greatly differed from ours, and that a poet was regarded as original for his or her capacity to twist and adapt recognized classics for his or her own ends. For our purposes, the content of the work is quite important in that it abounds in pugnacious feminist statements. The poet's clear, direct message is that women should devote themselves to scholarship and writing, rather than limiting themselves to a domestic role.

After a few years, she again capitalized on the same successful poetic scheme in her *Seconda parte de' Discorsi sopra le seconde stanze d'Orlando Furioso,* this time, as the title indicates, playing on the second stanza of each canto. This work was less successful. She later published a few more collections of poetry, all conveniently entitled *Quarte rime* (1550), *Quinte rime* (1552) and *Seste rime* (1558). These collections contain for the most part occasional and encomiastic poems — which were particularly successful due to their topicality — as well as some moralistic compositions.

Late in life, the poet married her relative Polidoro Terracina. In 1561, she published in Naples some elegiac stanzas, *Sovra tutte le donne vedove di questa nostra città di Napoli,* in which she reflects on the transitory nature of human affections and on the vanity of life, and comments on the state of widowhood in her time. She lived in Rome between 1570 and 1572, towards the end of her life, as attested by sonnets addressed to cardinals gathered there for the election of Pope Gregory XIII. Her last volume, which was not printed, contains poems imbued with mystical religious feelings.

Bacio Terracina enjoyed an immense popularity among her contemporaries because of the spirit and the wit of her vast literary production. Today, of all her large production of poetry, the *Prime rime* and the *Discorso* are the most appealing to the modern reader, for the clear feminist statements and messages they send.

We have selected a famous sonnet that shows Terracina's concern with the political state of Italy in her times, as well as her desire for moral and political change. We also present the best-known stanzas from Canto XXXVII of her *Discorso*. We have taken the original text of the sonnet from the de Blasi anthology, and the octaves from the *Discorso* from the 1608 Bonfadino edition.

BIBLIOGRAPHY

Works by Laura Bacio Terracina:
Rime. Venice: Giolito, 1548.
Rime seconde. Venice: (Giunti?), 1549.
Discorso sopra tutti i primi canti di 'Orlando Furioso.' Venice: Giolito, 1549.
Il discorso sopra il principio di tutti i canti di Orlando Furioso. Venice: Bonfadino, 1608.
Quarte rime. Venice: Valvassori, 1550.
Quinte rime. Venice: Valvassori, 1552.
Seste rime. Lucca: Busdrago, 1558.
Sovra tutte le donne vedove di questa città di Napoli. Naples: Cancer, 1561.
La seconda parte de' Discorsi sopra le seconde stanze de' Canti d'Orlando Furioso. Venice: Valvassori, 1567.
Rime della signora Laura Terracina detta nell'Accademia degl'Incogniti Febea. Naples: Bulifon, 1692.
Rime inedite. Biblioteca Nazionale di Firenze, Codex CCXXIX.

Anthologies containing works by Laura Bacio Terracina:
Bergalli, *op. cit.*
Costa Zalessow, *op. cit.*
Lirici del Cinquecento, op. cit., 475-78.

Poesia italiana del Cinquecento. Ed. G. Ferroni. Milan: Garzanti, 1978, 255-257.

Rime diverse di molti eccellentissimi autori. Venice: Giolito, 1549.

Studies and other works:

Borzelli, A. *Laura Terracina, poetessa napoletana del Cinquecento.* Naples: Marzano, 1924.

Costa-Zalessow, N. "Su due sonneti del Cinquecento attribuiti a L. Terracina," in *Forum Italicum* 1, vol. 15, (Spring 1981): 22-30.

Croce, Benedetto. "La casa di una poetessa" in *Storie e leggende napoletane.* Bari: Laterza, 1948, 275-289.

Dersofi, Nancy. "Laura Terracina." In *Italian Women Writers, op. cit.,* 422-430.

Dizionario enciclopedico, op. cit., 262.

Dizionario biografico, op. cit., V, 61-63.

Enciclopedia biografica bibliografica italiana, op. cit.

Maroi, Lucia. *Laura Terracina, poetessa napoletana del secolo XVI.* Naples: Perrella, 1913.

Russell, Rinaldina. "Laura Terracina." In *An Encylopedia of Continental Women Writers,* 2, *op. cit.*

Zancan, M. "La donna." In *Letteratura italiana,* 5. Turin: Einaudi, 1986, 765-827.

Veggo il mondo fallir, veggiolo stolto,
e veggio la virtute in abbandono;
e che le Muse a vil tenute sono,
tal che l'ingegno mio quasi è sepolto.

Veggio in odio ed invidia tutto vòlto   5
il pensier degli amici, e in falso tono
veggio tradito dal malvagio il buono,
e tutto a' nostri danni il ciel rivolto.

Nessun al ben comun tien fermo segno,
anzi al suo proprio ognun discorre seco,   10
mentre ha di vari affetti il petto pregno.

Io veggio, e nel veder tengo odio meco;
tal che vorrei vedere per disdegno
o me senz'occhi, o tutto il mondo cieco.

DA *IL DISCORSO SOPRA IL PRINCIPIO DI TUTTI I CANTI DI*
ORLANDO FURIOSO
    ALLA ECCELLENT. SIGNORA VERONICA DA GÀMBARA

Deh fosser molte al mondo come voi,
donne che a gli scrittor mettesser freno,
ch'a tutta briglia vergan contra noi
scritti crudeli e colmi di veleno:
ché forse andrebbe insino ai liti Eoi   5
il nome nostro e 'l grido d'onor pieno.
Ma perché contra a lor nulla si mostra,
però tengono vil la fama nostra.

    CANTO TRIGESIMOSETTIMO

Non credo, no, che gli scrittor, che in carte
han scritto in biasmo nostro e in poca lode,   10
ch'abbian sì ben compito il mondo e l'arte,
che non si possa oprar contra lor frode,
poi ch'hanno posto il ben nostro da parte

I see the world astray, I see it foolish,
I see that every virtue is abandoned
And that the Muses stand in low regard,
So that my talent is as good as buried.[1]
I see the thoughts of friends turned all to hatred   5
And envy; everywhere I see the good
Betrayed with ill intent by wicked people,
And heaven turned averse, to our destruction.
No one has firm respect for common good,
But all think only of their own advancement,   10
While every heart is filled with mundane thoughts.
And seeing this, my heart is full of hate;
So much, that from disgust, I'd rather be
Either without my eyes, or the world blinded.

FROM COMMENTARY ON THE BEGINNING OF ALL THE CAN-
TOS OF *ORLANDO FURIOSO*
DEDICATION TO VERONICA GÀMBARA

Were there more women here on earth like you
To put a halt to those too many writers
Who, unrestrained, publish against us women
Much cruel writing, filled with bitter venom:
Then might our names reach oriental shores —   5
Our names and fame, adorned with well-earned honors.
But since we have not ventured to oppose them,
They hold our writings in too low esteem.

CANTO 37

I can't believe that those industrious writers
Have written so much blame, so little praise   10
Of us, that all the world is so convinced
That no one can prevail against their frauds,
For they have set our good work to one side,

1. Matthew 25:25.

e il mal quanto si può per tutto s'ode.
Deh fossero almen dati a un atto buono   *15*
se come in acquistar qualch'altro dono.

Ché se da lor medesime potuto
avessero le donne scriver molto,
li scrittor forse non avrian taciuto
quel ch'or tacendo han più d'infamia ocolto.   *20*
Ma perché è vuopo mendicare aiuto
agli scrittor, per nostro viver stolto,
però si fan sì caldi in lor scrittura,
che senza industria non può dar natura.

Deh se lasciasser l'ago, il filo, il panno,   *25*
o dello studio togliesser la soma,
credo ch'a voi scrittor farebbon danno,
anzi, il più mal che non fer gli afri a Roma.
Ma perché poche son che questo fanno,
poca fama circonda nostra chioma.   *30*
Non molte donne al scriver qual ragiono,
affaticate notte e dì si sono.

Non restate perciò, donne ingegniose,
di por la barca di virtude al scoglio:
lasciate l'ago, fatevi bramose   *35*
sovente in operar la penna e il foglio,
ché non men vi farete gloriose
di questi tai di cui molto mi doglio.
Or state dunque attente in la lettura,
con somma diligenzia e lunga cura….   *40*

Or diamoci talmente alla virtute,
e diasi luoco a queste lingue oscure,
ché non saran le nostre così mute
che non bastino a vincer lor scritture.

And spread evil report on every hand.
Ah, had they only performed one good deed   15
So that we could acquire some other gift![1]

Because, if by themselves they had been able,
These women, to produce much more good writing,
Male writers would have not been silent,
Hiding feminine talent as a wrong.   20
But since today we must go beg for aid
From these male writers, just for our poor living,
They have become so heated in their writing,
Since nature gives no gifts without great labor.

If only women would give up their needles,   25
Their thread and cloth, and would take up their studies,
I think, then, they could wound you, o male writers,
More than the Carthaginians hurt the Romans.
But since few women have done this, so little
True fame has garlanded our heads with laurel.   30
Not many women take the pains I speak of,
To labor night and day and never rest.

And therefore do not cease, gifted women,
To launch your ships of talent on the ocean!
Forget your needles, make yourselves more eager   35
To labor frequently with pen and paper.
Thus you can win as glorious a fame
As men of whom I bitterly complain.
And also be attentive to your reading
With highest diligence and long endurance....   40

Let us devote ourselves so totally
To art and to the freeing of our tongues
That we will not be silenced to the point
Of ceding victory to men's productions.

1. The italicized verses correspond to Ariosto's verses in the first octave of
Canto 37 of *Orlando Furioso.*

Uscemo omai da questa servitute   45
in seguitar le sante alme letture.
Così si fosser poste a quelli studi,
ch'immortal fanno le mortal virtudi.

And let us free ourselves from servitude   45
But following holy, life-supportive reading.
If only we had devoted ourselves to studies
That make our mortal aptitudes immortal!

ISABELLA DI ᏟᎷORRA
(c.1520-1545?)

One of the few woman poets from southern Italy to be presented in this anthology, Isabella was born in approximately 1520 of an illustrious baronial family in the fief of Favale, between the regions of Calabria and Basilicata. We have little information on the Morra family, left to us by A. M. di Morra in *Familiae nobilissimae de Morra historia* (Naples, 1629). In Isabella di Morra's time, Italy was the battleground for a fierce conflict between the French dynasty (Francis I) and the Emperor Charles V, whose vast territories included Spain and dominated southern Italy. Isabella's father, Giovan Michele, had sworn allegiance to the French, and therefore was banished from the kingdom of Naples in 1527. He subsequently emigrated to the court of Francis I, leaving his family behind. The fief of Favale went to his firstborn son Marcantonio, and Isabella was left in the stern tutelage of her six brothers, uncultured and cruel men who did not understand her refined and poetic temperament, and who kept her isolated from any human contact.

The castle of Favale was situated on a peak in a very arid part of the region, near the small river Siri (today Sinni), a dismal site which in her poems Morra often compared to an infernal landscape. In spite of her brothers' surveillance, with her tutor as go-between, she became involved in a secret epistolary relationship with the Spanish nobleman Don Diego Sandoval de Castro, who was married to Donna Antonia Caracciolo of Naples. As soon as the correspondence between the two lovers was discovered, the tutor, while bearing a letter to Morra under Don Diego's wife's name, was murdered by three of the Morra brothers; soon after, they beat their sister to death in a fit of rage in order "to cleanse the family honor." The moral outrage caused by their sister being involved with a married man was surely compounded by the fact that the whole Morra family was pro-French, while Don Diego was Spanish. After Morra's death, having ambushed and killed Don Diego, the brothers were forced to flee and find refuge in France.

Morra was brought up without all the cultural and social advantages which benefited the women from central and northern Italy; rather, she was barred from any social and literary exchange. Paradoxically, this cultural isolation made her a more original and spontaneous poet, in that it effectively insulated her from too strict an adherence to the Petrarchan lyric mode prevailing in Italy. Her style, which she herself describes as "amaro, aspro e dolente" (bitter, harsh and grieving), is a strong, concise, direct style, which at its best reminds us of Dante, whose works she knew well. She had a special gift for poetic sound effects and for evocative imagery.

Morra left thirteen poems in all, reflecting her brief, intense and tragic life. They are perhaps the most autobiographical and artifice-free in all of Italian Renaissance women's poetry, and express in an eloquent, moving way Morra's sense of isolation, the terror of imprisonment, the hope for a freedom that never came, and the oppression of the stark, gloomy landscape around her. For the tragic events of her life as well as for the poignancy of her poetic expression, Morra has often been compared to a Romantic poet *ante litteram*. Her poetry appeared in several anthologies during the second half of the sixteenth century. Eight sonnets and one canzone appeared in *Rime di diversi illustri signori napolitani,* edited by Ludovico Dolce (Venice: Giolito, 1552). The rest of the poems appeared in 1556 in a reprint, also edited by Dolce. In 1559, the entire corpus was published in *Rime diversi d'alcune nobilissime e virtuosissime donne,* edited by Domenichi (Lucca: Busdrago, 1559). Later, her poetry appeared in two anthologies, both published in Naples by Antonio Bulifon: *Rime delle Signore Lucrezia Marinella, Veronica Gambara e Isabella di Morra* (1693), and *Rime di cinquanta illustri poetesse* (1695).

In 1929, the critic and philosopher Benedetto Croce brought Morra's poetry to light when he re-edited her *Rime,* printing them with a selection of poems authored by her lover Diego Sandoval de Castro and with the addition of a critical essay. Moreover, the

Comune of Valsinni, Morra's homeland in the Basilicata region, organized a convention in 1975 to honor the poet and to pay their respects.

We have taken the original text and numbering of the four sonnets and the *canzone* from Domenico Bronzini's edition, based on the Croce edition of 1929.

For further bibliographical and critical information, we refer the reader to the excellent work of Juliana Schiesari.

BIBLIOGRAPHY

Works by Isabella di Morra:
Rime. Intro. by A. de Gubernatis. Rome: Forzani, 1907.
Isabella di Morra con l'edizione del canzoniere. Ed. Domenico Bronzini. Matera: Montemurro, 1975.
Isabella di Morra e Diego Sandoval de Castro con l'edizione delle "Rime" della Morra. Ed. Benedetto Croce. Bari: Laterza, 1929, and Palermo: Sellerio, 1983 (reprint of the 1929 edition with the addition of critical and autobiographical essays).

Anthologies containing works by Isabella di Morra:
Costa-Zalessow, *op. cit.*
de Blasi, *op. cit.*
Rime delle Signore Lucrezia Marinella, Veronica Gambara e Isabella di Morra. Naples: Bulifon, 1693.
Rime diverse d'alcune nobilissime e virtuosissime donne. Ed. Ludovico Domenichi. Lucca: Busdrago, 1559.
Rime di cinquanta illustri poetesse. Naples: Bulifon, 1695.

Studies and other works:
Adler, Sara. "The Petrarchan Lament of Isabella di Morra." In *Donna: Women in Italian Culture.* Ottawa: Dovehouse, 1989, 201-21.
Caserta, G. *Isabella Morra e la società meridionale del Cinquecento.* Matera: META, 1976.
Croce, Benedetto. "Isabella di Morra e Diego Sandoval de Castro." In *Vite di avventure, di fede e di passione.* Bari: Laterza, 1947.
———."Sulle prime stampe delle 'Rime' di Isabella di Morra." In *Aneddoti di varia letteratura.* Bari: Laterza, 1953.

Dizionario enciclopedico, op. cit., 74.

Enciclopedia biografica bibliografica italiana, op. cit.

Finucci, Valeria. "Isabella di Morra." In *An Encylopedia of Continental Women Writers, op. cit.,* vol. 2, 876-77.

Maffia, Dante. "Isabella Morra." *Studi d'italianistica nell'Africa australe/ Italian Studies in Southern Africa 1990* 3, 4 (1991): 22-31.

Molinari, B. *Isabella di Morra poetessa del Cinquecento.* Naples: Gambella, 1907.

Russell, Rinaldina. "Intenzionalità artistica della 'disperata.'" In *Generi Poetici Medievali: Modelli e funzioni letterarie.* Naples: SEN, 1982, 163-82.

Schiesari, Juliana. "The Gendering of Melancholia: Torquato Tasso and Isabella di Morra." In *Refiguring Women: Perspectives on Gender and the Italian Renaissance.* Ed. Marilyn Migiel and Juliana Schiesari. Ithaca, N.Y.: Cornell University Press, 1991.

——. "Isabella di Morra." In *Italian Women Writers, op. cit.,* 279-285.

I

I fieri assalti di crudel Fortuna
scrivo, piangendo la mia verde etate;
me che in sì vili ed orride contrate
spendo il mio tempo senza loda alcuna.

    Degno il sepolcro, se fu vil la cuna,   5
vo procacciando con le Muse amate;
e spero ritrovar qualche pietate,
malgrado della cieca aspra importuna;

    e col favor delle sagrate dive,
se non col corpo, almen coll'alma sciolta,   10
esser in pregio a più felici rive.

    Questa spoglia, dov'or mi trovo involta,
forse tale alto re nel mondo vive,
che in saldi marmi la terrà sepolta.

3

D'un alto monte ove si scorge il mare
miro sovente io, tua figlia Isabella,
s'alcun legno spalmato in quello appare,
che di te, padre, a me doni novella.

    Ma la mia avversa e dispietata stella   5
non vuol ch'alcun conforto possa entrare
nel tristo cor, ma di pietà rubella
la salda speme in pianto fa mutare:

    ch'io non veggo nel mar remo né vela
(così deserto è l'infelice lito)   10
che l'onde fenda, o che la gonfi il vento.

    Contra Fortuna allor spargo querela,
ed ho in odio il denigrato sito,
come sola cagion del mio tormento.

1

I write about the fierce assaults of Fortune,
The cruel one, and mourn my hapless youth.
Living in such a base and ugly country,[1]
I waste my life without all recognition.
I seek a worthy sepulcher, though lowly   5
My cradle was, by following the Muses,[2]
And hope to find somewhere some sympathy
In spite of Fate, so cruel, harsh and blind.
And with the favor of those goddesses,[3]
Even without my body, with freed soul,   10
I hope on happier shores to be acclaimed.
Perhaps there lives a high king in this world
Who may preserve in everlasting marble
This mortal shroud in which I am confined.

3

From a high mountain top, where one can see
The waves, I, your sad daughter Isabella,
Gaze out for sight of any polished ship
Coming to bring me news of you, my father.[4]
But my adverse and cruel destiny   5
Permits no solace for my aching heart,
But, enemy to any thought of pity,
Turns all my firmest hopes into laments.
For I see neither oar cutting the sea,
Nor any sail that billows in the wind,   10
So solitary is this dismal shore.
So I can only curse my evil Fortune
And hold in hatred this unhappy place
The only source of my tormented life.

1. Favale, where she was confined without any social or intellectual life. 2. Goddesses of learning, music, poetry, etc. 3. The Muses again; she hopes to get recognition after death through her poetry. 4. The sonnet is addressed to her exiled father.

7

Ecco, che un'altra volta, o valle inferna,
   O fiume alpestre, o rovinati sassi,
   O ignudi spirti di virtute cassi,
   Udrete il pianto, e la mia doglia eterna.
Ogni monte udirammi, ogni caverna   5
   Ovunque arresti, ovunque io mova i passi;
   Che fortuna, che mai salda non stassi
   Cresce ognora il mio male, ognor l'eterna.
Deh mentre, ch'io mi lagno, e giorno, e notte,
   O fere, o sassi, o orride rovine,   10
   O selve incolte, o solitarie grotte;
Ulule, e voi del mal nostro indovine,
   Piangete meco, a voci alte interrotte,
   Il mio più d'altro miserando fine.

8

   Torbido Siri, del mio mal superbo,
or ch'io sento da presso in fine amaro,
fa' tu noto il mio duolo al padre caro,
se mai qui 'l torna il suo destino acerbo.
   Dilli com' io morendo, disacerbo   5
l'aspra fortuna e lo mio fato avaro,
e, con esempio miserando e raro,
nome infelice a le tue onde io serbo.
   Tosto ch'ei giunga a la sassosa riva
(a che pensar m'adduci, o fiera stella,   10
come d'ogni mio ben son cassa e priva!),
   inqueta l'onda con crudel procella,
e di': – M'accrebber sì, mentre fu viva,
non gli occhi no, ma i fiumi d'Isabella.

7[1]

Here once again, infernal rocky valley,
O Alpine rivers, ruinous high peaks,
O broken spirits stripped of every virtue,
You will now hear my plaints, my endless sorrow.
And every mountain, every cave shall hear me   5
Wherever I may stop, wherever go,
For Fortune, never stable, does not tarry,
But everlastingly adds to my pain.
While I lament, forever, night and day,
O beasts, o rocks, o melancholy ruins,   10
Uncultivated woods, o lonely caves,
Howl still with me, unriddling my grief,
And weep with me; in high continuous voices
Bewail my misery, worse than all others.

8

O turbid Siri,[2] careless of my grief,
Now that I feel so close to my life's end,
Make known my sorrow to my loving father[3]
If ever bitter Fate lets him return.
Tell him how, by my death, I will escape   5
My harsh misfortune and my niggard fate,
And, as a rare and piteous example,
I will entrust my sad name to your waves.
As soon as he[4] regains your rocky shoreline —
Why do you make me think of this, fierce star?   10
How I am robbed and shorn of every good! —
Stir up your restless currents with great storms
And say, "I grew so great while *she* was living,
Through — not the eyes — rivers of Isabella."

1. This sonnet shows her familiarity with Dante's *Inferno*. 2. The name of
the river flowing near the castle of Favale, now called Sinni. 3. Her father
has been exiled for political reasons. 4. Her exiled father.

CANZONE II

Poscia che al bel desir troncate hai l'ale,
che nel mio cor sorgea, crudel Fortuna,
sì che d'ogni suo ben vivo digiuna,
dirò, con questo stil ruvido e frale,
alcuna parte de l'interno male   5
causato sol da te, fra questi dumi,
fra questi aspri costumi
di gente irrazional, priva d'ingegno,
ove, senza sostegno,
son costretta a menar il viver mio,   10
qui posta da ciascuno in cieco oblio.

Tu, crudel, de l'infanzia in quei pochi anni,
del caro genitor mi festi priva,
che, se non è già pur ne l'altra riva,
per me sente di morte i grevi affanni: 15
ché 'l mio penar raddoppia gli suoi danni.
Cesar gli vieta il poter darmi aita
O cosa non più udita,
privar il padre di giovar la figlia!
Così, a disciolta briglia,   20
seguitata m'hai sempre, empia Fortuna,
cominciando dal latte e da la cuna.

Quella ch'è detta la fiorita etade,
secca ed oscura, solitaria ed erma,
tutta ho passato qui cieca ed inferma,   25
senza saper mai pregio di beltade.
È stata per me morta in te pietade,
e spenta l'hai in altrui, che potea sciôrre
e in altra parte porre
dal carcer duro il vel de l'alma stanca,   30
che, come neve bianca

CANZONE II

Since, cruel Fortune, you have clipped the wings
    Of that belov'd desire, born from my heart,
    So that I live deprived of every good,
    I shall speak out, though rough and weak my style,
    And tell a little of my inner pain   5
    Caused by you only, here among these thorns,
        Among the uncouth ways
    Of people lacking reason, short of wit,
        Where, robbed of any help,
I am constrained to live a narrow life,   10
Placed here alone, in blind oblivion.

Ah, cruel one, from childhood, those few years,
    You have deprived me of a loving father,
    Who, if he has not yet traversed the river[1]
    Must feel the pains of death on my account,   15
    Because my suffering doubles his grief.
    Caesar[2] forbids him yet to send me aid —
        Unheard-of cruelty!
    Keeping a father's heart from aid to daughter!
        And so, with loosened bridle,   20
    O cruel Fortune, you have followed me
Straight from my mother's breast and from the cradle.

This time of life, the so-called flowery age,
    I have spent here, alone, dried-out, obscure,
    Like a poor hermit, sightless, weak and ill,   25
    And knowing nothing of the gift of beauty.
    Pity for me indeed is dead in you
    And quenched in all those others who might loosen
        And carry clean away
    From its harsh jail the shadow of my soul,   30
        Which, as unsullied snow,

1. Acheron, river of death. 2. The Emperor Charles V, who exiled Isabella's father.

dal sol, così da te si strugge ogni ora,
e struggerassi infin che qui dimora.

    Qui non provo io di donna il proprio stato,
per te, che posta m'hai in sì ria sorte,   35
che dolce vita mi saria la morte.
I cari pegni del mio padre amato
piangon dintorno. Ahi ahi, misero fato,
mangiare il frutto, ch'altri colse, amaro
quei che mai non peccaro,   40
la cui semplicità faria clemente
una tigre, un serpente,
ma non già te, vêr noi più fiera e rea,
ch'al figlio Progne ed al fratel Medea.

    Dei ben, che ingiustamente la tua mano   45
dispensa, fatta m'hai tanto mendica,
che mostri ben quanto mi sei nemica
in questo inferno solitario e strano,
ogni disegno mio facendo vano.
S'io mi doglio di te sì giustamente,   50
per isfogar la mente,
da chi non son per ignoranza intesa
i' son, lassa, ripresa:
ché, se nodrita già fossi in cittade,
avresti tu più biasmo, io più pietade.   55

    Bastone i figli de la fral vecchiezza
esser dovean di mia misera madre;
ma, per le tue procelle inique ed adre,
sono in estrema ed orrida fiacchezza:
e spenta in lor sarà la gentilezza   60
da gli antichi lasciata a questi giorni,
se da gli alti soggiorni
pietà non giunge al cor del re di Francia,

Is melted by the sun, so it by you
Is melted while it sadly lingers here.

I'm not allowed the proper state of woman,
   Because of you, who set me in such straits   35
   That death would be a dearer goal than life.
   The sweet remembrances of my dear father
   Weep all around me. Ah, my wretched fate!
   To eat the bitter fruit gathered by others,
      Though I have done no wrong,   40
   My simple innocence would breed some pity
      In tigers or in serpents,
   But not in you, more pitiless than Procne[1]
   To her own son, Medea[2] to her brother.

Of all the goods your hand gives out unjustly,   45
   You have deprived me, leaving me a beggar.
   You prove yourself always my enemy;
   In this estranging, solitary hell,
   You render vain every design of mine.
   If I, with justice, do complain of you,   50
      Only to ease my mind,
   Those who, in ignorance, misunderstand me,
      Sharply rebuke me.
   Could I have only lived in some fair city,
   You would be blamed, people would pity me.   55

The sons, who should have been a strong support
   To my poor mother in her fragile age —
   Because of your unjust and wicked storms,
   Live in a state of helpless poverty.
   And quenched in them will be the noble spirit   60
   Left by our ancestors down to these days,
      Unless from highest heaven
   Pity rains down to touch the king of France,

1. She slew her own son to punish the infidelity of her husband. 2. She killed her brother in her attempt to escape from Colchis with Jason.

che, con giusta bilancia
pesando il danno, agguaglia la mercede   65
secondo il merto di mia pura fede.

   Ogni mal ti perdono
né l'alma si dorrà di te giammai,
se questo sol farai,
ahi ahi, Fortuna (e perché far no 'l déi?),   70
che giungan al gran Re gli sospir miei.

Who, with the scales of justice,
Weighing our wrongs, could match them
    with his mercy,   65
In true accord with my unspotted faith.
    Then I might pardon you,
And let my soul desist from its complaints,
    If you could do but this —
Ah, Fortune, why can you not do this much?   70
And let my sighs reach to that mighty king?

LUCIA BERTANI DELL'ORO
(1521-1567)

We do not know much about the early life of this woman poet, except that she belonged to the Bolognese family Dell'Oro, and that she married a Gurone Bertani of Modena. She was a learned woman, well-versed in literature, painting, and the sciences, and was held in high esteem both as a critic and as a poet. She actively participated in the famous literary dispute between Annibal Caro and Ludovico Castelvestro, and vainly attempted to reconcile the two warring scholars. She was also friends with Lodovico Domenichi, who praised her highly, and with Alessandro Melani.

Lucia wrote little, and was more important for her role in literary salons than as a poet. Much of her production is of an occasional encomiastic nature, such as the rhymes included in *Rime di diversi in morte della Signora Irene delle Signore di Spilimbergo* (1561) written for that famous noblewoman, and those for Lucrezia Gonzaga, included in *Rime in lode di Lucrezia Gonzaga* (1565).

According to Bandini Buti, she died in 1557 at the age of 46.

She must be remembered, however, for her active and vivacious participation in the intellectual life of her time, and for her contribution to literary criticism. As evidenced in her rhymes, she regarded herself as a literary mouthpiece for her times, celebrating, chastising and bestowing praise. We present two panegyric poems: one to Veronica Gàmbara, in which she shows appreciation for another *gentildonna* of great talent, and another, dedicated to both Veronica Gàmbara and Vittoria Colonna, in which she confesses her desire to emulate the acknowledged greatest women poets of her time.

BIBLIOGRAPHY

Anthologies containing works by Lucia Bertani Dell'Oro:
Bergalli, *op. cit.*
de Blasi, *op. cit.*
Rime di diversi in morte della Signora Irene delle Signore di Spilimbergo.
    Venice: n.p., 1561.
Rime di cinquanta illustri poetesse. Naples: Bulifon, 1695.
Rime di tre gentildonne del secolo XVI, op. cit.

Studies and other works:
Enciclopedia biografica bibligrafica italiana, op. cit.

La santa veramente unica ebrea,
  Di cui v'adorna il nome, e di cui l'orma
  Seguite sì che 'l piè vostro riforma
  I vestigi qua giù, ch'ella premea,
Non ammirare ed adorar facea   5
  Ne' bianchi lini la divina forma
  Di colui che salvò l'umana torma
  Quanto voi fate me, celeste dea.
Col vostro degno e grave aspetto santo,
  La cui stampa vegg'io nel'alme rime   10
  Vostre che fanno al maggior Tósco scorno;
Tal ch'io v'adoro in terra tra le prime
  Alme dotte, che fan tra noi soggiorno,
  E di tutte portate il pregio e 'l vanto.

The touching Hebrew saint, truly unique,[1]
Whose name adorns you, in whose holy steps
You follow, till your footprint takes the form,
Down here on earth, even as she impressed it,
Makes me no more admire and adore   5
The Holy Face, printed on her white linen,
Of Him who was the Savior of mankind,
Than you make me adore you, heavenly goddess,
With your respected, grave and holy face
Whose imprint I behold in your high verses,   10
Putting the greatest Tuscan bard[2] to shame;
So much do I adore you here on earth.
Among the wisest souls who live among us,
You bear away the prize and boast of all.

1. "Veramente unica," a pun on the name Veronica. According to legend, Saint Veronica wiped the face of Christ on His way to Golgotha, and her handkerchief retained a perfect imprint of His face. The poem is dedicated to Veronica Gàmbara, who is here compared to St. Veronica. For the use of the same pun to contrary effect, see Veronica Franco, *Terze Rime*, 16, pp. 192-93 below. 2. Dante, of course; the panegyric tone of this poem is not out of character with the style of the period. It also shows the respect of aspiring women writers towards those who had already succeeded artistically.

❦

Ebbe l'antica e gloriosa etade
   Saffo e Corinna, che con dotte piume
   S'alzaro insino al bel celeste lume
   Per molte, degne e virtuose strade.
Or due, che allor il crin cinge e bontade,   5
   Non pur fan d'Aganippe nascer fiume;
   Ma spengono ogni falso e rio costume
   Con opre eccelse, eterne, uniche e rade;
Tal che l'alta lor fama i pregi ingombra
   De le due prime; e in questa e quella parte   10
   Sonar si sente Gàmbara e Pescara.
Quest'alme illustri son cagion che ogni arte
   Tento per tôrre alla mia luce d'ombra,
   Sol perchè al mondo un dì si mostri chiara.

The glorious days of old were glad to own
Both Sappho and Corinna, whose wise pens
Raised them as high as to the light of heaven
Through many honorable, virtuous ways.
And now these two, whose hair is bound with laurel,   5
Not only pour out new streams from Aganippe[1]
But quench all impious and evil customs
With their high works, eternal and rare.
Such that their fame not only overshadows
The ancient two, but everywhere the names   10
Of Gàmbara and Pescara[2] resound.
These noble souls inspire me to strive
To bring my little light out of the shadow,
Only that it may shine forth to the world.

1. A fountain in Greece, sacred to the Muses.   2. Veronica Gàmbara and
Vittoria Colonna, who was the marchionness of Pescara.

GASPARA STAMPA
(1523-1554)

In the first of the Duino Elegies, Rainer Maria Rilke remembers
Gaspara Stampa thus:

> But Nature, spent and exhausted, takes lovers back
> into herself, as if there were not enough strength
> to create them a second time. Have you imagined
> Gaspara Stampa intensely enough so that any girl
> deserted by her beloved might be inspired
> by that fierce example of soaring, objectless love
> and might say to herself, "Perhaps I can be like her"?
> Shouldn't this most ancient of sufferings finally grow
> more fruitful for us? Isn't it time that we lovingly
> freed ourselves from the beloved and, quivering, endured:
> as the arrow endures the bowstring's tension, so that
> gathered in the snap of release it can be more than
> itself. For there is no place where we can remain.[1]

The greatest and most creative poet of the Italian Renaissance,
Gaspara Stampa was born in 1523 in Padua, of a Venetian mother
and the impoverished Milanese nobleman Bartolomeo Stampa,
who had become a jeweler. The three Stampa children, Cassandra,
Baldassarre and Gasparina (as she was also called) received an excellent education, and were taught Latin, Greek, metrics and music.
When her father died in 1531, her mother, Cecilia, moved the family
back to her native Venice, where the children were to become very
active in the social, literary and especially musical life of the city.
Cassandra and Gasparina soon became famous for their talent in
singing as well as for their expertise in accompanying themselves
on the lute.

Their popularity in musical circles was such that many madrigals were dedicated to them, and many specifically to Gaspara,
the more talented of the two sisters. Perissone Cambio, one of the

greatest composers of the Renaissance, stated: "No lady in the world loves music more than she, and none has a rarer degree of mastery over it." He added, addressing her, "there are thousands upon thousands of gentle and noble spirits who have heard your sweet harmonies and have given you the name of heavenly siren" (in A. Einstein, *The Italian Madrigal.* Princeton, 1971, vol. 1, p. 439).

When young Baldassarre died at the age of twenty, there was no male protection or guidance in the Stampa household, which was headed by a mother regarded by many as too indulgent and too open-minded for the good of her daughters' reputation. The two sisters were left to lead their lives with the freedom of move-ment and expression that their artistic careers could grant them; a freedom, however, which cost them not only their reputation, but caused many to speculate that they had in fact belonged to the throng of courtesans flourishing in the Venice of their time. The critic Abdelkader Salza, who in 1913 published Gaspara's *Rime* together with those of the courtesan Veronica Franco, tried in vain to find conclusive proof that Stampa had been a courtesan. The truth may be that she was maligned much like the free and artistic women of any age. We have, however, a letter written to Gaspara by a relative, Sister Angelica, the Abbess of the Convent of San Paolo in Milan, begging her to make sure that the "conversazioni" (conversations in literary salons) and the free life she led would not "endanger her beautiful chastity."

Benedetto Croce, who had a special appreciation of Stampa's poetry, called her "l'appassionata" (the passionate woman), adding that "she was not a courtesan by trade, as some contemporaries classified her, but certainly a woman outside the rules, probably a *virtuosa* of music and singing, with the free and easy attitudes of life and the equivocal relationships that the [musical] profession brought with itself, and almost justified." (*Poesia popolare e poesia d'arte.* Bari: Laterza, 1967).

She was befriended by scholars of the stature of Varchi, Domenico Venier, Alamanni and Luigi Domenichi, and was ac-cepted in the *Accademia dei Dubbiosi* with the literary name of "Anassilla," from the Anaxum, the Latin name of the river Piave, flowing through the lands of Count Collaltino di Collalto, the man whom she passionately loved and celebrated in her poetry.

Gaspara started to write poetry when she was in her twenties. Although she wrote within the tenets of the Petrarchan tradition, she distinguished herself through the special sense of rhythm provided by her musical education, and through the spontaneity which came from a passionate and headstrong temperament. Her *Rime* represent a poetic diary of her love for Collaltino. Gaspara met this nobleman on Christmas day, 1548, when she was twenty five. In a manner reminiscent of Petrarch's love for Laura, she fell in love with him instantly. This love, ecstatic and tormented in its vicissitudes, possessed her until 1551.

Collaltino undoubtedly loved Stampa, as he remained in turbulent liaison with her for over three years. He did not, however, seem to have the capacity to reciprocate her love with the same intensity. This imbalance in their relationship caused her to write lyrics filled alternately with ecstasy and sorrow, with the remembrance of happy moments shared, but also with jealousy and anxiety. Between them, moreover, there was an unbridgeable social gap. Stampa was painfully conscious that she was "lowly" in comparison with his status, and attempted to bridge this gulf with her poetry. Some of the most famous lyrics of the *Rime* are those in which Gaspara acknowledges a passionate, carnal relationship with Collaltino in an open manner unheard of in her day.

After the stormy relationship with Collaltino, she fell in love again, with the patrician Bartolomeo Zen, with whom she had a tender relationship based on a correspondence of interests and sensibilities.

In 1553, however, Gaspara's health took a turn for the worse. She went to Florence to recover in a less humid climate, but soon after her return to Venice, she caught a high fever which killed her in a few days. The same year, her beloved sister Cassandra had her *Rime* published, with a dedication to Monsignor Della Casa. Owing to the originality of Stampa's poetry, which did not follow Petrarchan tradition closely enough, her Rime was not very successful in her century. Stampa's poetry had to wait two centuries before being published again, by Luisa Bergalli, commissioned by Count Antonio Rambaldo di Collalto, a descendent of that same Collaltino who had caused Stampa so much pain — some sort of poetic justice. She is now hailed as one of the greatest Italian poets.

Stampa's *Rime* represents one of the largest and most varied *Canzonieri* in Italian literature, comprising 311 poems in all, which the poet had arranged in chronological order. Salza, the editor of the 1913 critical edition, made major changes to the structure of the original Stampa texts, dividing it into Love Poems and Occasional Poems. The first, larger section, Love Poems, includes 245 poems, most of them sonnets. It contains the lyrics for Count Collaltino, as well as the love poems for Bartolomeo Zen. The second section includes poems for male and female friends and *literati*, and ends with several religious sonnets. We have taken the text of our originals from the Salza critical edition.

From her poetry, the twentieth century poet D'Annunzio extracted the verse "Viver ardendo e non sentire il male" (to live burning and not to feel the pain), which he used as a motto.

Gaspara did in fact free herself from her obsessive love by sublimating her pain into some of the greatest poetry in Italian literature. For a greater selection of her poetry in translation, as well as a more extensive introduction, we refer the reader to our *Gaspara Stampa, Selected Poems* (New York: Italica Press, 1994).

BIBLIOGRAPHY

Works by Gaspara Stampa:

Rime di Madonna Gaspara Stampa. Ed. Cassandra Stampa with Giorgio Benzone. Venice: Plinio Pietrasanta, 1554.

Rime di Madonna Gaspara Stampa con alcune altre di Collaltino e di Vinciguerra conti di Collalto, e di Baldassarre Stampa. Ed. Luisa Bergalli with Apostolo Zeno. Venice: Piacentini, 1738.

Rime di Gaspara Stampa. Ed. P. Mestica Chiappetti. Florence: Barbèra, 1877.

Rime di tre gentildonne del secolo XVI: Vittoria Colonna, Gaspara Stampa e Veronica Gambara. Ed. O. Guerrini. Milan: Sonzogno, 1883.

Rime di Gaspara Stampa e di Veronica Franco. Ed. A. Salza. Bari: Laterza, 1913.

Rime. Ed. Rodolfo Ceriello. Milan: Rizzoli, 1954; new ed. 1976 with intro. by Maria Bellonci.

Gaspara Stampa: Selected Poems. Ed. Laura Stortoni and Mary Prentice Lillie. New York: Italica Press, 1994.

Anthologies containing works by Gaspara Stampa:

Costa-Zalessow, *op. cit.*

Le più belle pagine di Gaspara Stampa, Vittoria Colonna, Veronica Gambara, Isabella di Morra. Ed. Giuseppe Toffanin. Milan: Treves, 1935.

Lirici del Cinquecento, op. cit., 332-337.

Poesia del Quattrocento e del Cinquecento, op. cit., 1293-1296.

Studies and other works:

Bandini Buti, M. "Gaspara Stampa." *Poetesse e scrittrici,* vol. II. In *Enciclopedia Bibliografica e Bibliografia Italiana,* ser. 4, pt. 6. Milan: Istituto editoriale italiano, 1941, 278-283.

Bassanese, Fiora. "*A Feminine Voice: Gaspara Stampa.*" Canadian Journal of Italian Studies 3,2 (Winter 1980): 81-88.

——. *Gaspara Stampa.* Boston: Twayne, 1983.

——. "Gaspara Stampa's Poetics of Negativity." *Italica* 61 (Autumn 1984): 335-46.

——. "Gaspara Stampa." In *Italian Women Writers, op. cit.,* 404-413.

Bellonci, Maria. "La vita e gli amori della poetessa padovana Gaspara Stampa." In *Supplemento del Corriere della Sera,* Sept. 26, 1976.

Croce, B. "Gaspara Stampa." *Rassegna degli interessi femminili* I, (1887): vols. 2 and 3.

Dizionario enciclopedico, op. cit., I, 163-165.

Dolci, Giulio. "Gaspara Stampa." In *Letteratura Italiana: I Minori*, vol. 2. Milan: Marzorati, 1961, 315-25.

Flora, Francesco. *Gaspara Stampa e altre poetesse del '500*. Milan: Nuova Accademia, 1962.

Innocenzi Gregio, Elisa. "In difesa di Gaspara Stampa." *Ateneo Veneto* 38,1 (1915): 1-160, 280-99.

Jones, Ann Rosalind. "'New Songs for the Swallow:' Ovid's Philomela in Tullia d'Aragona and Gaspara Stampa. In *Refiguring Women: Gender Studies and the Italian Renaissance*. Ed. Marilyn Migiel and Juliana Schiesari. Ithaca: Cornell University Press, 1991.

Lawner, Lynn. "Gaspara Stampa and the Rhetoric of Submission." In *Renaissance Studies in Honor of Craig Hugh Smith*, vol. I. Florence: Giunti Barbera, 1985, 345-62.

Malagoli, Luigi. *La lirica del Cinquecento e Gaspara Stampa*. Pisa: Editrice Goliardica, 1966.

——. "La nuova sensibilità e il nuovo stile: Gaspara Stampa." In *Le contraddizioni del Rinascimento*. Florence: La Nuova Italia, 1968, 105-23.

Rilke, Rainer Maria. *The Notebooks of Malte Laurids Briggs*. Transl. Stephen Mitchell. New York: Vintage, 1985, 134, 235.

Vassalli, Donati Chimenti. "Emancipazione e schiavitù in Gaspara Stampa." *Osservatore Politico Letterario* 19, 9 (1972): 70-85.

Vitiello, Justin. "Gaspara Stampa: The Ambiguities of Martyrdom." *Modern Language Notes* 90 (January 1975): 58-71.

2

Era vicino il dí che 'l Creatore,
che ne l'altezza sua potea restarsi,
in forma umana venne a dimostrarsi,
dal ventre virginal uscendo fore,
    quando degnò l'illustre mio signore,   5
per cui ho tanti poi lamenti sparsi,
potendo in luogo piú alto annidarsi,
farsi nido e ricetto del mio core.
    Ond'io sí rara e sí alta ventura
accolsi lieta; e duolmi sol che tardi   10
mi fe' degna di lei l'eterna cura.
    Da indi in qua pensieri e speme e sguardi
volsi a lui tutti, fuor d'ogni misura
chiaro e gentil, quanto 'l sol giri e guardi.

7

Chi vuol conoscer, donne, il mio signore,
miri un signor di vago e dolce aspetto,
giovane d'anni e vecchio d'intelletto,
imagin de la gloria e del valore:
    di pelo biondo, e di vivo colore,   5
di persona alta e spazioso petto,
e finalmente in ogni opra perfetto,
fuor ch'un poco (oimè lassa!) empio in amore.
    E chi vuol poi conoscer me, rimiri
una donna in effetti ed in sembiante   10
imagin de la morte e de' martíri,
    un albergo di fé salda e costante,
una, che, perché pianga, arda e sospiri,
non fa pietoso il suo crudel amante.

2

It was about the day¹ when the Creator,
Who could have stayed in His sublime abode,
Came down to show Himself in human form,
Issuing from the Holy Virgin's womb,
When it occurred that my illustrious lord²   5
For whom I wrote so many love laments,
Who could have found a nobler resting place,
Made his own nest and refuge in my heart.
So I embraced this rare and lofty fortune
With joy, only regretting that so late   10
I was made worthy by Eternal Care.³
Since then I turned my hopes and thoughts and glances
On him alone, so noble, brave, and gentle,
Beyond all others that the sun beholds.

7

If, ladies, you desire to know my lord,⁴
Look for a gentleman with sweet expression,
Though young in years, old in his intellect;
Image of valor and of warlike glory;
His hair is blond, and his complexion light,   5
He's tall in stature, with a manly chest,
Seeming perfection in his every act,
But, ah, in love not faithful to his word.
If you should care to know me, you might see,
A lady in her manner and appearance   10
Like Death herself and every kind of sorrow,
An inn of steady faith and constancy,
One who, for all her tears, her ardent sighs,
Can win no pity from her cruel lover.

1. Stampa met Collaltino on Christmas Day, 1548. A Petrarchan echo (*Rime* 3): Petrarch fell in love with Laura on Holy Friday, 1327; Stampa, with an obvious parallel, on Christmas Day. 2. Collaltino. 3. God, who made her worthy of such a noble love. 4. Collaltino.

10

 Alto colle, gradito e grazioso,
novo Parnaso mio, novo Elicona,
ove poggiando attendo la corona,
de le fatiche mie dolce riposo;
 quanto sei qui tra noi chiaro e famoso,   5
e quanto sei a Rodano e a Garona,
a dir in rime alto disio mi sprona,
ma l'opra è tal, che cominciar non oso.
 Anzi quanto averrá che mai ne canti,
fia pura ombra del ver, perciò che 'l vero   10
va di lungo il mio stil e l'altrui innanti.
 Le tue frondi e 'l tuo giogo verdi e 'ntero
conservi 'l cielo, albergo degli amanti,
colle gentil, dignissimo d'impero.

43

 Dura è la stella mia, maggior durezza
è quella del mio conte: egli mi fugge,
i' seguo lui; altri per me si strugge,
i' non posso mirar altra bellezza.
 Odio chi m'ama, ed amo chi mi sprezza;   5
verso chi m'è umíle il mio cor rugge,
e son umíl con chi mia speme adugge;
a cosí stranio cibo ho l'alma avezza.
 Egli ognor dá cagione a novo sdegno,
essi mi cercan dar conforto e pace: 10
i' lasso questi, ed a quell'un m'attegno.
 Cosí ne la tua scola, Amor, si face
sempre il contrario di quel ch'egli è degno:
l'umíl si sprezza, e l'empio si compiace.

10

High hill,[1] so pleasing and so beautiful,
My new Parnassus, my new Helicon,[2]
Resting on which I now await my crown,[3]
Sweet place of rest from my poetic labors,
How bright and famous you are, here among us,   5
And famous, too, beside Garonne and Rhone,[4]
Lofty desire spurs me to say in rhyme,
Yet the work is so great, I daren't begin —
But if it happens that I sing of it,
It will be just a shadow of the truth,   10
Which far surpasses both my art and others'.
May heaven keep your leaves and summit safe,
Preserve this hill, sojourn of royal lovers,
O gentle hill, most worthy of a ruler!

43

Harsh is my fortune, but still harder fate
Is dealt me by my lord[5]; he flees from me.
I follow him, while others pine for me,
But I cannot admire another's face.
I hate the one who loves, love him who scorns me.   5
Against the humble ones, my heart rebels,
But I am humble toward the one who spurns me.
So my soul starves for such a harmful food!
He gives me cause for anger every day,
The others try to give comfort and peace.   10
Those I deny, but cling to my tormentor.
Thus, in your school, O Love, the scholars win
The opposite of that which they deserve:
The humble are despised, the proud are praised.

1. Collalto, or "high hill," is the name of the estate of her lover, Collaltino di Collalto. 2. Mountains in Greece, sacred to the Muses. 3. The crown of laurel, bestowed on poets. 4. Rivers in France marking the limits of Languedoc, where Collaltino was serving the king of France. 5. Collaltino.

60

Quinci Amor, quindi cruda empia Fortuna
m'affligon sí, che non so com'io possa
riparar questa e quell'altra percossa,
che mi dánno a vicenda or l'altro or l'una.

Aer, mar, terra, ciel, sol, stelle e luna,   5
con quant'ha piú ciascuna orgoglio e possa
a danno mio, a mia ruina mossa,
lassa, mi si mostrò fin da la cuna.

E quel ch'è sol il mio fido sostegno,
per accrescermi duol, fra sí brev'ora   10
partirassi da me senza ritegno.

Almen venisse acerba morte ancora,
mentr'io dolente mi lamento e sdegno,
da le man di tant'oste a trarmi fòra!

69

Mentre, signor, a l'alte cose intento,
v'ornate in Francia l'onorata chioma,
come fecer i figli alti di Roma,
figli sol di valor e d'ardimento,

io qui sovr'Adria piango e mi lamento,   5
si da' martír, si da' travagli doma,
gravata si da l'amorosa soma,
che mi veggo morir, e lo consento.

E duolmi sol che, sí come s'intende
qui 'l suon da noi de' vostri onor, ch'omai   10
per tutta Italia si chiaro si stende,

non s'oda in Francia il suono de' miei lai,
che cosí spesso il ciel pietoso rende,
e voi pietoso non ha fatto mai.

60

On one side Love, the other, cruel Fortune
Afflict me so that I can never tell
How to protect myself from either blow
Dealt to me by the one or by the other.
Air, sea, earth, sky, and sun, and stars and moon — 5
With whatsoever pride and power each has
To injure me and send me to my ruin,
Have worked against me even from the cradle;
And that one, who's my only true support,
Just to increase my sorrow, in brief time 10
Will leave me comfortless, without regret.[1]
May bitter death at least come to my aid
While I, repining, mourn but do not try
To flee out of my enemy's harsh hands.

69

While you, my lord, intent on lofty ventures,
Win for your head, in France, the victor's crown,
As did the noble sons of ancient Rome,
Sons of high courage and of dauntless valor,
I, by the Adriatic Sea lament, 5
Tamed as I am by suffering and pain,
Weighed down so by the burden of my love.
I see myself as dying; and I am glad.
I only grieve that everybody here
Has heard the news of your distinguished honors 10
Spread through all Italy with such acclaim.
But there in France, the sound of my laments
Is never heard,[2] though heaven itself feels pity;
But you have never pitied me at all.

1. Collaltino is about to leave for France. 2. Stampa in this sonnet appears
to be almost jealous of Collaltino's fame.

89

Ma che, sciocca, dich'io? perché vaneggio?
perché sí fuggo questo chiaro inganno?
perché sgravarmi da si util danno,
pronta ne' danni miei, ad Amor chieggio?

    Come, fuor di me stessa, non m'aveggio   5
che quante ebber mai gioie, e quante avranno,
quante fùr donne mai, quante saranno,
co' miei chiari martír passo e pareggio?

    Ché l'arder per cagion alta e gentile
ogni aspra vita fa dolce e beata   10
piú che gioir per cosa abietta e vile.

    Ed io ringrazio Amor, che destinata
m'abbia a tal foco, che da Battro a Tile
spero anche un giorno andar chiara e lodata.

89

I'm such a fool! Why do I talk such nonsense!
Why do I flee from such a clear[1] deception?
Why do I ask Love to unburden me
Of this useful[2] distress, to my own damage?
I am beside myself, if I don't see   5
That, with my clear torments, I have now equaled
Even surpassed, all women who have ever
Had joy in their past life and yet will have.
Burning of love for such a noble cause[3]
Makes every life of hardship high and worthy,   10
More than enjoying low and abject things.
And I thank Love, who destined for my life
Such ardor, that from Bactria to Thule[4]
I hope one day to win both fame and honor.

1. Used here also in the sense of noble. 2. The pain that makes her write; therefore, she would be damaging herself in freeing herself from such pain. 3. The love for Collaltino — noble because of his status and because it gives her inspiration to write. 4. Bactria was the name of part of Persia and represents the far south-east; "Thule" a semi-mythical island in the northwest — possibly Iceland. Cf. Goethe's *Es war ein Koenig in Thule.*

107

Or che ritorna e si rinova l'anno,
passato il verno e la stagion più fresca,
l'amoroso disir mio si rinfresca,
e la mia dolce pena, e 'l dolce affanno.

E qual i novi umor gravidi fanno   5
gli arbori, onde lor frutto a suo tempo esca,
tal umor nel mio petto par che cresca,
al qual poi pensier dolci a dietro vanno.

Ed è ben degno che gioia ed umore,
or ch'egli è meco la mia primavera,   10
mi rinovelli e mi ridesti Amore.

Oh pur non giunga a si bel giorno sera!
oh pur non cangi il bel tempo in orrore,
dipartendo da me l'alma mia sfera!

112

Se voi poteste, o sol degli occhi miei,
qual sète dentro donno del mio core,
veder coi vostri apertamente fuore,
oh me beata quattro volte e sei!

Voi più sicuro, e queta io più sarei: 5
voi senza gelosia, senza timore;
io di due sarei scema d'un dolore,
e più felicemente ardendo andrei.

Anzi aperto per voi, lassa, si vede,
più che 'l lume del sol lucido e chiaro,   10
che dentro e fuori io spiro amor e fede.

Ma vi mostrate di credenza avaro,
per tôrmi ogni speranza di mercede,
e far il dolce mio viver amaro.

148

107

Now that the year returns and is renewed,
Winter is past, the coldest time[1] is over,
Desire for love is freshly born in me,
And my sweet pain, even my sweetest trials.
And as the rising sap brings out the blossoms   5
From which sweet fruit arises in due time,
It seems that just such sap will fill my breast,
Following which sweet thoughts come close behind.
And it is right that joy and flowing sap —
Now that my lord of spring is here beside me[2] —   10
That Love should be renewed and laugh within me.
Never may evening come to this bright day!
Oh, may this lovely time[1] not turn to horror!
Parting me from my shining well-loved sphere![3]

112

If you could only see, sun of my eyes,[4]
That you are solely master of my heart —
If you could see this clearly in the open,
How happy I should be — four or six times!
You would be more secure, I more serene,   5
You free from jealousy and free from fear;
I should be freed from one grief of the two[5]
And I would burn with a more joyous flame.
But openly for you, alas, one sees
More plainly than the clear and shining sunlight,   10
That both inside and out I breathe pure love.
But you still show yourself lacking in faith,[6]
Taking from me all hope and all compassion,
Making my former sweet life sadly bitter.

1. "Time" and "weather" are the same in Italian. 2. Collaltino has returned to Stampa. 3. Meaning "sun" also stands for Collaltino. The poet is afraid that he will leave again. 4. Collaltino. 5. That he does not love her any more, and that he is jealous of her without cause. 6. He does not trust her as she trusts him.

124

Signor, io so che 'n me non son piú viva,
e veggo omai ch'ancor in voi son morta,
e l'alma, ch'io vi diedi, non sopporta
che stia piú meco vostra voglia schiva.

E questo pianto, che da me deriva,   5
non so chi 'l mova per l'usata porta,
né chi mova la mano e le sia scorta,
quando avien che di voi talvolta scriva.

Strano e fiero miracol veramente,
che altri sia viva, e non sia viva, e pèra,   10
 e senta tutto e non senta niente;

 si che può dirsi la mia forma vera,
da chi ben mira a sí vario accidente,
un'imagine d'Eco e di Chimera.

132

Quando io dimando nel mio pianto Amore,
che cosí male il mio parlar ascolta,
mille fiate il dí, non una volta,
ché mi fere e trafigge a tutte l'ore:

— Come esser può, s'io diedi l'alma e 'l core   5
al mio signor dal dí ch'a me l'ho tolta,
e se ogni cosa dentro a lui raccolta
è riso e gioia, è scema di dolore,

ch'io senta gelosia fredda e temenza,
e d'allegrezza e gioia resti priva,   10
s' io vivo in lui, e in me di me son senza?

— Vo' che tu mora al bene ed al mal viva —
mi risponde egli in ultima sentenza; —
questo ti basti, e questo fa' che scriva.

124

My lord, I know that I no longer live
Within myself, and in you I am dead.
The soul I gave to you cannot endure
The slackening of your desire to see me,
And this complaint that pours out of my eyes —   5
I do not know who pulls it through these gates[1]
Or who directs my hand and makes it move
Whenever I may chance to write of you.
Surely a rare, wild miracle it is
That one can live and yet not be alive.   10
I feel it all, and yet not feel at all.
So that this form of mine could be perceived
By the beholder of this strange event
As images of Echo[2] and Chimera.[3]

132

When in my weeping I inquire of Love
(Who so unwillingly gives ear to me)
A thousand times a day – never just once –
Why he[4] will wound and pierce me all the time:
"How can it be, since I gave heart and soul   5
To him,[5] the day I took them both[6] from me,
If everything enclosed within his breast
Is only joy and laughter, never sorrow,
How can I feel cold jealousy and fear
And be deprived of all my joyfulness,   10
Living in him, and never in myself?"
"I bid you die to joy and live in grief,"
Love answers me in his hard final sentence:
"Let this suffice you, that it makes you write."

1. The eyes are the gates of her tears. 2. Her state is similar to that of Echo, a nymph who languished for the unrequited love of Narcissus. 3. A mythical monster — Stampa compares herself to an image without true existence. 4. Love. 5. Collaltino. 6. Her heart and soul.

208

Amor m'ha fatto tal ch'io vivo in foco,
qual nova salamandra al mondo, e quale
l'altro di lei non men stranio animale,
che vive e spira nel medesmo loco.

Le mie delizie son tutte e 'l mio gioco   5
viver ardendo e non sentire il male,
e non curar ch'ei che m'induce a tale
abbia di me pietà molto né poco.

A pena era anche estinto il primo ardore,
che accese l'altro Amore, a quel ch'io sento   10
fin qui per prova, più vivo e maggiore.

Ed io d'arder amando non mi pento,
pur che chi m'ha di novo tolto il core
resti de l'arder mio pago e contento.

243

Dettata dal dolor cieco ed insano,
vattene al mio signor, lettera amica,
baciando a lui la generosa mano.

E digli che dal dí, che la nimica
mia stella me lo tolse, il cibo mio   5
è sol noia, dolor, pianto e fatica.

Ben fu 'l ciel al mio ben contrario e rio,
ch'a pena mi mostrò l'amato obietto,
che, misera, da me lo dipartio.

O brevi gioie, o fral uman diletto!   10
o nel regno d'Amor tesor fugace,
subito mostro e subito intercetto!

208

Love has made me live in ceaseless fire
Like a strange salamander[1] come to earth
Or like that bird of fable,[2] no less strange,
That lives and breathes in this same element.
All my delight it is, and all my joy,   5
To live, endlessly burning, with no pain,[3]
Not caring whether he who caused my grief
Takes pity on me, either great or small.
Barely had I put out my heart's first flame
Than Love kindled a second, which I feel   10
As sharper, livelier than the first had been.
This ardency of love I don't repent,
So long as he who lit my heart anew
Remains at peace, contented in my love.

243[4]

Dictated by my sorrow, blind and mad,
    Dear Letter, go to my belovèd lord,
    Kissing his hand, always so generous,
And tell him, from the day when that unfriendly
    Star of my fate took him away from me,   5
    My food is only boredom, tears, and trouble.
Heaven has indeed made war against my welfare,
    Having but barely shown me the loved object
    When it, alas, stole him away from me.
O short-lived joy! O frail delights of earth!   10
    O fleeting treasures in the realm of Love
    Shown me so briefly, suddenly removed!

1. A mythical creature who could only live in fire. 2. The phoenix. 3. The great Italian poet Gabriele D'Annunzio (1863-1938) chose this verse as his motto. 4. A *capitolo*.

Il bel paese, che superbo giace
fra 'l Rodano e la Mosa, or mi contende
la suprema cagion d'ogni mia pace.   15

    Mentre ivi il mio signor gradito intende
a l'onorate giostre, a' pregi, a' ludi,
di cui sí chiara a noi fama s'estende,

    io, misera, che 'n lui tutti i miei studi,
tutte le voglie ho poste, essendo lunge,   20
conven che disiando agghiacci e sudi.

    E sí fiero il martír m'assale e punge,
ch'io mi vivo sol d'esso e vivrommi anco
fin che 'l ciel, conte, a me vi ricongiunge.

    Voi, qual guerrier vittorioso e franco,   25
ferite altrui con l'onorata lancia;
io son ferita qui dal lato manco.

    O per me poco aventurosa Francia!
o bel paese, avverso a' miei disiri,
che 'mpallidir mi fai spesso la guancia!   30

    Dovunque avien che gli occhi volga e giri,
non vi trovando voi, conte, mi resto
senza speranza, preda de' sospiri.

    Voi prometteste ben di scriver presto,
non possendo tornar, per porger ésca   35
fra tanto al mio disir atro e funesto:

    e, poi che non lo fate, temo ch'esca
da la memoria vostra la mia fede,
e che del mio dolor poco v'incresca.

    È questa de l'amor mio la mercede?   40
e de la vostra fede è questo il pegno?
Misera donna ch'ad amante crede!

    Credetti amar un cavalier piú degno

That lovely country, lying in its pride
　　Between Moselle and Rhone, now steals from me
　　The highest source of all my joy and peace.　　　　15
While there,[1] my lord delightedly takes part
　　In honorable jousts, prizes and games,
　　The fame[2] of which shines brilliantly down here.[3]
While I, unhappy, placing all my thoughts,
　　All my desires on him, so far away,　　　　20
　　That I both freeze and sweat, desiring him,
And such fierce torment stabs and pierces me
　　That I exist and only live for it,
　　And shall, till heaven, Count, shall reunite us.
You, like a warrior, brave and victorious,　　　　25
　　Strike others with your highly-honored lance,
　　While I am wounded on my left-hand side.[4]
O France! Ill-omened and unkind to me!
　　Beautiful country, adverse to my joy!
　　How often do you make my cheeks turn pale!　　　　30
Wherever I may turn my eyes to look,
　　Not seeing you, my Count, I must remain
　　Forever hopeless, victim of my sighs.
You promised me that you would write me, soon,
　　Since you cannot return to bring me bait　　　　35
　　To feed my dark funereal desire;
Since you cannot come back to offer food,
　　At least of memory, to serve my faith,
　　While you take little pity on my grief.
Is this the compensation for my love?　　　　40
　　Is this the token of your faithfulness?
　　Unhappy woman, to believe her lover!
I thought I loved the worthiest of knights,

1. France, where Collaltino is. 2. The fame of his exploits is reaching
Italy. 3. Venice, where Stampa is staying. At his departure, Collaltino had
promised to write to her. 4. The side of the heart.

e 'l piú che mai fosse, ed or m'aveggio
che la credenza mia non giunge al segno....   45

   Deh, dolce conte mio, per quelle e queste   65
fra noi ore lietissime passate,
ond'io mi piacqui e voi vi compiaceste,

   piú lungamente omai non indugiate
a scrivermi due versi solamente,
se 'l mio diletto e la mia vita amate....

   244

   De le ricche, beate e chiare rive
d'Adria, di cortesia nido e d'Amore,
ove sí dolce si soggiorna e vive,

   donna, avendo lontano il suo signore,
quando il sol si diparte, e quando poi   5
a noi rimena il matutino albore,

   per isfogar gli ardenti disir suoi,
con queste voci lo sospira e chiama;
voi, rive, che l'udite, ditel voi.

   Tu, che volando vai di rama in rama,   10
consorte amata e fida tortorella,
e sai quanto si tema e quanto s'ama,

   quando, volando in questa parte e 'n quella,
sei vicina al mio ben, mostragli aperto
in note, ch'abbian voce di favella: 15

   digli quant'è 'l mio stato aspro ed incerto,
or che, lassa, da lui mi trovo lunge
per ria fortuna mia e non per merto.

   E tu, rosignuolin, quando ti punge
giusto disio di disfogar tuoi lai   20
con voce ove cantando non s'aggiunge,

   digli, dolente quanto fossi mai,

The handsomest who ever lived, but now
   I must confess that I have missed my mark!...   45
Sweet Count, for past and present joyful hours
     Exchanged between us in more happy times,   65
     When I pleased you, and you delighted me,
Do not delay or put off any longer
     To write two verses only for my sake,
     If you do truly love me, and my life....

244[1]

On the rich, blessèd, and unclouded banks
Of Adria,[2] nest of courtesy and love,
Where one can stay and live so sweet a life,
     A woman, whose dear lord is far away,
Whether the sun has set, or when again   5
It brings to us the dawn of a new day,
     In order to express her ardent love
With words like these she sighs and calls to him:
"You, seashores, you who hear, speak out to him,
     And you who lightly flit from branch to branch,   10
Beloved companion, faithful turtle dove,
You know how much one fears, how much one loves,
     When you, flying from one place to the other,
Come close to my dear lord, show openly
In singing just as plainly as in words;   15
     Tell him how harsh is my uncertain state,
Now that, alas, I am so far from him,
Because of evil fortune, not my fault;
     And you, sweet nightingale, when you are spurred
by the desire to vent your inner sorrow,   20
wherever with your voice you cannot reach
     Go tell him, pray, how lonely I have been

1. A *capitolo*. 2. The Adriatic; Stampa is in Venice, Collaltino is in
France.

che la mia vita è tutta oscura notte,
essendo priva di quei dolci rai.

    E tu, che 'n cave e solitarie grotte,   25
Eco, soggiorni, il suon de' miei lamenti
rendi a l'orecchie sue con voci rotte.

    E voi, dolci aure ed amorosi venti,
i miei sospir accolti in lunga schiera
deh fate al signor mio tutti presenti.   30

    E voi, che lunga e dolce primavera
serbate, ombrose selve, e sète spesso
fido soggiorno a questa e a quella fèra,

    mostrate tutte al mio signore espresso
che non pur i diletti mi son noia,   35
ma la vita m'è morte anco senz'esso.

    Ei si portò, partendo, ogni mia gioia,
e, se, tornando omai, non la rimena,
per forza converrá tosto ch'io moia.

    La speme sola al viver mio dá lena,   40
la qual, non tornand'ei, non può durare,
da soverchio disio vinta e da pena.

    Quell'ore, ch'io solea tutte passare
liete e tranquille, mentre er'ei presente,
or ch'egli è lunge son tornate amare.   45

    Ma, lassa, a torto del suo mal si pente,
a torto chiama il suo destin crudele,
chi volontario al suo morir consente....

    E, se rimena il sole un di quel giorno,
non pensate mai piú da me partire,
ch'io non vi sia da presso notte e giorno,   60
    poi ch'io mi veggo senza voi morire.

and that my life is one perpetual night,
as I am deprived of his luminous rays.
    And you who live in solitary caves,
Echo, bring to his ears, in broken tones,   25
The very sound of my lonely laments.
    And you, sweet breezes, and you amorous airs,
Bring to the presence of my lord, collected
In one long flight, my many loving sighs.
    And you, who keep a long and pleasant springtime,   30
Shadowy woods, and who often preserve
Safe dwelling-places for wild animals,
    Let all of them together show my lord
Not only that all pleasures simply bore me,
But life itself is death, deprived of him.   35
    He took with him on parting, all my joy,
And if he does not bring it back, returning,
I will be forced to die, before too long.
    Hope only gives me strength to keep on living;
If he does not return, it won't endure,   40
Destroyed by much desire and still more pain.
    Those hours, which I was used to pass with him,
Tranquil and happy, while he stayed with me,
Now he is gone, have turned to bitterness.
    But oh, in vain, one mourns her suffering,   45
In vain bewails her cruel destiny
She who voluntarily consents to die!…
    And if, my lord, you come to me some time,
Do not think you will lightly get away,
For I'll be at your side both day and night,   50
    Before, without you, I'll consent to die!

LAURA BATTIFERRI AMMANNATI
(1523-1589)

Laura was born in 1523 in Urbino, a town made famous by Baldassar Castiglione's *The Book of the Courtier*. She was the illegitimate daughter of the nobleman Giovanni Antonio Battiferri. Having been legally recognized by her father, she received an excellent education and soon distinguished herself for her knowledge and wisdom. She married Vittorio Sereni, who left her a widow at an early age (Cf. *When from the Rugged Mountains…*).

In 1550 she was married again to architect and sculptor Bartolomeo Ammannati, with whom she lived the rest of her life in a villa in Maiano, near Florence. She accompanied Bartolomeo in his travels, and her life was very active. She corresponded with prominent *literati* of her time, such as Bernardo Tasso, Annibal Caro, Benedetto Varchi, and was friends with the famous painter Bronzino. Her portrait by Bronzino — now at Palazzo Vecchio in Florence — depicts her as a dignified, if less than attractive, matron, with an austere aquiline profile, her head wrapped in white veils, her delicate hands holding a book of poetry, most probably her own, open as an example to the beholder. For her vast and varied literary production, she was admitted to the *Accademia degli Assorditi* in Urbino, and to the *Accademia degli Intronati* in Siena. She led an upright life, devoting herself to charity and exerting a deep moralizing influence on her husband's artistic conception. Although she cannot be regarded as a truly great poet, she enjoyed great renown and esteem in her times for her knowledge and for her integrity.

Her first book, *Il primo libro delle opere toscane,* which was first published in Florence in 1560, and later reprinted in Naples with the more general title of *Rime,* includes lyric compositions such as sonnets, madrigals and sestinas. She loved living in the countryside and her poetry is particularly effective when describing nature in touching elegiac tones. She thought very highly of her poetic mission, and her lofty conception of poetry is expressed in the sixteen letters she wrote to Benedetto Varchi, published by Gargiolli in 1879 in *Scelte di curiosità inedite e rare.* The poem *When the Sun Stoops to Hide…* reflects her concern with being remembered by posterity — a concern shared with many other Renaissance women — as well as a feeling of urgency to complete the task of collecting and publishing her poems, so that she could become "eternally illustrious." In *Before the Color of the Hair…* she calls for fame, praying to Apollo to bestow laurel wreaths on her forehead.

She died in 1589, having donated all of her assets to the Collegio di San Giovannino in Florence, an institution for the education of poor young men. Her husband outlived her by only three years.

We have taken the Italian text of *When from the rugged mountains, damp and dark…,* and *Between these sunny shores and untamed landscapes…,* from the de Blasi anthology; the original of *When the sun stoops to hide his lofty forehead…* from the Costa-Zalessow anthology, and the original of *Before the color of the hair that Nature…* from *Lirici del Cinquecento,* edited by D. Ponchiroli.

BIBLIOGRAPHY

Works by Laura Battiferri Ammannati:
Il primo libro delle opere toscane. Florence: Giunti, 1560.
I sette salmi penitenziali del Santissimo Profeta David, tradotti in lingua toscana. Florence: Giunti, 1563.
Rime. Naples: Bulifon, 1694.

Anthologies including works by Laura Battiferri Ammannati:
Bergalli, *op. cit.*
Costa-Zalessow, *op. cit.*
Croce, B. "La lirica cinquecentesca." In *Poesia popolare e poesia d'arte, op. cit.*
de Blasi, *op. cit.*
Lirici del Cinquecento, op. cit., 354-357.

Studies and other works:
Bertoni, G. "Luisa Bertani e Laura Battiferri." *Giornale storico della letteratura italiana* 85 (1925): 379-380.
Dizionario enciclopedico, op. cit., I, 289.
Dizionario biografico, op. cit., VII, 242-244.
Enciclopedia biografica bibliografica italiana, op. cit.
Rabitti, Giovanna. "Laura Battiferri Ammannati." In *Italian Women Writers, op. cit.,* 44-49.
Zaccagnini, G. "Lirici urbinati del secolo XVI." *Le Marche* III (1903): 1-3.

Quando nell'ocean l'altera fronte
inchina il sole e 'l nostro mondo imbruna
e dal più basso ciel la fredda luna
sormonta e fa d'argento ogni alto monte,
    partesi il buon pastor dal chiaro fonte   5
e la sua greggia alla sua mandra aduna,
e 'l stanco pellegrin raccoglie in una
le forze stanche al suo voler mal pronte;
    et io che veggio avvicinar la notte
e volar l'ore e i giorni, gli anni e i lustri,   10
e già dal quinto indietro mi rivolgo,
    il passo affretto, e prima che s'annotte,
lo stuol de' pensier miei sparsi raccolgo
per fargli in ciel eternamente illustri.

❦

Pria che la chioma che mi diè natura,
e quel vigor ch'ancor riserbo intero
si cangi e scemi al trapassar leggero
di lui, che 'l men ne lascia e 'l più ne fura;
    spero, quest'acqua e sì chiara e sì pura,   5
e quest'ombrosa valle e quest'altero
monte tanto cantar, quanto il pensiero
per lor posto ha in non cale ogni altra cura;
    s'altrui volere e cruda invida stella,
usi a giusti desii far danno e scorno,   10
non mi vietin fornire opra sì bella.
    Apollo, tu che a queste piagge intorno
sai ch'ombreggia la fronde tua novella,
scendi talor nel dolce mio soggiorno.

Stortoni & Lillie

When the sun stoops to hide his lofty forehead
In the deep ocean, darkening our world,
And from the lowest circle the cold moon
Advances, silvering each mountain top,
The careful shepherd leaves his crystal fountain   5
And drives his flock to shelter in their fold;
The weary pilgrim gathers up his powers,
So weak they hardly answer to his will;
So I, seeing the night come ever closer,
The flying hours and days, the years and lusters,[1]   10
Aware that five have passed me by already,
Hasten my step, before the darkness thickens,
To gather up my throng of scattered thoughts[2]
And make them shine in heaven evermore.

Before the color of the hair that Nature
Gave, with the vigor that I still keep whole,
May change[3] and weaken with the careless passing
Of him[4] who leaves but few, and steals the rest,
I hope to sing so well of this clear river   5
And of this shady valley, and the lofty
Mountain above it, that all other thoughts
Are put aside out of regard for this.
If other's will, and cruel, envious stars
Are wont to harm and scorn our just desires,
Let them not hinder me in this high work.   10
Apollo, you who know that on these shores
Your fresh new laurel leaves will cast their shade,
Descend to me at times in my sweet sojourn.

1. A luster was a Roman measure of five years: she is now twenty-five.
2. She is beginning to collect her poetry for posterity. 3. While her hair
becomes white, in her youth still. 4. Time.

❧

Quando dagli alti monti umida e bruna,
da voi partendo il Sol, l'ombra discende,
e che l'umane cure ad una ad una
sgombra chi i petti altrui tranquilli rende,
di noiosi pensier morte e fortuna   5
m'empie, e riposo al cor lasso contende,
onde dentro col cor per gli occhi fuore
piangendo spendo le mie notti e l'ore.

Nel tempo poi che l'alte stelle erranti
sparir fa il Sol che in oriente appare   10
cinto il crin d'ôr de' suoi bei raggi santi,
sicchè la terra si rallegra e il mare,
e gli augei per le frondi alte e tremanti
s'odon dolce garrir, dolce cantare,
sola al mondo son io che piango allora,   15
che mie tenèbre mai non sgombra aurora.

Che mi val, lassa, se l'aurate corna
scalda del Tauro il gran pianeta ardente,
e quinci e quindi di bel verde adorna
fa la terra fiorir, gioir la gente,   20
e la schiera pennuta, quando aggiorna,
dolci note d'amor cantar sovente,
se la mia speme morta unqua non sorge
nè la nova stagion gioia mi porge?…

Quando si veggon le campagne intorno,   25
in vece d'erba e di fior bianchi e gialli,
sparse di brina, e tempestoso il giorno
girsene e breve, e che nell'ime valli

Stortoni & Lillie

When from the rugged mountains, damp and dark,
Shadows descend as the sun leaves the sky,
And night lifts human troubles one by one,
And brings repose and peace to others' breasts,
Death and my fate bring painful thoughts to me,   5
Denying rest and peace to my worn heart,
So that within myself and from my eyes
Despair and tears consume my nights and hours.

When dawn draws near to pale the wandering stars,
Before the sun arises in the East,   10
His golden locks bound with fair, holy rays,
And makes the earth and ocean to rejoice,
While birds among the lofty trembling boughs
Are heard sweetly to chatter, sweetly sing;
Alone in all the world I still must weep,   15
For dawn does not relieve my heavy shadows.

Alas, how does it help me if the sun
Warms the gold horns of Taurus[1] with his rays,
And, near and far, adorns the earth with green,
Bringing forth blossoms, making men rejoice,   20
While feathered flocks, as morning light appears,
Are often heard singing their song of love —
If my dead hope can never be revived,
Nor the new season bring me joy again?…

And when I see the countryside around   25
Covered with frost instead of verdant grass
And colored flowers, and when the days pass by
Stormy and brief, and in the valley depths

1. The astrological sign that governs the period from April 21st to May
20th.

la neve e il ghiaccio fa lungo soggiorno,
e s'indurano i liquidi cristalli,   *30*
sento in me fare un freddo, umido verno,
nebbia di duol, pioggia di pianto eterno.

❀

Fra queste piagge apriche e chiusi orrori,
presso un bel rio che mormorando stilla,
lungi dal volgo in solitaria villa,
compart'io il tempo e i giorni miei migliori;
   e più m'aggrada udir ninfe e pastori,   *5*
quando Apollo da noi lontan sfavilla,
che desti al suon dell'amorosa squilla,
ven palesando i lor graditi amori,
   e Maiano veder con tanti intorno
folti boschi, alti monti e verdi campi,   *10*
e Mensola ch'al par dell'Arno corre,
   che quante melodie, palazzi et ampi
tetti rendon Fiorenza e 'l mondo adorno,
che 'nvidia e reo destin non mi pon torre.

The snow and ice make ever longer sojourn,
And when the flowing crystal streams turn hard,   30
I feel within myself a cold, wet winter,
A fog of sorrows, rain of constant tears.

❧

Between these sunny shores and untamed landscapes,
Where sweetly flows the murmuring stream nearby,
Far from the crowd, here in my lonely villa,
I spend my time, the best of all my days.
I love to live among the nymphs and shepherds   5
While high Apollo showers them with song,
Wakening them to tell their amorous stories
And open to the world their happy loves.
Where cool Maiano[1] rests by woods and mountains
Amid green fields, and Mensola[2] runs by   10
Parallel to the famous river Arno —
Rather than concerts, palaces, high halls,
Gracing the town of Florence and the world —
Lest envy and ill fortune steal my peace.

1. The poet's country villa was near Maiano, in Tuscany.   2. Maiano is crossed by the little river Mensola.

VERONICA FRANCO
(1546-1591)

Daughter of a courtesan, who started her on this career, Veronica
Franco (or Franca, as she was sometimes called in her time) was
born in Venice in 1546. She became one of the most celebrated
courtesans, famous for her wit and talent, as well as for her beauty
and amatory skills. Although legally married to the physician Paolo
Panizza, she continued to practice her profession until 1580, when
she was tried by the Pope's *Santo Uffizio* for immoral behavior. Her
name, address and fee, together with those of her mother, were listed
in the Official List of Prostitutes of Venice.

In her prime, she belonged to the circle of the famous scholar
Domenico Venier. It is easy to imagine her as one of the opulent,
sensual Titian-haired beauties appearing in the paintings of many
of the Venetian masters of her time, such as Tintoretto, Carpaccio
and Titian. Her fame was such that in 1574 she was hired by the
Republic of Venice to entertain young King Henry III of Valois on
his way to Paris to receive the crown of France. It is reported that
Veronica gave him a portrait of herself done in precious enamel, and
composed a letter and two sonnets for the illustrious visitor.

She exchanged a literary correspondence with Guglielmo
Gonzaga, Duke of Mantua, and was friends with Cardinal Luigi
d'Este, to whom she dedicated her letters in 1575. Montaigne in
his *Journal de voyage en Italie* recorded having received a gift of
letters from her.

In 1580, as a result of increased religious supervision after the
Council of Trent, the Inquisition brought charges against her for
practising magic. During the trial, she confessed to having given
birth six times, but managed to defend herself and was absolved.
In 1570, she first entertained the idea of founding a shelter for
"fallen women." The Hospice of Santa Maria del Soccorso that
was to shelter abandoned maidens and reformed or aging courtesans was founded in 1577, partly as a result of her efforts. Much

has been written about her deep religious conversion in later years; but the repentance sonnet *Ite pensier fallaci* belongs, as Croce pointed out, to another Veronica, that is, to Veronica Gàmbara. Franco had the merit of having contributed to the shelter for destitute women, therefore demonstrating a social conscience towards women in difficulties, and is regarded by some as one of Italy's first social workers. We do not have many details about the end of her colorful life. She died in her native Venice in 1591.

Franco's literary production, as in the case of many *cortegiane honeste* of her times, was used first as a tool of the trade, since it was necessary for a successful courtesan in her times to be musical and to be able to turn out a good poem. Later, her poetry became a frank, spirited, and unhibited expression of her feelings. Bravely following in Dante's footsteps, she chose to write poetry in *terza rima* (tercets), which had been used earlier by Gaspara Stampa in her more discursive and narrative compositions. Some of her poems are addressed to specific people for specific purposes of communication. She is, perhaps, one of the few Renaissance women poets to reject Petrarchism and its lyric formats and tenets. She wrote in *terza rima* or in prose, echoing at times Ludovico Ariosto, who was the first to use tercets for lyric poetry. The fast tempo and the concatenation of the tercets suits her salty and vivacious speech.

Although she appears proud of her amatory skills, there are moments, especially in her letters, when she writes with sadness about the risks, the degradation and the health hazards of a courtesan's life (see *Letter to a mother who wanted her daughter to become a courtesan*). In fact, in spite of her success in her career, like most other Renaissance courtesans she died young, aged forty-five.

Her *Terze rime*, which were also called *Capitoli,* were first published in 1575, and are comprised of 25 *capitoli* (that is, compositions in tercets), eighteen written by Veronica herself, and the other seven by authors addressing themselves to her. The critic Salza reprinted her *Terze Rime* in a critical edition in 1913, together with the *Rime* of Gaspara Stampa. Of these compositions, the most challenging and interesting one is addressed to Maffio Venier, a patrician who, punning on her name, had ungallantly called her "verunica puttana" (a truly unique harlot). In this poem, she does not deny her profession as Tullia d'Aragona had done, and, while vehemently defending herself, she makes a spirited and combative defense of women in general.

Her fifty letters, *Lettere familiari a diversi*, were published in 1580, and in 1949 were reprinted by Benedetto Croce who had a special appreciation of Veronica as a poet. Most of them are simple invitations or occasional compositions; in some she expresses her feelings about her home town, Venice. The most famous letter, Letter XXII— of which we have translated the greater part — is written to a woman who had asked Veronica to help her daughter become a courtesan. In this letter, in which Veronica talks in stark and realistic tones about the profession of a courtesan, we can hear echoes of Aretino, and a veiled accusation of her own mother, who had started her early in this trade.

Veronica is, for the independence of her spirit and for the openness of her expression, one of the brightest feminist spirits of the Renaissance. Dacia Maraini, the greatest female writer and feminist of Italy today, recently wrote a play about her and her life, *Veronica, meretrice e scrittora* (Milan: Bompiani, 1992).

For an in-depth, scholarly study of Veronica Franco, we refer the reader to Margaret Rosenthal's *The Honest Courtesan: Veronica Franco, Citizen and Writer in Sixteenth-Century Venice.* (Chicago & London: University of Chicago Press, 1992). Rosenthal is now in the process of translating Franco's *Terze rime* and selected letters from the *Lettere familiari* in collaboration with Ann Rosalind Jones for the University of Chicago Press.

We have taken the original texts of the poems we present from the 1913 Salza critical edition, and Letter XXII from the 1949 Croce volume.

BIBLIOGRAPHY

Works by Veronica Franco:
Terze Rime di Veronica Franca al Serenissimo Signor Duca di Mantova et di Monferrato. Venice, N.P.: c. 1575.
Lettere familiari a diversi della Signora Veronica Franco. Venice: n.p., c.1580.
Terze rime e sonetti. Ed. Gilberto Beccari. Lanciano: Carabba, 1912.
Rime di Gaspara Stampa e di Veronica Franco. Ed. A. Salza. Bari: Laterza, 1913.
Lettere familari a diversi della S. Veronica Franco. Ed. B. Croce. Bari: Laterza, 1949.

Anthologies containing works by Veronica Franco:
Costa-Zalessow, *op. cit.*
de Blasi, *op. cit.*
Lirici del Cinquecento, op. cit., 332-337.
Poesia del Quattrocento e del Cinquecento, op. cit., 1293-1296.

Studies and other works:
Aguzzi-Barbagli. "Note per una nuova interpretazione delle *Lettere familiari* di Veronica Franco." Atti del Pacific Northwest Council on Foreign Languages, (PNCFL), vol. 28. Seattle: University of Washington, 1977.
Croce, B. "Veronica Franco." In *Poeti e scrittori del pieno e del tardo Rinascimento.* Bari: Laterza, 1952, III, 218-234 (reprint of the *Proemio* of Franco's *Lettere*).
———. "La Lirica cinquecentesca." In *Poesia popolare e poesia d'arte, op. cit.*
Dazzi, Manlio. *Il libro chiuso di Maffio Venier. (La tenzone con Veronica Franco).* Venice: Neri Pozza, 1956.
Dizionario enciclopedico, op. cit., I, 163-165.
Frugoni, A.G. "I 'Capitoli' della cortigiana Veronica Franco." *Belfagor* 3,1 (1948): 44-59.
Graf, A. "Una cortigiana fra mille: Veronica Franco." In *Attraverso il Cinquecento.* Turin: Loescher, 1888.
Leigh, Marcella Diberti. *Veronica Franco: Donna, poetessa e cortigiana del Rinascimento.* Ivrea: Priuli & Verlucca, 1988.
Maraini, Dacia. *Veronica, meretrice e scrittora.* Milan: Bompiani, 1992.
Migiel, Marilyn. "Veronica Franco." In *Italian Women Writers, op. cit.,* 138-144.
Milani, Marisa. "'L'incanto' di Veronica Franco." *Giornale storico della letteratura italiana* 162 (1985): 250-63.

Niccoli, Gabriel A. "Veronica Franco: a profile of a *cortigiana letterata* of the late Renaissance." Thesis. University of British Columbia, 1973.

Palluchieri, Rodolfo e Paola Rossi. *Tintoretto. Le opere sacre e profane.* Milan: Alfieri, 1982.

Richter, Bodo L.O. "Une courtisane venitienne au temps de la Renaissance, Veronica Franco."*Nouvelle Revue* 88 (1984).

Rosenthal, Margaret.*The Honest Courtesan: Veronica Franco, Citizen & Writer in Sixteenth-Century Venice.* Chicago & London: University of Chicago Press, 1992.

Rossi, Paola. *Jacopo Tintoretto. I ritratti.* Venice: Alfieri, 1973.

Scrivano, R. "La poetessa Veronica Franco." *Rassegna della letteratura italiana,* 64, VIII (1960): 50-68.

Tassini, G. *Veronica Franco, celebre poetessa e cortigiana del secolo XVI.* Venice: Tip. Fontana, 1888.

———. *Curiosità veneziane (Veronica Franco).* Venice: Grimaldo, 1872.

Zorzi, Alvise. *Cortigiana veneziana. Veronica Franco ed i suoi poeti.* Milan: Camunia, 1986.

LETTERA 22

*E, se ben primieramente si tratta l'interesse di vostra figliuola,
io parlo della vostra persona, perchè la rovina di lei non può essere separata dalla vostra, e perché le sète madre, e perché, s'ella
diventasse femina del mondo, voi diventereste sua messaggiera
col mondo e sareste da punir acerbamente, dove forse il fallo di
lei sarebbe non del tutto incapace di scusa, fondata sulle vostre
colpe. Voi sapete quante volte io v'abbia pregata e ammonita ad
aver cura della sua virginità; e, poi che il mondo è così pericoloso
e così fragile e che le case delle povere madri non sono punto sicure
dall'insidie amorose dell'appetitosa gioventù, vi mostrai la via di
liberarla dal pericolo e di giovarle nella buona istituzione della
vita e nel modo di poterla onestamente maritare, e m'offersi
d'adoper-armi con ogni mezo possibile perch'ella fosse accettata
nella Casa delle citelle, e di più, d'aiutarvi, nell'occasion dell'
ac-compagnarla, con le mie proprie facoltà. Da principio mi
ringraziaste e mostraste di darl'orecchie, e di aver l'animo ai
miei amorevoli conforti. Tra noi convenimmo del modo che si
devea tenere perch'ella fosse ricevuta, ed era la cosa in procinto di
esseguirsi, quando, non so da quale spirito mossa, dove prima la
facevate andar schietta d'abito e d'accon-ciamenti nella maniera
che conviene ad onesta donzella, co' veli chiusi dinnanzi al petto
e con altre circostanze di modestia, a un tratto l'avete messa sulla
vanità del biondeggiarsi e del lisciarsi, e d'improvviso l'avete fatta*

LETTER 22 (*EXCERPT*)[1]

Although we are primarily dealing with your daughter's interest, I am talking about yourself, since her ruin cannot be separated from yours, because you are her mother, and, if she became a courtesan, you would become her go-between[2] with the world, and you would deserve to be punished severely, whereas her own error would be more easily excusable, since it was based on your guilt. You know how many times I have begged and admonished you to protect her virginity; and, since the world is so dangerous and fragile, and since the houses of poor mothers are not at all safe from the amorous ambushes of lusty youths, I showed you the way to free her from danger and to be of profit to her in setting her up well in life, and in marrying her honorably. I offered to do all I could so that she would be accepted into the House of Unmarried Maidens; in addition, I offered to help with my own means on the occasion of her entrance. At first you thanked me, seemed to listen to me, and to be receptive to my loving advice. We decided between us how we should go about having her accepted in the House; everything was going according to plan when, moved by I do not know what spirit, while you before made her go around dressed simply and like a chaste young lady, with veils covering her breasts, and with other modest accoutrements, suddenly, you started encouraging her vanity, bleaching her hair, and making her

1. This letter is written to a mother who wanted her daughter to become a courtesan. The woman to whom this letter is addressed had been complaining that Franco no longer received her. Franco states that she is writing to warn her "with loud cries" that she is "near a great precipice." 2. Franco's own mother had been her go-between. They were listed together, with address and fee, in the catalog of courtesans for the city of Venice. This letter has been rightly interpreted as a condemnation of her mother.

comparer co' capegli inanellati dintorno alla fronte e 'l collo, col petto spalancato e ch'esce fuori dei panni, con la fronte alta e scoperta e con tutte quell'altre apparenza e con tutti quegli altri abbellimenti che s'usano di fare perchè la mercanzia trovi concorrenza nello spedirsi. E vi giuro per mia fede che, quando da prima me la conduceste davanti così travestita, penai a riconoscerla e vi dissi quello che conveniva all'amicizia e alla carità....

Or finalmente non ho voluto mancar di farvi queste righe, essortandovi di nuovo ad avvertire al caso vostro, a non uccider in un medesimo colpo l'anima e l'onor vostro insieme a quello di vostra figlia, la quale, per considerar la cosa carnalmente ancora, è così poco bella, per non dir altro, perchè gli occhi n'ingannano, e ha così poca grazia e poco spirito nel conversar che le romperete il collo credendola far beata nella professione de le cortegiane, nella quale ha gran fatica di riuscire chi sia bella e abbia maniera e giudizio e conoscenza di molte virtù; nonché una giovane che sia priva di molte di queste cose e in alcune non ecceda la mediocrità.... Ma poi soggiungo che, presupposto che la fortuna sia per esservi in ciò tutta favorevole e benigna, non è questa vita tale che in ogni essito non sia sempre misera. Troppo infelice cosa e troppo contraria al senso umano è l'obligar il corpo e l'industria di una tal servitù che spaventa solamente a pensarne, darsi in preda in tanti, con rischio d'esser dispogliata, d'esser derubata, d'esser uccisa, ch'un solo dì ti toglie quanto con molti in molto tempo hai acquistato, con tant'altri pericoli d'ingiuria e d'infermità contagiose e spaventose; mangiar con l'altrui bocca, dormir con gli occhi altrui, muoversi secondo l'altrui desiderio, correndo in manifesto naufragio sempre della

up, making her appear in public with her hair curled on her forehead and neck,[1] with her neck and breasts uncovered and bursting out of her bodice, walking boldly with an unveiled forehead: briefly, with all the appearance and embellishments used to show off one's merchandise for profit. And I swear on my honor that, when you first brought her to me so disguised, I hardly recognized her, and I told you what was demanded by friendship and charity....

Now finally I cannot help sending you these lines, exhorting you again to take care of this matter, not to ruin at one blow your own honor and soul, together with your daughter's, who — to look at this matter from a purely physical point of view — is so unattractive, to put it mildly, since my eyes do not deceive me, and has so little grace and spirit in conversation, that you might break her neck in the hope of making her succeed in the courtesan's profession, in which even women who have beauty, allure, judgment, and knowledge of many subjects can succeed only with great difficulty, let alone a young woman who lacks most of these qualities, and, in others, does not exceed mediocrity.... Then I must add that even if Fortune were only benign and favorable to you in this endeavor, this life is such that in any case it would always be wretched. It is such an unhappy thing, and so contrary to human nature, to subject one's body and activity to such slavery that one is frightened just by the thought of it: to let oneself be prey to many, running the risk of being stripped, robbed, killed, so that one day can take away from you what you have earned with many men in a long time, with so many other dangers of injury and horrible contagious diseases[2]: to eat with someone else's mouth, to sleep with someone else's eyes, to move

1. This type of coiffure, with frizzed bleached hair, was typical of Venetian courtesans and can be seen in paintings of the time. 2. At this time, syphilis was rampant in Europe, causing many deaths. In Renaisance times, its origins were commonly attributed to the Americas. Girolamo Fracastoro wrote a treatise on the subject in 1530, *Syphilis, Sive Morbus Gallicus*.

facoltà e della vita; qual maggiore miseria? quai ricchezze, quai comodità, quai delizie possono acquistare un tanto peso? Credete a me: tra tutte le sciagure mondane questa è l'estrema. Ma poi, se s'aggiungeranno ai rispetti del mondo quei dell'anima, che perdizione e che certezza di dannazione è questa?... Non sostenete che non pur le carni della misera vostra figliuola si squarcino e si vendano, ma d'esserne voi stessa il macellaio.... Né trascorrerà forse molto tempo che vostra figliuola medesima, avvedutasi della grandissima offesa da voi fattale, vi fuggirà più d'ogn'altro quanto più, dovendo voi, sì come madre, aiutarla, l'avrete oppressa e rovinata. E questo potrebbe essere il principio del vostro supplizio, dal quale Nostro Signor vi guardi col rimanervi dalla mala intenzione che mostrate avere di guastare e corrempere la fattura del vostro proprio sangue e delle vostre proprie carni....

SONETTO *1*

   Come talor dal ciel sotto umil tetto
Giove tra noi qua giú benigno scende,
e perché occhio terren dall'alt'oggetto
non resti vinto, umana forma prende;
   cosí venne al mio povero ricetto,   5
senza pompa real ch'abbaglia e splende,
dal fato Enrico a tal dominio eletto,
ch'un sol mondo nol cape e nol comprende.
   Benché sí sconosciuto, anc'al mio core
tal raggio impresse del divin suo merto,   10
che 'n me s'estinse il natural vigore.
   Di ch'ei di tant'affetto non incerto,
l'imagin mia di smalto e di colore
prese al partir con grato animo aperto.

according to someone else's whim, running always towards the inevitable shipwreck of one's faculties and life. Can there be greater misery than this? What wealth, what comforts, what delights, can be worth all this? Believe me, among all the misfortunes that can befall a human being in this world, this life is the worst. But then, if you add to the considerations of the world, those of the soul, what perdition and what certainty of damnation is this?... Do not allow the flesh of your wretched daughter to be torn apart and sold, being you yourself the butcher.... Maybe it will not be long before your own daughter, having realized the great injury that you have done her, will flee from you since you, her mother, who should have helped her, have instead oppressed her and ruined her. And this could be the beginning of your punishment, and may the Lord keep you from persisting in the evil intention you show of spoiling and corrupting the product of your own flesh and of your own blood....

SONNET I[1]

As when great Jove came down from heaven
To be the guest beneath some mortal roof,
And so that earthly eyes should not be blinded
By his appearance, he took human form,
And thus he came to my modest abode,   5
Without his royal pomp that shines and blinds,
Henry, elect by Fate to such high power
That one word could not hold, nor comprehend —
Although thus in disguise, he touched my heart
With such a ray of his supernal merit   10
As quite extinguished all my native vigor,
So that, confiding in such great affection,
He took my image, in enameled color,
On his departure, with a willing heart.

1. Addressed to Henry III of France, with the gift of a portrait of herself.

Terza Rima 2

S'esser del vostro amor potessi certa
per quel che mostran le parole e 'l volto,
che spesso tengon varia alma coperta;
    se quel, che tien la mente in sé raccolto,
mostrasson le vestige esterne in guisa,   5
ch'altri non fosse spesso in frode còlto.
    quella téma da me fôra divisa,
di cui quando perciò m'assicurassi,
semplice e sciocca, ne sarei derisa:
    "a un luogo stesso per molte vie vassi,"   10
dice il proverbio; né sicuro è punto
rivolger dietro a l'apparenzie i passi.
    Dal battuto camin non sia disgiunto
chiunque cerca gir a buona stanza,
pria che sia da la notte sopragiunto.   15
    Non è dritto il sentier de la speranza.
che spesse volte, e le piú volte, falle
con falsi detti e con finta sembianza:
    quello de la certezza è destro calle,
che sempre mena a riposato albergo,   20
e refugio ha dal lato e da le spalle:
    a questo gli occhi del mio pensier ergo,
e da parole e da vezzi delusa,
tutti i lor vani indizi lascio a tergo.
    Questa con voi sia legitima scusa,   25
con la qual di non creder a parole,
né a vostri gesti, fuori esca d'accusa.
    E, se invero m'amate, assai mi duole

Stortoni & Lillie

TERZE RIME 2[1]

If I could be convinced by what you show me
    In words and face — for both can be a cover
    For fickle heart — that you do truly love;
If what your mind keeps well concealed within you
    Could be brought out in open by such actions   5
    By which the other cannot be deceived,
The fear I feel could easily be lifted,
    Fear that, if I proceed without full surety
    I might be laughed at for a simple fool.
The proverb says, "By many different pathways   10
    One comes to the same place," nor is it wisdom
    To follow in the steps of outward show.
From the well-trodden path no one should wander
    Who hopes to find himself a pleasant lodging
    Before the shadows of the night descend.   15
The road of hope is difficult to follow,
    For many times — most times — it will deceive you
    With lying words and false appearances.
The way of certainty lies to the right
    And leads one always to an inn of safety,   20
    A refuge for the shoulders and the sides,
And toward this way my eyes and steps are turning —
    Having been fooled by blandishments too often —
    All these inducements I now leave behind.
Let such be my legitimate excuse   25
    For not believing in your words and gestures:
    Thus I escape your charge of faithlessness.
I do regret that, if you truly love me,

1. The poem is addressed to Marco Venier, who had written a verse epistle to Franco praising her beauty. She returns his love, and asks him to do deeds and works suitable to the virtue of the soul; only then will she bestow upon him the pleasures she has learnt from Venus.

che con effetti non vi discopriate,
come, chi veramente ama, far suole: 30
    mi duol che da l'un canto voi patiate,
e da l'altro il desio, ch'o d'esser grata
al vostro vero amor, m'interrompiate.
    Poi ch'io non crederò d'esser amata,
né 'l debbo creder, né ricompensarvi   35
per l'arra, che fin qui m'avete data,
    dagli effetti, signor fate stimarvi:
con questi in prova venite, s'anch'io
il mio amor con effetti ho da mostrarvi;
    ma, s'avete di favole desio,   40
mentre anderete voi favoleggiando,
favoloso sará l'accetto mio;
    e, di favole stanco e sazio, quando
l'amor mi mostrerete con effetto,
non men del mio v'andrò certificando.   45
    Aperto il cor vi mostrerò nel petto,
allor che 'l vostro non mi celerete,
e sará di piacervi il mio diletto;
    e, s'a Febo si grata mi tenete
per lo compor, ne l'opere amorose   50
grata a Venere piú mi troverete.
    Certe proprietati in me nascose
vi scovrirò d'infinita dolcezza,
che prosa o verso altrui mai non espose,
    con questo, che mi diate la certezza   55
del vostro amor con altro che con lodi,
ch'esser da tai delusa io sono avezza:
    piú mi giovi con fatti, e men mi lodi,
e, dov'è in ciò la vostra cortesia
soverchia, si comparta in altri modi.   60
    Vi par che buono il mio discorso sia,

You don't express this clearly in your actions,
  As one who truly loves is wont to do.   30
On one hand, I don't want to make you suffer,
  But on the other hand, you block my wishing
  To be compliant — if your love's sincere.
Since I cannot believe you really love me —
  Nor ought I think so, or give compensation   35
  For the slight pledge you've given me so far —
Let yourself gain esteem, sir, by your actions
  And come to me with deeds I can confide in;
  Then I will show my love to you in acts.
But if you only look for fairy stories,   40
  As long as you keep up this kind of nonsense
  I can be just as fanciful as you.
When you have had enough of fantasizing
  And prove your love to me with something solid,
  Then I shall certify my love no less.   45
You'll see my heart then open in my bosom —
  Whenever you stop hiding yours from me—
  Pleasing you then will be my great delight.
Now, if you think I should give praise to Phoebus
  For helping me write verse, the art of loving   50
  Reveals me more a devotee of Venus.
Then I shall show you traits in me, well hidden
  Till now, distinguished by infinite sweetness,
  Which neither verse nor prose has shown you yet,
When you have given me your assurance   55
  Of love, with tokens other than sweet nothings —
  For I am used to being fooled by those —
I need from you more deeds and less fine phrases
  (your courtesy in this way is unbounded):
  Let me perceive your love by other means.   60
Do you believe my reasons to be right,

o ch'io m'inganni pur per aventura,
non bene esperta de la dritta via?

    Signor, l'esser beffato è cosa dura,
massime ne l'amor; e chi nol crede   65
ei stesso la ragion metta in figura.

    Io son per caminar col vostro piede,
ed amerovvi indubìtatamente,
sí com'al vostro merito richiede.

    Se foco avrete in sen d'amor cocente,   70
io 'l sentirò, perch'accostata a voi
d'ardermi il cor egli sarà possente:

    non si ponno schivar i colpi suoi,
e chi si sente amato da dovero
convien l'amante suo ridamar poi;   75

    ma 'l dimostrar il bianco per lo nero
è un certo non so che, che spiace a tutti,
a quei, ch'anco han giudicio non intiero.

    Dunque da voi mi sian mostrati i frutti
del portatomi amor, ché de le fronde   80
dal piacer sono i vani uomini indutti.

    Ben per quanto or da me vi si risponde,
avara non vorrei che mi stimaste,
ché tal vizio nel sen non mi s'asconde;

    ma piaceriami che di me pensaste   85
che ne l'amar le mie voglie cortesi
si studian d'esser caute, se non caste:

    né cosi tosto d'alcun uom compresi
che fosse valoroso e che m'amasse,
che 'l cambio con usura ancor gli resi.   90

    Ma chi per questo poi s'argomentasse
di volermi ingannar, beffa se stesso;

Or is my logic wholly wrong perchance
   Being that I am not expert in the right way?[1]
It's not a pleasant thing, this being fooled,
   Chiefly in love — and if you don't believe me,   65
   Imagine how you'd feel it for yourself.
I am about to venture where you lead me
   And I shall love you very well — no question —
   But only as your merit may deserve.
If you have fires of love scalding your bosom   70
   I'll surely feel them, lying by your side,
   Their heat will burn right through into my heart.
From the attack of love there's no escaping,
   For one who feels truly beloved by someone
   Must in all equity return that love.   75
But to show white where black's the honest color
   Is somehow — I don't know — always displeasing
   Even to those whose judgment's not too strong.
Do show me then the fruits of love you bear me.
   The buds alone — which may appear attractive   80
   To empty minds — don't hold much weight with me.
However much you offer in your answer,
   I don't want you to think me avaricious —
   I do not hide that vice within my breast —
But it would please me if you understood this: 85
   My courteous wishes in this case of loving
   Urge me, "Be cautious, if not always chaste."
Nor have I learned from any man of valor,
   With full conviction that he truly loved me,
   But that I paid him back with interest.   90
Anyone, then, who comes to the conclusion
   That it is safe to cheat me, fools himself,

1. This verse, laden with several layers of meanings and double entendre, obviously echoes the first tercet of Dante's Inferno ("dritta via"). Franco here could allude to the fact that her logic may not be right, or openly acknowledge the fact that she may not have led the "right" life.

e tale il potria dir, chi 'l domandasse.
    E però quel, che da voi cerco adesso,
non è che con argento over con oro   95
il vostro amor voi mi facciate espresso;
    perché si disconvien troppo al decoro
di chi non sia piú che venal, far patto
con uom gentil per trarne anco un tesoro.
    Di mia profession non è tal atto;   100
ma ben fuor di parole io 'l dico chiaro,
voglio veder il vostro amor in fatto.
    Voi ben sapete quel che m' è piú caro:
seguite in ciò com'io v'ho detto ancora,
ché mi sarete amante unico e raro.   105
    De le virtuti il mio cor s'innamora,
e voi, che possedete di lor tanto,
ch'ogni piú bel saver con voi dimora,
    non mi negate l'opra vostra in tanto,
che con tal mezzo vi vegga bramoso   110
d'acquistar meco d'amador il vanto:
    siate in ciò diligente e studioso,
e per gradirmi ne la mia richiesta
non sia 'l gentil vostro ozio unqua ozioso.
    A voi poca fatica sará questa,   115
perch'al vostro valor ciascuna impresa,
per difficil che sia, facil vi resta.
    E, se sí picciol carico vi pesa,
pensate ch'alto vola il ferro e 'l sasso,
che sia sospinto da la fiamma accesa: 120
    quel che la sua natura inchina al basso,
piú che con altro, col furor del foco
rivolge in su dal centro al cerchio il passo;
    onde non ha 'l mio amor dentro a voi loco,
poi ch'ei non ha virtú di farvi fare   125

And I can say this to whomever asks.
Nevertheless, what I am now demanding
    Is not that you express your love overtly   95
    By any gift of silver or of gold,
Because it is unfitting and improper
    For anyone not venal to make compact
    With a true gentleman, to take his wealth.
Such action is no part of my profession.   100
    But, more than just with words — I tell you plainly —
    I want to see your love freely expressed.
You know well what it is I love most dearly:
    Follow the way that I have often shown you;
    You'll be my lover then, unique and rare.   105
My heart above all else loves all the virtues,
    And you possess them in so full a measure
    That all fine learning makes its home in you.
Do not deny me your authentic effort
    To such a point as proves you to be eager   110
    To win true-lovers' fame along with me.
Be diligent in this, and always willing
    To please me in the way I have requested.
    Let not your noble leisure make you lax.
And this should cause you very little trouble,   115
    For every challenge to a proven hero,
    However hard it be, is light as air.
But, if so small a burden weighs upon you,
    Think to how high a flight a stone or iron
    May be cast up by an explosive fuse.   120
That which lies in the lowest place by nature,
    Below all else, with fury of the fire
    Flies upward from the center to the rim.
It seems my love has little hold upon you
    Since it lacks strength enough to make you freely   125

quel ch'anco senz'amor vi saria poco.
    E poi da me volete farvi amare?
quasi credendo che, cosí d'un salto,
di voi mi debba a un tratto innamorare?
    Per questo non mi glorio e non m'essalto;   130
ma, per contarvi il ver, volar senz'ale
vorreste, e in un momento andar troppo alto:
    a la possa il desir abbiate eguale,
benché potreste agevolmente alzarvi
dov'altri con fatica ancor non sale.   135
    Io bramo aver cagion vera d'amarvi,
e questa ne l'arbitrio vostro è posta,
si che in ciò non potete lamentarvi.
    Dal merto la mercé non fia discosta,
se mi darete quel che, benché vaglia   140
al mio giudicio assai, nulla a voi costa;
    questo fará che voli e non pur saglia
il vostro premio meco a quell'altezza,
che la speranza col desire agguaglia.
    E, qual ella si sia, la mia bellezza,   145
quella che di lodar non sète stanco,
spenderò poscia in vostra contentezza:
    dolcemente congiunta al vostro fianco,
le delizie d'amor farò gustarvi,
quand'egli è ben appreso al lato manco;   150
    e 'n ciò potrei tal diletto recarvi,
che chiamar vi potreste pur contento,
e d'avantaggio appresso innamorarvi.
    Cosí dolce e gustevole divento,
quando mi trovo con persona in letto,   155
da cui amata e gradita mi sento,
    che quel mio piacer vince ogni diletto,
si che quel, che strettissimo parea,

Do that which, even loveless, would be slight.
Now, do you really want to make me love you?
   Or do you think that you will catch me leaping
   Out of myself to fall in love with you?
I do not boast of this, or sing my praises,   130
   But I must tell you truly, flying wingless
   Involves a risk of venturing too high.
You have the power, equal to your wishes,
   So much that you might easily soar upwards
   To where no other man could ever reach.   135
I yearn for any good excuse to love you:
   The matter stands wholly within your judgment,
   So you can have no reason to complain.
Reward will not be missing from your merit,
   If you will give me the one thing I value   140
   Above all else — and it will cost you nothing.
This act will make your merit fly, not merely
   Climb up, in my regard, to such a summit
   That hope will surely equal your desire,
And then, for what it's worth, my famous beauty,   145
   Which you seem never to be tired of praising,
   I shall expend for your content alone.
Then, lying at your side in perfect concord
   I shall provide you with the joy Love renders
   When he is on the side where beats the heart.   150
And in this way I'll give you so much pleasure
   That you may call yourself fully contented
   And close to falling even more in love.
I can become so lovely and delicious
   Whenever I'm in bed with any person   155
   To whom I feel myself pleasing and loved,
That then my sweetness will surpass all others',
   So that the knot of love, which seemed already

nodo de l'altrui amor divien piú stretto.
   Febo che serve a l'amorosa dea,   *160*
e in dolce guiderdon da lei ottiene
quel che via piú, che l'esser dio, il bea,
   a rivelar nel mio pensier ne viene
quei modi, che con lui Venere adopra,
mentre in soavi abbracciamenti il tiene;   *165*
   ond'io instrutta a questi so dar opra
sí ben nel letto, che d'Apollo a l'arte
questa ne va d'assai spazio di sopra,
   e 'l mio cantar e 'l mio scriver in carte
s'oblia da chi mi prova in quella guisa,   *170*
ch'a' suoi seguaci Venere comparte.
   S'avete del mio amor l'alma conquisa,
procurate d'avermi in dolce modo,
via piú che la mia penna non divisa.
   Il valor vostro è quel tenace nodo   *175*
che me vi può tirar nel grembo, unita
via piú ch'affisso in fermo legno chiodo:
   farvi signor vi può de la mia vita,
che tanto amar mostrate, la virtute,
che 'n voi per gran miracolo s'addita.   *180*
   Fate che sian da me di lei vedute
quell'opre ch'io desio, ché poi saranno
le mie dolcezze a pien da voi godute;
   e le vostre da me si goderanno
per quello ch'un amor mutuo comporte,   *185*
dove i diletti senza noia s'hanno.
   Aver cagion d'amarvi io bramo forte:
prendete quel partito che vi piace,
poi che in vostro voler tutta è la sorte.
   Altro non voglio dir: restate in pace.   *190*

So firmly tied, will tighten all the time.
Phoebus, attendant on the amorous goddess,   160
   Obtained from her a most delightful guerdon,
   Blessing him more than his divinity.
This strikes my fancy with a revelation
   Of skills Venus possessed for giving pleasure,
   Holding him closely in a sweet embrace.   165
So now I know — being so well instructed —
   Ways to behave in bed, by far surpassing
   The art the god Apollo taught to me.
My singing and my verse, inscribed on paper,
   Will be forgotten, when you learn what Venus   170
   Has taught to her most faithful followers.
So, if your soul is vanquished by this goddess,
   You will succeed in having me so fully
   That neither poetry nor love is lost.
Your valor, sir, and that firm bond of loving,   175
   Will pull me to your breast and there transfix me
   More firmly than a nail in knotty wood.
Your virtue in so loving me will make you
   Lord of my life, till everyone who sees it
   Will point it out as a great miracle.   180
Let me but see in you, moved by that virtue,
   The deeds I so desire, for they will give you
   The full enjoyment of my sweetest gifts.
And I shall equally enjoy your sweetness
   In all the ways that mutual love embraces   185
   Where joy is felt, unshackled by constraint.
I greatly yearn to have this cause to love you —
   Choose the alternative your heart desires:
   The outcome is entirely in your will.
I say no more: you may remain at peace.   190

191

Terza Rima 16

D'ardito cavalier non è prodezza
(concedami che 'l vero a questa volta
io possa dir, la vostra gentilezza),
　　da cavalier non è, ch'abbia raccolta
ne l'animo suo invitto alta virtute,　　　　　　　　　　5
e che a l'onor la mente abbia rivolta,
　　con armi insidiose e non vedute,
a chi piú disarmato men sospetta,
dar gravi colpi di mortal ferute.
　　Men ch'agli altri ciò far poi se gli aspetta　　　10
contra le donne, da natura fatte
per l'uso che piú d'altro a l'uom diletta:
　　imbecilli di corpo, ed in nulla atte
non pur a offender gli altri, ma se stesse
dal difender col cor timido astratte.　　　　　　　　　15
　　Questo doveva far che s'astenesse
la vostra man da quell'aspre percosse,
ch'al mio feminil petto ignudo impresse.
　　Io non saprei giá dir onde ciò fosse,
se non che fuor del lato mi traeste　　　　　　　　　20
l'armi vostre del sangue asperse e rosse.
　　Spogliata e sola e incauta mi coglieste,
debil d'animo, e in armi non esperta,
e robusto ed armato m'offendeste;
　　tanto ch'io stei per lungo spazio incerta　　　　25
di mia salute; e fu da me tra tanto
passion infinita al cor sofferta.
Pur finalmente s'e stagnato il pianto,

Stortoni & Lillie

In a bold knight I cannot call it prowess —
  Let us concede that I may speak out freely
  For just this once, at least, about your knighthood —
It is no noble deed in one who garnered
  In his unconquered spirit such high virtues   5
  As turned his mind to honor — hitherto —
To strike with unseen and insidious weapons
  At one unarmed and therefore unsuspecting
  Such heavy blows, inflicting mortal wounds.
Such an attack is the more unexpected   10
  Against us women, who are made by nature,
  More than all else, for giving joy to men;
Weak in our bodies, very ill adapted
  For doing harm to others, hardly daring
  At heart even to defend ourselves.   15
This fact alone should make you be more careful
  And not strike blows so cruel and so bitter
  With your own hand upon my naked breast.
I cannot even tell how this can happen,
  But that I know that you withdrew your weapon,   20
  Dripping red blood, from my afflicted side.
Helpless, alone, incautious, you had caught me,
  One not adept at weapons, weak by nature,
  When you, armed and robust, made your attack,
So fierce, that I for a while was uncertain   25
  Of living on in health, for I had suffered
  Infinite pain within my woman's heart.
But in the end, my weeping spell was over,

1. In which she answers at length a slanderer who insulted her in his verses, and refutes the injustices with which he attacked her way of life. (The slanderer is said to have been one Maffio Venier, who addressed a scurrilous sonnet to her, calling her "Ver' unica puttana" – "a truly unique harlot.")

e quella piaga acerba s'e saldata,
che da l'un mi passava a l'altro canto.   30

    Quasi da pigro sonno or poi svegliata,
dal cansato periglio animo presi,
benché femina a molli opere nata:

    e in man col ferro a essercitarmi appresi,
tanto ch'aver le donne agil natura,   35
non men che l'uomo in armeggiando intesi:

    perché 'n ciò posto ogni mia industria e cura,
mercé del ciel, mi veggo giunta a tale,
che piú d'offese altrui non ho paura.

    E, se voi dianzi mi trattaste male,   40
fu gran vostro diffetto, ed io dal danno
grave n'ho tratto un ben, che molto vale.

    Cosí nei casi avversi i savi fanno,
che 'l lor utile espresso alfin cavare
da quel, che nuoce da principio, sanno: 45

    e cosí ancor le medicine amare
rendon salute; e 'l ferro e 'l foco s'usa
le putrefatte piaghe a ben curare:

    benché non serve a voi questa per scusa,
che m'offendeste non giá per giovarmi,   50
e 'l fatto stesso parla e si v'accusa.

    Ed io, poi che 'l ciel volse liberarmi
da sí mortal periglio, ho sempre atteso
a l'essercizio nobile de l'armi,

    si ch'or, animo e forze avendo preso,   55
di provocarvi a rissa in campo ardisco,
con cor non poco a la vendetta acceso.

    Non so se voi stimiate lieve risco
entrar con una donna in campo armato;
ma io, benché ingannata, v'avvertisco   60

    che 'l mettersi con donne è da l'un lato

My bitter wound eventually mended,
   Though I was stricken through from side to side.   30
Awakened then as from an idle slumber
   I found new courage in averted peril,
   Although a woman, born for woman's work,
And taught my hands to wield an iron weapon —
   For women are by nature just as agile   35
   As men, and so I learned to arm myself.
I have put so much industry and labor
   Into learning to fight — thank heaven for it! —
   That I no longer fear to be attacked.
And if, before now, you had used me badly,   40
   It was your own defect, but from the damage
   I have derived a good of highest worth.
So, mighty sages from contrary fortune
   Derive great value, winning good from evil,
   Even from that which caused them former pain,   45
And so, again, medicines harsh and bitter
   Bring health, and so it is that the red-hot iron
   Will give relief to putrefying sores.
And yet, for you this is no mitigation —
   You did not wound me for my own advantage —   50
   This fact speaks loudly and accuses you.
And I, because high heaven chose to heal me
   From such a mortal danger, learned to practice
   The difficult but noble art of arms.
So now, having regained both power and courage,   55
   I burn to challenge you to field of battle
   With a full heart kindled for my revenge.
You think, perhaps, the risk is very little —
   Entering in armed conflict with a woman —
   But I, although betrayed, announce to you   60
That for a man to fight against a woman

biasmo ad uom forte, ma da l'altro è poi
caso d'alta importanza riputato.

    Quando armate ed esperte ancor siam noi,
render buon conto a ciascun uom potemo,   65
ché mani e piedi e core avem qual voi;

    e, se ben molli e delicate semo,
ancor tal uom, ch'è delicato è forte:
e tal, ruvido ed aspro, è d'ardir scemo.

    Di ciò non se ne son le donne accorte;   70
che, se si risolvessero di farlo,
con voi pugnar porían fino a la morte.

    E per farvi veder che 'l vero parlo,
tra tante donne incominciar voglio io,
porgendo essempio a lor di seguitarlo.   75

    A voi, che contra tutte sète rio,
con qual'armi volete in man mi volgo,
con speme d'atterrarvi e con desio;

    e le donne a difender tutte tolgo
contra di voi, che di lor sète schivo,   80
si ch'a ragion io sola non mi dolgo.

    Certo d'un gran piacer voi sète privo,
a non gustar di noi la gran dolcezza;
ed al mal uso in ciò la colpa ascrivo.

    Data è dal ciel la feminil bellezza,   85
perch'ella sia felicitate in terra
di qualunque uom conosce gentilezza.

    Ma dove 'l mio pensier trascorre ed erra
a ragionar de le cose d'amore,
or ch'io sono in procinto di far guerra?   90

    Torno al mio intento, ond'era uscita fuore,
e vi disfido a singolar battaglia:
cingetevi pur d'armi e di valore,

    vi mostrerò quanto al vostro prevaglia

Brings heavy shame to him, but for the other
    Can be a case of great and high import.
When we are armed and practiced well, we women
    Can answer for ourselves as well as men can —   65
    Have we not hands and feet and arms like you?
Although we may be delicate and fragile,
    Some men are gentle, too, and yet courageous,
    And others cowards, although rough and harsh.
But, for a fact, most women do not know this;   70
    If only they would set their minds upon it
    They certainly could fight you to the death.
And, to persuade you that I speak out truly,
    I want to be the first of many women
    To set a brave example for the rest,   75
I challenge you, to all of us so cruel,
    To fight, and you may have your choice of weapon —
    Still, I shall hope and wish to throw you down.
So, to defend us all, I'll undertake it
    Against your body — you so hateful to us —   80
    I'm not the only one who should complain.
Surely you've robbed yourself of many pleasures,
    Unable as you are to taste our sweetness —
    The fault in this I lay to your misuse.
Heaven itself created women's beauty   85
    To make of us an earthly source of pleasure
    For any man practiced in courtesy.
Tell me why, thoughts of mine, do you so wander
    Turning to speak of gentle love and beauty
    Now that I've girded myself up for war?   90
I turn back to my purpose where I left it:
    Again I challenge you to single combat,
    So brace yourself with courage and with arms!
And I will show you how much we women

il sesso femminil: pigliate quali   95
volete armi, e di voi stesso vi caglia,
    ch'io vi risponderò di colpi tali,
il campo a voi lasciando elegger anco,
ch'a questi forse non sentiste eguali.
    Mal difender da me potrete il fianco,   100
e stran vi parrá forse, a offenderne uso,
da me vedervi oppresso in terra stanco:
    cosí talor quell'uom resta deluso,
ch'ingiuria gli altri fuor d'ogni ragione,
non so se per natura, o per mal uso.   105
    Vostra di questa rissa è la cagione,
ed a me per difesa e per vendetta
carico d'oppugnarvi ora s'impone.
    Prendete pur de l'armi omai l'eletta,
ch'io non posso soffrir lunga dimora,   110
da lo sdegno de l'animo costretta.
    La spada, che 'n man vostra rade e fora,
de la lingua volgar veneziana,
s'a voi piace d'usar, piace a me ancora:
    e, se volete entrar ne la toscana,   115
scegliete voi la seria o la burlesca,
ché l'una e l'altra è a me facile e piana.
    Io ho veduto in lingua selvaghesca
certa fattura vostra molto bella,
simile a la maniera pedantesca: 120
    se voi volete usar o questa o quella,
ed aventar, come ne l'altre fate,
di queste in biasmo nostro la quadrella,
    qual di lor piú vi piace, e voi pigliate
ché di tutte ad un modo io mi contento,   125
avendole perciò tutte imparate.
    Per contrastar con voi con ardimento,

Prevail against you, letting you choose freely   95
  Whatever arms you wish — you still will quail;
For I shall answer you with such great vigor,
  (Although I let you pick the field of battle)
  That you'll not be my equal even then!
You can defend yourself from me but poorly,   100
  However strange it seems, against all custom,
  To find yourself thrown to the ground by me.
A man like you should really be embarrassed —
  Having hurt others, with no show of reason —
  By nature or bad habit, I can't say.   105
Yours is the fault that lies behind this quarrel,
  So, in my own defense, as well as vengeance,
  The task of fighting you I claim as mine.
Take up the arms, that you have freely chosen,
  For I can't stand delay in this much longer,   110
  Pressed as I am with anger in my soul.
Choose if you will the common speech of Venice —
  A sword you've taken in your hand too often —
  If that's your choice, I will accept it too.
Or, if you wish, enter the lists in Tuscan —   115
  Be just as serious as you like, or comic —
  For either mode's an easy one for me.
I've seen, expressed in somewhat uncouth language,
  A piece of yours that struck me as pedantic —
  And yet it was a pretty bit of work —   120
So, if you wish to use this style or that one —
  To threaten me as you have done to others,
  (Using a cross-bow shaft for your offense),
Whatever pleases you, what style you fancy —
  They're all the same to me — I'll be contented —   125
  I've mastered all of them quite well by now.
With perfect confidence I can defy you.

in tutte queste ho molta industria speso:
se bene o male, io stessa mi contento;
    e ciò sarà dagli altri ancora inteso,   *130*
e 'l saperete voi, che forse vinto
cadrete, e non vorreste avermi offeso.
    Ma, prima che si venga in tal procinto,
quasi per far al gioco una levata,
non col ferro tagliente ancora accinto,   *135*
    de la vostra canzone, a me mandata,
il principio vorrei mi dichiaraste,
poi che l'opera a me vien indrizzata.
    "Verunica" e 'l restante mi chiamaste,
alludendo a Veronica mio nome,   *140*
ed al vostro discorso mi biasmaste;
    ma al mio dizzionario io non so come
"unica" alcuna cosa propriamente
in mala parte ed in biasmar si nome.
    Forse che si direbbe impropriamente,   *145*
ma l'anfibologia non quadra in cosa
qual mostrar voi volete espressamente.
    Quella, di cui la fama è gloriosa,
e che 'n bellezza od in valor eccelle,
senza par di gran lunga virtuosa,   *150*
    "unica" a gran ragion vien che s'appelle;
a l'arte, a l'ironia non sottoposto,
scelto tra gli altri, un tal vocabol dielle.
    L'unico in lode e in pregio vien esposto
da chi s'intende; e chi parla altrimenti   *155*
dal senso del parlar sen va discosto.
    Questo non è, signor, fallo d'accenti,
quello, in che s'inveisce, nominare
col titol de le cose più eccellenti.
    O voi non mi voleste biasimare,   *160*

In all these modes I've had sufficient practice —
    With good results or bad, I've pleased myself.
And this will soon be clear to other people: 130
    You'll feel it, too, when finally defeated
    You fall, and haven't injured me at all.
But first, before we venture on this action —
    Preliminary practice for our duel,
    For we're not yet equipped with cutting steel —   135
I wish you'd tell me truly, what's the reason
    For that rude song of yours, which was directed
    At me — at least it was addressed to me —
"Verunica," and so forth, you addressed me
    Alluding to "Veronica," as rightly   140
    I'm called, slandering me here in your text.
But in my dictionary there's no entry
    Making the word "unique" derogatory —
    It's not a word to use in speaking blame,
Unless by some rhetorical extension —   145
    But double meanings are fallacious weapons
    And don't tell clearly what you want to say.
A lady with a glorious reputation,
    Excelling both in dignity and beauty,
    Without a rival for her spotless name —   150
"Unique" she should be called with perfect reason:
    The art of irony would not be chosen
    In her case, if you put that word to her.
"Unique" is said in praise and admiration
    By those who mean it; those who twist its meaning   155
    Strike far away from the right use of words.
This, sir, is not a case of different accents —
    Turning against one whom he would discredit
    A title better fit for excellence.
Either you did not really want to shame me,   160

o in questo dir menzonga non sapeste.
Non parlo del dir bene e del lodare,
    ché questo so che far non intendeste;
ma senz'esser offeso da me stato,
quel che vi corse a l'animo scriveste,   *165*
    altrui volendo in ciò forse esser grato;
benché me non ingiuria, ma se stesso,
s'altri mi dice mal, non provocato.

    E 'l voler oscurar il vero espresso
con le torbide macchie degli inchiostri   *170*
in buona civiltá non è permesso;
    e spesso avien che 'l mal talento uom mostri,
giovando in quello onde piú nuocer crede:
essempi in me piú d'una volta mostri,
    si come in questo caso ancor si vede,   *175*
che voi, non v'accorgendo, mi lodate
di quel ch'al bene ed a la virtú chiede.

    E, se ben "meretrice" mi chiamate,
o volete inferir ch'io non vi sono,
o che ve n'en tra tali di lodate.   *180*

    Quanto le meretrici hanno di buono,
quanto di grazioso e di gentile,
esprime in me del parlar vostro il suono.

    Se questo intese il vostro arguto stile,
di non farne romor io son contenta,   *185*
e d'inchinarmi a voi devota, umile;
    ma, perch'al fin de la scrittura, intenta
stando, che voi mi biasimate trovo,
e ciò si tocca e non pur s'argomenta,
    da questa intenzion io mi rimovo,   *190*
e in ogni modo question far voglio,
e partorir lo sdegno ch'entro covo.

    Apparecchiate pur l'inchiostro e 'l foglio,

Or in this case you're not a clever liar —
I don't refer to kind words and true praise —
For *that* I know was not what you intended,
    Although I never harmed you in my lifetime —
    You only wrote what first came to your mind.   165
Perhaps you wished to please some other people —
    But here, not I, but you, incur the damage
    By speaking ill without the slightest cause.
For, wishing to distort the truth expressly
    With sordid inky blots in careless writing   170
    Is not allowed in good society.
It often happens that a man shows malice,
    Pleasing himself by giving others heartache —
    You've done this to me many times, I know.
But anyone can see by this example   175
    How you, not understanding words, have praised me
    With an expression suited to the best.
And, if indeed you labeled me a harlot,
    Perhaps you meant to say that I am *not* one,
    Or, there are some of them deserving praise.   180
How much of good is found in so-called harlots,
    How much gentility and graceful manners,
    You have implied of me in what you wrote.
If this is what you meant, writing so subtly,
    Not spreading tales of me, I'm very happy,   185
    And humbly bow before you, with good grace.
But since I find the end of all your writing
    Is your intent to slander and debase me —
    This much is plain and cannot be disproved —
I shall abstain from such a lowly gesture.   190
    Now, in the end, I take you to task,
    And vent the anger nesting in my heart.
Therefore prepare yourself with ink and paper,

e fatemi saper senz'altro indugio
quali armi per combatter in man toglio.   *195*
    Voi non avrete incontro a me rifugio,
ch'a tutte prove sono apparecchiata,
e impazientemente a l'opra indugio:
    o la favella giornalmente usata,
o qual vi piace idioma prendete,   *200*
chè 'n tutti quanti sono essercitata;
    e, se voi poi non mi risponderete,
di me dirò che gran paura abbiate,
se ben cosí valente vi tenete.
    Ma, perché alquanto manco dubitiate,   *205*
son contenta di far con voi la pace,
pur ch'una volta meco vi proviate:
    fate voi quel, che piú vi giova e piace.

TERZA RIMA 24

    ...Povero sesso, con fortuna ria   *55*
sempre prodotto, perch'ognor soggetto
e senza libertà sempre si stia!
    Né però di noi fu certo il diffetto,
che, se ben come l'uom non sem forzute,
come l'uom mente avemo ed intelletto.   *60*
    Né in forza corporal sta la virtute,
ma nel vigor de l'alma e de l'ingegno,
da cui tutte le cose son sapute:
    e certa son che in ciò loco men degno
non han le donne, ma d'esser maggiori   *65*
degli uomini dato hanno piú d'un segno.
    Ma, se di voi si reputiam minori,
fors' è perché in modestia ed in sapere

And let me know without delaying further
    What weapons I shall take in fighting you.   195
You'll find there's no escaping from my challenge,
    For I'm prepared for any sort of trial,
    And wait impatiently for the event.
Take if you wish our ordinary language,
    Or any form of dialect that suits you,   200
    For I am practiced in all kinds of speech.
And if you do not dare send me your answer,
    I'll say aloud you're nothing but a coward,
    Though you may think yourself so brave and bold.
Still, if you fear to own this kind of weakness,   205
    I'll gladly sign a pact of concord with you,
    So long as you will give me one more chance.
Do as you like — whatever suits you best.

Terza Rima 24 (*EXCERPT*)[1]

…Poor female sex, you are forever troubled   55
    With evil fortune, held in base subjection
    And forced to live deprived of liberty!
This does not come from any fault of ours,
    Because, though we fall short of men's robustness,
    We are the same in mind and intellect.   60
For virtue does not lie in strength of body,
    But in soul's vigor and the force of genius
    By which anything known can be possessed.
And I am certain that in such endeavors
    Women are not in any way less worthy,   65
    But often show a greater aptitude.
But if we think ourselves inferior,
    Perhaps from modesty and greater knowledge,

1. Courteous reproach to someone who angrily insulted a woman, and almost physically assaulted her.

di voi siamo piú facili e migliori....

    E cosí noi, che siam di voi piú sagge,   76
per non contender vi portamo in spalla,
com'anco chi ha buon piè porta chi cagge.

    Ma la copia degli uomini in ciò falla;
e la donna, perché non segua il male,   80
s'accomoda e sostien d'esser vassalla.

    Ché, se mostrar volesse quanto vale,
in quanto a la ragion, de l'uom saria
di gran lunga maggiore, e non che eguale.

    Ma l'umana progenie mancheria,   85
se la donna, ostinata in sul duello,
foss'a l'uom, com'ei merta, acerba e ria.

    Per non guastar il mondo, ch'è sí bello
per la specie di noi, la donna tace,
e si sommette a l'uom tiranno e fello,   90

    che poi del regnar tanto si compiace,
si come fanno 'l piu quei che non sanno
(ché 'l mondan peso a chi piú sa piú spiace),

    che gli uomini perciò grand'onor fanno
a le donne, perché cessero a loro   95
l'imperio, e sempre a lor serbato l'hanno....

We are superior in every way....
And therefore we, better than you in wisdom,   76
    To avoid conflict, bear you on our shoulders,
    As those with stronger feet bear those who fall.
But the majority in this thinks wrongly,
    And woman, since she will not practice evil,   80
    Lets herself be reduced to vassalage.
Because, if she but wished to prove her value
    In power of mind, she could by far excel
    The men, not merely prove herself their equal.
But since the human race could not continue   85
    If women, obstinate in this great duel,
    Should treat men coldly and with bitterness,
So, not to spoil the world, which is so lovely
    For all of us, we women must be silent;
    Though men be evil tyrants, we submit.   90
They are delighted with their empty power,
    For the most part, not knowing what they do
    (For mortal weight is felt most by the wise),
And therefore men should show the greatest honor
    To women, since they freely have surrendered   95
    All earthly rule, leaving it up to men....

MODERATA FONTE
(1555-1592)

Modesta da Pozzo, known under the transparent pseudonym of Moderata Fonte (moderate fountain), was born in 1555 of an upper class Venetian family, and married Filippo dei Giorgi (or Zorzi in Venetian). We have a comparative wealth of biographical material on her, since her relative and mentor, Nicolò Doglioni, wrote an extensive biography of her life, which was published in 1600, with Fonte's treatise *Il merito delle donne*.

Orphaned in 1556, she became the ward of her grandmother and was schooled in a convent, where she distinguished herself through her scholarship and talent. Doglioni tells us that she also learned from her brother's grammar school education: unable to attend herself, she would ask her brother what he had learned when he came home from school each day. After his marriage, Doglioni invited Fonte to live with his familiy, and became a supportive patron for her, encouraging her to write. He also arranged her marriage to Filippo dei Giorgi, a well-to-do official in the Venetian Republic. Fonte bore three children, and died at the age of thirty-seven at the birth of the fourth. She did most of her writing when she was single, although she also wrote during the ten years of her marriage. According to Doglioni, she had barely completed *Il merito delle donne* before she died. Throughout her work, the reader can sense the frustration that she felt when household responsibilities took her away from studies and literary endeavors.

Her poetry does not follow the canons or forms of Petrarchism; rather, she used *ottava rima* for most of her work, following the examples of Poliziano, Ariosto, Bernardo and Torquato Tasso. Writing in *ottava rima* was a way, so to speak, of invading the poetic field of epic and chivalric poetry that had been hitherto dominated by men poets. But she used the situations, poetic forms and conventions of chivalric poetry to convey particular feminine insights. In the epic poem *Floridoro* (Venice, 1581), which is composed of thirteen cantos of approximately one hundred octaves each, Fonte shows a preference for the description of exploits of female characters. The musical quality of her poetry, as well as her fierce feminist sentiments, are evident in Canto X, where she casts herself as a *giovane romita* (a young woman hermit), a virgin with *alti pensieri accesi* (high burning ambitions), equating the solitude of her virginal status with the loftiness of her ambitions. *Floridoro* also contains a *novella* that warns women against men's seductive ploys, a theme that she later enlarged upon in *Il merito delle donne* (The Merits of Women). Living as she did during the strictly pious Counter-Reformation, Fonte nevertheless managed to show a streak of independence and unconventionality in dedicating this work to Bianca Cappello, a young Venetian woman of outrageously free mores, who married Francesco de' Medici, thus becoming the Duchess of Tuscany. However, she twisted the tradition of chivalric and epic poems by presenting male protagonists who are unable to live up to their status as heroes and rescuers of damsels in distress.

Like many other poets during the times of renewed religious fervor immediately following the Council of Trent, she wrote religious poems, also in *ottava rima*, one of which was on the passion of Christ, *La passione di Gesù Cristo* (Venice, 1582). She is best known, however, for her original feminist work published posthumously in 1600, *Il merito delle donne, ove chiaramente si scuopre quanto siano elle degne e più perfette degli uomini* (The merits of women, in which it is clearly shown how women are more worthy and perfect than men). In this work, we have alternately a *laudatio mulierum* and a *vituperatio virorum*. This work, a medley of prose, poetry, and science, had been written between 1587 and 1592, and clearly shows that Fonte had dramatic talent. The book was published several years after the poet's death, almost contemporaneously with Marinelli's *The Nobility of Women*, at a time when there was an immediate necessity to respond to Giuseppi Passi's libel against women entitled *I donneschi difetti* (The vices of women). Fonte's unpublished treatise came to light, and Doglioni added lyrics to the manuscript as well as a dedication by two of her children. *Il merito delle donne* is divided into two parts: *Giornata Prima* (first day), in which the women protagonists form a tribunal to judge men's behaviour, and *Giornata Seconda* (second day), where they demonstrate their knowledge of science and the properties of herbs and plants.

In the work's frame — reminding us of Boccaccio's *Decameron* — seven women, Adriana, Virginia, Leonora, Lucrezia, Cornelia, Elena, and Corinna, meet in a garden, the typical *locus amoenus,* to talk freely "without having men in the way to make remarks about them or inhibit them." For two days, the women converse about feminine virtues and masculine faults. It is clear that the author wrote not only about the merit of women in general, but also about her own merits. Corinna appears to be the author's persona: she plays the harpsichord, she is single, and her emblem is the Phoenix. She resembles Ariosto's Marfisa, the woman warrior who wanted to be "unica al mondo forte" (the only strong woman in the world). Corinna had been foreshadowed in *Floridoro*:

Io, che d'entrar fra li sentier diversi
e fra l'immense vie bramo et ardisco,
Per qual hor deggio incamminar miei versi?

(And I, who through diverse and immense ways
dare enter paths with courage and with zeal,
in which direction must I now turn my verses?)

In *Il merito delle donne,* written while she was married, Fonte reflected with longing on the peace of mind of her youth, when she lived "stando rinchiusa infra l'anguste mura" (being enclosed within narrow walls). Her thirst for knowledge was outstanding. Somewhat bookish and reserved, she would probably have remained celibate had she been left to her own devices. Her marriage, dictated by the norms of society, interrupted her literary endeavors, and it is no surprise that in *Il merito delle donne* she expresses such a negative opinion of married life. Fonte was a contemporary of Veronica Franco and lived in the same city, yet her life was diametrically opposed to that of the outspoken and sensual courtesan, and we have no evidence that they ever crossed paths. They knew the same artists and *literati*, though in different ways: Veronica in person, often in bed, while Moderata's knowledge of men and their ideas came mostly through their books or their art.

Recently, Fonte has received a lot of attention both from Italian scholars, such as Ginevra Conti Odorisio and Adriana Chemello (who has given the most extensive consideration to Fonte's work), as well as by the American critics Patricia Labalme, Paola Malpezzi Price and Margaret King. The latter, in *Women of the Renaissance,* selects Fonte as one of three women who best analyze and write about the problematics of women's social status.

The excerpt from *Il merito delle donne* we present here is taken from Adriana Chemello's critical edition (Venice: Eidos, 1988). We are also presenting four octaves from the fourth canto of *Floridoro,* containing statements so favorable to women that Luisa Bergalli quoted them in the introduction to her anthology.

BIBLIOGRAPHY

Works by Moderata Fonte:
Le feste. Rappresentazione avanti il Serenissimo Prencipe di Venetia Nicolò Ponte il giorno di S. Stefano. Venice: Guerra, 1581.
Tredici canti del Floridoro di Mad. Moderata Fonte. Venice: Rampazzetto, 1581.
La Passione di Christo descritta in ottava rima da Moderata Fonte. Venice: Guerra, 1582.
Il merito delle donne scritto da Moderata Fonte in due giornate ove chiaramente si scopre quanto siano elle degne più perfette de gli huomini. Venice: Imberti, 1600.
Il merito delle donne. Ed. A. Chemello. Venice: Eidos, 1988.

Anthologies containing works by Moderata Fonte:
Bergalli, *op. cit.*
Le stanze ritrovate. Ed. A. Arslan, A. Chemello and G. Pizzamiglio. Venice: Eidos, 1991.

Studies and other works:

Chemello, Adriana. "Donna di palazzo, moglie, cortigiana; ruoli e funzioni sociali della donna in alcuni trattati del Cinquecento." In *La corte e il "Cortigiano."* Ed. A. Prosperi. Rome: Bulzoni, 1980, 113-132.

———. "La donna, il modello, l'immaginario: Moderata Fonte e Lucrezia Marinella." In *Nel cerchio della luna*. Ed. M. Zancan. Venice: Marsilio, 1983, 95-170.

———. "Giochi ingegnosi e citazioni dotte: immagini del femminile." *Nuova DWF* 25-26 (1985): 39-56.

———. Introduction to *Il merito delle donne*. Venice: Eidos, 1988.

———. "Il 'genere femminile' tesse la sua 'tela.' Moderata Fonte e Lucrezia Marinelli." In *Miscellanea di studi*. Ed. R. Cibin and A. Ponziano. Venice: Multigraf, 1993, 85-107.

Collina, Beatrice. "Moderata Fonte e *Il merito delle donne*." *Annali d'italianistica* 7 (1989): 142-64.

Conti Odorisio, Ginevra. *Donna e società nel Seicento*. Rome: Bulzoni, 1979.

King, Margaret. *Women of the Renaissance*. Chicago: University of Chicago Press, 1991.

Labalme, Patricia. "Venetian Women on Women: The Early Modern Feminists." *Studi Veneziani* 5, 197 (1981): 81-109.

Malpezzi Price, Paola. "A Woman's Discourse in the Italian Renaissance: Moderata Fonte's *Il merito delle donne*." *Annali d'italianistica* 7 (1989): 165-81.

———. "Moderata Fonte." In *Italian Women Writers, op. cit.,* 128-137.

Pilot, Antonio. "Sette gentildonne veneziane a conciliabolo in due giornate dell'estremo Cinquecento e quel che ne seguì." *Ateneo Veneto* 33, 3 (1910): 281-317.

Smarr, Janet L. "The Uses of Conversation: Moderata Fonte and Edmund Tilney." *Comparative Literature Studies* 32, 1 (1995): 1-25.

Zanette, Emilio. "Bianca Capello e la sua poetessa." *Nuova Antologia* 458 (1953): 455-68.

IL MERITO DELLE DONNE: PRIMA GIORNATA

*"O felice Corinna — disse allora Lucrezia — e quale altra
donna al mondo è che vi possa agguagliare? Certo niuna: non
vedova, poiché non può vantarsi di non aver prima pennato
un pezzo; non maritata, poiché stenta tuttavia, non donzella
che aspetti marito, poiché aspetta di penare e si suol dire per
proverbio che marito è mal'anno non manca mai. Felice e
beatissima dunque voi e chi segue il vostro stile e molto più
poiché vi ha Dio dato così sublime ingegno che vi dilettate ed es-
sercitate nelle virtuose azioni e impiegando i vostri alti pensieri
nei cari studi delle lettere, così umane, come divine, cominciate
una vita celeste, essendo ancora nei travagli e pericoli di questo
mondo, li quali voi rifiutate, rifiutando il comercio delli fallacis-
simi uomini, dandovi tutta alle virtù che vi faranno immortale.
E certo che voi, mediante il vostro sublime intelletto dovereste
scriver un volume in questa materia, persuadendo per carità alle
povere figliuole che non sanno ancora discernere il mal dal bene,
quello che sia il loro meglio e così voi diverreste a doppio gloriosa
e fareste servizio a Dio ed al mondo intieramente"….*
[*Corinna canta:*]
  Libero cor nel mio petto soggiorna,
Non servo alcun, né d'altri son che mia,
Pascomi di modestia, e cortesia,
Virtù m'essalta, e castità m'adorna.
  Quest'alma a Dio sol cede, e a lui ritorna,

Stortoni & Lillie

The Merit of Women: First Day (*Excerpt*)[1]

"O happy Corinna," Lucrezia said then, "what woman in the world can equal you? Certainly none: not a widow, since she cannot boast (of freedom) without having first gone through the pain (of marriage) for a while; not married, because she still suffers; not like a maiden waiting for a husband, because she expects to suffer in the future; the proverb says that husband and mishap never fail to come.... Happy and most blessed are you then, and those who follow your way of life; and much more, because God has given you such a sublime talent that you delight in and practice virtuous acts; and, employing your lofty thoughts in the cherished studies of letters, both human and divine, you start leading a celestial life while still in the vicissitudes and dangers of this world, which you reject, rejecting commerce with fallible men, giving yourself entirely to the virtues that will make you immortal. And certainly, by means of your sublime intellect, you should write a volume on this matter, convincing, out of charity, the poor maidens, who still cannot distinguish good from evil, that maidenhood is in their best interest; thus you would become doubly glorious, and you would be of service to God and to the whole world....[2]
[Corinna sings:]

A free heart makes its home within my breast,
servant to no one but myself alone.
I feed on modesty and courtesy,
virtue exalts me, chastity adorns.
This soul serves only God, returns to Him,

1. Seven women are gathered in a garden. Among them special attention is given to Corinna, the poet's persona. Corinna (the name is from the Greek poet who surpassed Pindar in eloquence) is free from matrimonial bonds and well versed in science and literature. She is praised by Lucrezia.
2. The women now gather around Corinna and beg her to recite a sonnet. Corinna, with "gracious modesty," agrees, and starts to recite, accompanying herself on the harpsichord.

Benché nel velo uman s'avolga, e stia;
E sprezza il mondo, e sua perfidia ria,
Che le semplici menti inganna, e scorna.
    Bellezza, gioventù, piaceri, e pompe,
Nulla stimo, se non ch'a i pensier puri,
Son trofeo, per mia voglia, e non per sorte.
    Così negli anni verdi, e nei maturi,
Poiché fallacia d'uom non m'interrompe,
Fama e gloria n'attendo in vita, e in morte.

     Il Floridoro
       Canto 4

Le donne in ogni età fûr da natura
   Di gran giudicio e d'animo dotate,
   Né men atte a mostrar con studio, e cura
   Senno, e valor degli uomini son nate.
   E perchè, se comune è la figura,   5
   Se non son le sostanze variate,
   S'hanno un simile cibo, e un parlar, denno
   Differente aver poi l'ardir e 'l senno?

Sempre s'è visto, e vede, pur ch'alcuna
   Donna v'abbia voluto il pensier porre,   10
   Nella milizia riuscir più d'una,
   E il pregio, e il grido a molti uomini tôrre.
   E così nelle lettere, e in ciascuna
   Impresa, che l'uom pratica, e discorre
   Le donne sì buon frutto han fatto, e fanno,   15
   Che gli uomini a invidiar punto non hanno.

E benchè di sì degno, e sì famoso
   Grido di lor non sia numero molto
   È perchè ad atto eroico, e virtuoso
   Non hanno il cor, per più rispetti volto   20

although, for now, wrapped in human veil,
it scorns the world with its perfidious ways
which carelessly deceive the simple souls.

　　Beauty and youth, pleasure and foolish pomp
I count as nothing; only pure, high thoughts
are trophies for my will, not gifts of fate.

　　Thus, in my green years and maturer age,
if man's deceitful ways do not prevent,
I hope for fame and glory after death.

FLORIDORO
　　CANTO 4

Women in every age are blessed by Nature
　　With highest gifts of judgment and of courage,
　　Nor are they born less apt, with zeal and study,
　　To equal men in wisdom and in daring.
　　So why — since they are similar in body,　　　　5
　　Not differing in substance or proportion,
　　Eating the same food, speaking the same language —
　　Should they be less in bravery or wit?

It has been seen before, and may be seen still,
　　That if a woman sets her mind upon it,　　　　10
　　She may — and more than once — succeed in warfare,
　　Winning acclaim and praise from many men.
　　Likewise, in letters and in other exploits
　　That men have undertaken and made much of,
　　Women have borne good fruit, and still may do so,　　15
　　So that they have no cause to envy men.

Although deserving fame, the cry of glory
　　Has not been won by many in times past —
　　Perhaps because their hearts have not been in it,
　　Nor on heroic deeds of martial courage.　　　　20

L'oro, che sta nelle miniere ascoso
Non lascia d'esser or, benchè sepolto;
E quando è tratto, se ben fa lavoro,
È così ricco, e bel, come l'altr'oro.

Se quando nasce una figliola il padre   25
    La ponesse col figlio a un'opra uguale,
    Non saría nelle imprese alte, e leggiadre
    Al frate inferior, nè disuguale;
    O la ponesse in fra l'armate squadre
    Seco, o ad impar qualch'arte liberale;   30
    Ma perchè in altri affar viene allevata,
    Per l'educazione poco è stimata.

But gold, although still hidden in deep mines,
Is none the less true gold, though it lies buried.
When brought to light and wrought by skillful workmen,
It is as rich and fine as other gold.

So when the father has a little daughter,   25
    Let him set her to tasks just like his sons',
    And not consign her to a lower station
    In terms of noble wit or deeds of daring.
    Let her stand at his side in martial squadrons,
    Or let her set her mind to liberal arts.   30
    For, when confined to ordinary training,
    Her education brings her small esteem.

ISABELLA ANDREINI
(1562-1604)

Isabella Andreini was the most famous *comica* (dramatic actress) of her times, as well as a talented writer of prose and poetry. She was born in Padua in 1562 of the Venetian Canali family. Although we know nothing about her childhood, we can tell that she received a thorough classical education, and could express herself fluently in several languages. Her writings were judged to be of a high enough quality to admit her to Academy of the Intenti in Pavia, with the literary name of Accesa. According to the chronicles of her times, she was a great beauty, endowed with a lively and graceful temperament.

At the tender age of fourteen, she joined the well-known *commedia dell'arte* company *I gelosi,* where she acted the role of *prima donna innamorata,* or romantic prima donna. In 1578, she married Francesco Andreini, a fellow actor, to whom she bore four daughters and three sons. Francesco was himself a famous *commedia dell'arte* actor, and she often appeared with him on stage. She enjoyed great success acting under her own name in a series of plays featuring her, such as *La Fortunata Isabella* (Lucky Isabella) and *La gelosa Isabella* (Jealous Isabella). Her best-known piece seems to have been *La Pazzia di Isabella* (Isabella's Madness), which she performed at the wedding of Ferdinand I de' Medici and Christine of Lorraine in 1589. In 1603-4 the Gelosi performed in France at the court of Henry IV, where Isabella's acting talent was praised by Queen Marie de' Medici. Andreini was fluent and could act in several languages, and she enjoyed the admiration of the great poets Tasso, Marino and Chiabrera.

At the age of forty-two, on June 1st 1604, Andreini died on her journey back to Italy, near Lyon; she was pregnant for the eighth time. Luisa Bergalli, in the biographical notes to her anthology, laconically states that her death was caused by an abortion or a miscarriage (the same word in Italian). After her death, the company *I gelosi* dissolved, and Andreini was deeply mourned by the public, the theatrical and literary world, as well as by her family. A medal was coined for her, with her effigy and the inscribed Latin words *Aeterna fama* (eternal fame). In *commedia dell'arte,* the name *Isabella* remained the name of the type of role she had preferred to play, the beautiful and witty *innamorata.* One of her sons, Giovanni Battista, an actor and a writer, dedicated to his mother's memory a collection of his poetry, *Pianto di Apollo* (Apollo's Tears), published in 1606. Her husband wrote about his grief and paid homage to the achievements of his wife by collecting her letters and dialogues.

Although Andreini is remembered more for her great acting talent, we should not overlook her literary production. In 1588, she published *Mirtilla,* a pastoral play in verse, written in imitation of Tasso's *Aminta,* which had been performed in 1573 by the Gelosi company, and was published in 1590. As evidenced by the many editions (1588, 1594, 1598, 1602, 1605, 1616), this play enjoyed enormous success, capitalizing as it did on the popularity of Tasso's work and of the pastoral play in general. *Mirtilla* is a pastoral fable based on tragi-comic conventions, but it cleverly reverses some of the roles: the would-be ravisher satyr is tricked and captured, while the potential victim, the nymph, takes a humorous and titillating revenge.

Andreini's *Rime* appeared in 1601-3; it is a collection of over three hundred poems which shows a considerable ability for diverse poetic forms, such as sonnets, madrigals, eclogues, *capitoli, scherzi,* and more. Andreini's style was musical and delicate, going far beyond Petrarchism to complex Baroque themes prevailing in Italy at the time. Like other Baroque poets, she used unusual similes and startling conceits. Hers, however, is a very musical and delicate style, which reminds us of Tasso's and Chiabrera's poetry, especially in the madrigals and in the *canzonette. (See how dewy morning glows...)* Her lyric production, evident in the sonnet *If anyone should read...,* reflects the Baroque concern about the tenuous line of demarcation between fiction and reality.

Andreini's *Lettere* (letters), which Luisa Bergalli found *graziosissime* (very lovely), were published posthumously by her grieving husband in 1607. They consist of one hundred and forty-eight epistolary compositions, reflections and musings on various themes and subjects, several of which were written in defense of women. From the letters, we present the most famous, *Del nascimento della donna* (On the Birth of Women) addressed to a gentleman who was distressed for having sired a daughter, in which the author presents an eloquent defense of women, expressing also her concern over their sad lot in the society of her time. In the play *Mirtilla*, Andreini also shows her feminist sympathies when the nymph turns the tables on her attacker.

Andreini's husband also collected her dialogues which appeared in 1620 under the title of *Fragmenti di alcune scritture della Signora Isabella Andreini comica gelosa e academica intenta*. This work consists of thirty-one dialogues or debates between a man and a woman, on lyric subjects such as love, passion and jealousy, as well as on literary and theatrical topics, such as comedy or dramatic art in general, and on the superiority of letters over arms. These scenes, quarrels or debates between a man and a woman, were set pieces performed on stage as needed, and mark the transition from the improvisation of *commedia dell'arte* to the written script. For an interesting study of one of these dialogues, as well as for an English translation, we refer the reader to the work of Louise George Clubb, who, in *Italian Drama in Shakespeare's Time,* studied the similarities between the Eudosia-Manlio exchange and the language of Shakespearean comedy.

We have taken the original texts of the sonnets and the *scherzo* from *Rime d'Isabella Andreini Padovana Comica Gelosa.* (Milan: G. Bordone & P. Locarni, 1601). We have taken the original text of the letter *Del nascimento della donna* from *Lettere della Signora Isabella Andreini Padovana, Comica Gelosa et Academica Intenta, nominata l'Accesa.* (Venice: G.B. Combi, 1634, pp. 32-35). We also present here the hilarious climax of the play *Mirtilla*, which we have taken from the Verona 1588 edition, portions of which have been reprinted in *Le stanze ritrovate.*

BIBLIOGRAPHY

Works by Isabella Andreini:

Frammenti d'alcune scritture della Sign. Isabella Andreini comica gelosa e accademica Intenta, raccolti da Francesco Andreini comico geloso. Venice: Combi, 1617

Lettere Aggiuntovi di Nuovo li Ragionamenti Piacevoli. Venice: G.B. Combi, 1638

Lettere d'Isabella Andreini Padovana, comica gelosa. Venice: M.A. Zaltieri, 1607.

Mirtilla, pastorale d'Isabella Andreini, comica gelosa. Verona: Sebastiano Dalle Donne e Camilli Franceschini, 1588.

Rime d'Isabella Andreini Padovana, comica gelosa. Milan: G. Bordone & P. Locarni Compagni, 1601.

Rime d'Isabella Andreini comica gelosa & academia intenta detta l'Accesa. Parte seconda. Milan: Girolamo Bordone & Pietromartire Locarni, 1605.

Anthologies containing works by Isabella Andreini:

Costa-Zalessow, *op. cit.*

de Blasi, *op. cit.*

Raya, G. *Lirici del Cinquecento.* Milan and Naples: S.A. Editrice Dante Alighieri, 1993, 173.

Le stanze ritrovate, op. cit.

Studies and other works:

Clubb, Louise George. "The State of the Arts in the Andreinis' Time." In *Studies in the Italian Renaissance: Essays in Memory of Arnolfo B. Ferruolo.* Eds. Gian Paolo Biasin, Albert Mancini and Nicholas Perella. Naples: Perella, 1985, 263-81.

——. *Italian Drama in Shakespeare's Time.* New Haven: Yale University Press, 1989.

Costa-Zalessow, Natalia. "Among the Treasures of the Frank de Bellis Collection: Isabella Andreini's *Rime* and *Lettere*." San Francisco State University's College of Humanitites Magazine, vol 13 (Fall 1994): 124-143.

Croce, B. "Studi sulla letteratura cinquecentesca: Isabella Andreini." *Quaderni della critica* 17-18 (1950): 85-90.

De Angelis, Francesca Romana. *La divina Isabella.* Florence: Sansoni, 1991.

De Cerro, E. "Un'attrice di tre secoli fa: Isabella Andreini." *Natura ed arte* 17 (1908): 458-461, 529-532.

Dersofi, Nancy. "Isabella Andreini." In *Italian Women Writers, op. cit.,* 18-25.

Dizionario biografico, op. cit., XVII, 704-705.

Dizionario enciclopedico, op. cit., I, 128-130.

Enciclopedia biografica bibliografica italiana, op. cit.

Falena, U. "Isabella Andreini." *La rassegna nazionale* 27 (May 15 1905): 267-279.

Longman, Stanley. "Isabella Andreini." In *Encyclopedia of Continental Woman Writers, op. cit.,* 38-39.

MacNeil, Anne. "Music and the Life and Work of Isabella Andreini: Humanistic Attitudes Towards Music, Poetry and Theater in the Late Sixteenth and Early Seventeenth Centuries." Ph.D. dissertation, University of Chicago, 1994.

Molinare, Cesare. *La commedia dell'arte.* Milan: Mondadori, 1985.

Newcomb, Anthony. "Courtesans, Muses, or Musicians?" In *Women Making Music.* Ed. Jane Bowers and Judith Tick. Chicago: University of Illinois Press, 1987, 90-115.

Smith, Winifred. *Italian Actors of the Renaissance.* New York: Coward-McCann, 1930.

Taviani, F. and M. Schino. *Il segreto della Commedia dell'arte, La memoria delle compagnie italiane del XVI, XVII e XVIII secolo.* Florence: La Casa Usher, 1982.

Tessari, Roberto. "Sotto il segno di Giano: La Commedia dell'arte di Isabella e di Francesco Andreini." In *The Commedia dell'arte from the Renaissance to Dario Fo.* Ed. C. Cairns. Lewiston, Queenstown, Lampeter: Edwin Mellen Press, 1989.

Vescovo, Piermario. "Isabella Andreini." In *Le stanze ritrovate, op. cit.,* 83-94.

LETTERA DEL NASCIMENTO DELLA DONNA

Con mio grandissimo piacere ho inteso che la Sig. N., vostra moglie, ha partorito una bellissima figlia, la quale, crescendo in bellezza (come si dèe sperare), sarà perfettissima d'animo e di corpo, poichè la bellezza del corpo è chiaro inditio della bellezza dell'animo: si come l'una bellezza argomentar fa l'altra, così tutte due fanno argomentar perfettione; poichè secondo l'openione del Savio, altro non è bellezza del corpo, che perfettione del corpo, e altro non è la bellezza dell'animo, che perfettione dell'animo: ma quanto mi son allegrata di questo felice natale, tanto mi son attristata della vostra ingiusta mestizia. M'è stato detto che grandemente v'affliggete per esservi nata una femina, quasi che per esser tale, ella non sia vostra carne, vostro sangue e vostr'ossa, non men di quello che sarebbe stato un maschio, et è possibile che voi, che siete uomo di tanta esperienza, non vogliate pigliar con allegrezza d'animo quel che vi manda Iddio sapientissimo, Facitor delle cose? Non sapete voi che per commune opinion de i dotti le donne son al mondo in maggior numero de gli uomini? Chiaro segno della feminil perfezione, essendo che l'eterna et infallibil Providenza Divina si compiace d'adornar sempre questa bella machina del mondo del suo maggior e più chiaro splendore, e se non fosse che molte, anzi infinite carte si veggono fregiate de i meriti delle donne, con ordine e con stile molto più degno e molto più alto ch'io non saprei non solo descriver con la penna, ma né pur imaginarmi con l'idea, m'ingegnerei, per levarvi così folle passione dal cuore, d'accennare scrivendo, o pur qual insperto pitore ombreggiar alcuna feminil lode. Dunque, se la vostra figlia è nata non solo per accrescer questo perfettissimo sesso, ma, chi sa, per far voi col tempo felicissimo padre, a che tanto attristarvi? A che contra 'l voler del Cielo, che sempre opera bene, desiderar un maschio? O quanti padri ci sono stati e tuttavia ci sono, i quali e sono stati e sono infelicissimi e miserissimi per li maschi. Oh quante case, oh

LETTER ON THE BIRTH OF WOMEN

It was with great pleasure that I heard that Mrs. N., your wife, has given birth to a very beautiful daughter, who, as she grows in beauty (as is to be expected), will be perfect in body and soul, since corporal beauty is a clear sign of the beauty of the soul. Since one beauty leads to the other, they both lead to perfection, since, according to the opinion of the Sage, the beauty of the body is but the perfection of the body, and the beauty of the soul is but the perfection of the soul. But as much as I rejoiced over this happy event, I was grieved by your unjust sadness. I was told that you are upset because a daughter was born to you, almost as if by being such, she was not your flesh, your blood and your bones, as much as a son would be; and is it possible that a man of such great experience as you would not want to accept with a joyful heart that which is sent to you by God the most wise, Maker of all things? Do you not know that, according to the common opinion of learned men, there are more women than men in this world? This is a clear sign of feminine perfection, since the eternal and unerring Divine Providence always delights in adorning with its principal and clearest splendor this beautiful machine that is our world. And if it were not for the fact that a lot of, or rather innumerable, papers have been written about the merits of women, with an order and style much nobler and higher than I could ever achieve or even envision with my pen, I would attempt with my writing to discuss it, or to make a sketch of women's merits like an inexperienced painter, in order to remove such an insane notion from your heart. So, why be so saddened, since your daughter was born not only to increase the numbers of this very perfect sex, but also (who knows) to make you, in time, a very happy father? Why desire a boy against the wish of heaven that works always for the best? Oh, how many fathers there were, and still are, who were and are very unhappy and miserable on account of their

quante famiglie per essi poverite, infamate, e dessolate. Le pazienti donne si contentano di viver in quella soggezione, nella qual nascono ad una vita regolata e modesta, si contentano d'aver il breve confine della casa per dolce prigione, godendo della continua servitù, non è lor grave d'esser sottoposte all'altrui severo arbitrio, lor non dispiace lo star in continuo timore, e quando la conoscenza delle cose umane vien loro da gli anni permessa, come quelle che portano dal nascimento la modestia e la riverenza, non osano di volger pur un sguardo in alcuna parte, se prima non concede chi d'esse ha cura. Quante ci sono che per far la volontà de' parenti, senz'alcuna replica si rinchiudono per sempre tra solitarie mura, e quante ve n'ha che dovendo sopporre il collo al giogo maritale, per non dispiacer alle altrui voglie, senza dir parola in contrario, pigliano tal'uno che meritava di morire prima che nascesse, e con quanta pazienza sopportano poi la maggior parte de' diffetti insopportabili de i mariti? I maschi non son così tosto usciti fuor della disciplina de' precettori, che vogliono esser compagni del padre, poi fratelli e poi assolutamente padroni. Oh quanti ci sono che bramando maschi et ottenendogli, bramano et ottengono o la morte o la ruina loro. Il nascimento d'Edippo fu cagion della morte violenta di Laio suo Padre, poich'egli di sua mano l'uccise. Quando nacque Paride, nacque l'incendio di Troia & Hecuba, mentre di lui haveva grave il seno, sognò di partorir (come sapete) una fiamma grandissima. Sono infiniti gli esempi ch'io lascio, per non essere prolissa: basta, che le femine, o tutte, o per lo più, apportano contento, & onore alle famiglie. Non vi pare, che si potessero chiamare fortunati appieno que' padri, da i quali nacquero le sempre famose Corinna, Saffo, Erinna, Aspasia, Prasilla, Amaltea, Manto, Areta, Carmenta, e tan'altre, che di sapere non sol agguagliarono, ma superarono gli uomini? Non furono

male children? How many houses, how many families have been impoverished, disgraced and desolated by their doing? The patient women are happy to live under that subjection into which they are born and to lead a regimented and modest life; they contentedly regard the limited confines of their houses as a sweet prison, enjoying the continuous servitude; it does not burden them to be subjected to the strict command of others; it does not displease them to live in constant fear; and when knowledge of the things of the world is allowed them with age, as women who from birth have carried a modest and reverent demeanor, they do not dare to cast a glance anywhere unless their guardians allow it. How many women are there who, to obey the will of their parents, lock themselves up forever within solitary walls without protest? And how many women are there who, having to submit their neck to the marital yoke in order not to displease others, without any contradictions, marry a man who deserved to die before being born? And with what patience do they later bear the greatest part of the unbearable faults of their husbands?

No sooner are boys free from the discipline of their teachers, than they want to be their fathers' companions, then their brothers, and then their absolute masters. Oh how many men are there who, yearning to have male offspring and having obtained them, desire and obtain either their death or their ruin? The birth of Oedipus caused the violent death of his father Laius, whom he killed with his own hands. When Paris was born, the fire of Troy was born too, and Hecuba while pregnant with him, dreamed (as you know) that she was giving birth to a huge flame. There are infinite examples that I won't mention in order not to be verbose. It is enough to say that girls, all or most, bring happiness and honor to their families. Don't you think we could call most fortunate those fathers from whom were born such eternally famous daughters

avventuratissimi quelli, del cui ceppo uscirono le valorose Ca-
milla, Hippolita, Zenobia, Hipsicratea, Tomiri, Tiburna, e altre
infinite? Non chiameremo noi felicissimi quegli, per cui vennero
al Mondo le castissime Penelope, Lucretia, Artemisia, & altre,
che sono innumerabili? certo sì. Hor che sapete voi, che non
voglia farvi gratia il Cielo, che questa vostra figlia sia un'altra
Saffo di sapere, ovvero una Tomiri di valore, e una Penelope di
castità, e potrebbe anch'essere, che per farla più maravigliosa, in
lei sola unisse tutte queste gratie singolari: onde la vostra patria
havesse molto più da pregiarsi di lei, che Lesbo della sua Saffo,
Scithia della sua Tomiri, & Itaca della sua Penelope; consolatevi
dunque, e fate grandissima festa del nascimento di questa vostra
figlia, da quale spero, che debbia a portarvi infinito contento, e
spero ancora, che mi ricorderete nel colmo de' vostri piaceri per
indovina. Vi bacio le mani, e prego Iddio, che per sua bontà ci
dia lunga vita, accoicchè possiam godere delle molte e meravigliose
attioni di vostra figlia.

as Corinna,[1] Sappho, Erinna, Aspasia, Diotima, Praxilla, Amalthea, Manto, Arete, Carmenta, and others, who not only were equal but even surpassed men in knowledge? Weren't those men fortunate from whose lineage descended the brave Camilla, Hippolyte, Zenobia, Hypsicratea, Tamiris, Tiburna, and others? Wouldn't we call most fortunate those men who gave this world the chaste Penelope, Lucretia, Artemisia and others who are innumerable? Certainly we would. But you do not yet know if heaven meant to grant you a favor by making this daughter of yours another Sappho in knowledge, or a Tamiris of bravery or a Penelope of chastity, or even unite in her alone all of these singular qualities in order to create a greater marvel, so that your country could value her more than Lesbos its Sappho, Scythia its Tamiris and Ithaca its Penelope. Therefore console yourself, celebrate the birth of this daughter of yours, who, I hope, will bring you infinite joy. I also hope that you will remember me in the future as the one who foresaw your happiness. I kiss your hands and pray to God that through his kindness He will give us a long life, so that we can enjoy the many and marvelous actions of your daughter.

1. Andreini here uses *exampla* of famous women of antiquity: Sappho, lyric poetess from Lesbos; Corinna, lyric poetess of Tanagra, contemporary of Pindar; Erinna, poetess of the Dorian island of Telos; Aspasia, refined and literary Athenian courtesan, mistress of Pericles; Diotima, priestess at Mantinea, teacher of Socrates, who, in Plato's *Symposium,* espouses the metaphysics of love; Praxilla, poetess of Sicyon, who wrote hymns and drinking songs; Amalthea, the mythological nurse of Zeus who was transformed into the star Capella; Manto, daughter of the seer Tiresias, diviner and prophetess of Apollo; Arete, wife of Alcinoüs, king of the Phœacians; Carmenta, the mythological prophetess who, according to legend, taught the Aboriginies how to write; Camilla, a legendary warrior heroine who, in Vergil's *Aeneid,* joined the forces of Turnus and was killed by the Etruscans; Hippolyta, mythological queen of the Amazons; Zenobia, historical queen of Palmyra; Ipsicratea, Tamiris and Tiburna, great heroines of antiquity; Penelope, chaste wife of Odysseus; Lucretia, model of fortitude, raped by Sextus, who took her life rather than live with dishonor; Artemisia II, wife of Mausolus of Caria, who erected the Mausoleum at his death.

MIRTILLA PASTORALE
ATTO TERZO, SCENA SECONDA. SATIRO E FILLI

Filli: *Parrà forse ad alcun che degna io sia*
d'ogni grave castigo non amando
chi ama me. No 'l nego, ma che posso
far'io s'Amor non vol ch'io pensi o faccia
se non quel che a lui piace?...
Satiro: *Vè, che ti giunsi, or non potrai fuggire!*
Filli: *Ahimé, ch'è quel ch'io sento? Chi mi tiene?*
Chi mi fa violenza?
Satiro: *Ah, dispietata,*
or non ti gioverà l'esser crudele,
né l'adequar nel corso
i più veloci venti.
Di qui non partirai, s'a le mie pene
non dai qualche mercede.
E quando tu non voglia a l'arso core
dar qualche refrigerio, ingrata voglio
nuda legarti a quella dura roccia,
ove con strazio finirai tua vita.
Filli: *Mercede, ahimé, mercede*
nume caprigno! Ascolta
prima le mie preghiere,
deh, che gloria ti fia
di vincere una ninfa
ch'abbattuta è di già da tuoi begl'occhi?

Stortoni & Lillie

MIRTILLA: A PASTORAL (*EXCERPT*)
ACT 3, SCENE 2. SATYR AND PHYLLIS[1]

Phyllis: Some may believe that I am worthy
of every great punishment for not loving
him who loves me. I don't deny it, but what can I do
if Love does not allow me to think or do
but what he pleases?...   5

Satyr: Aha, I finally found you, you will not be able to
escape me!

Phyllis: Alas, what is this I hear? Who is grabbing me?
Who is raping me?

Satyr: Ah, heartless one,
your disdain will no longer help you,   10
nor will your running
as fast as the swiftest winds.
You will not leave from here unless you give
some relief to my suffering.
And if you do not want to relieve   15
my burning heart, ungrateful one, I plan to
tie you naked to that hard rock,
where you will end your life in anguish.

Phyllis (*pretending to be in love with him*):
Mercy, oh mercy,
oh goat-like god! Listen   20
first to my prayers!
Oh, what honor could come to you
from conquering a nymph
who has already been vanquished by your beautiful
eyes?

---

1. The Satyr has fallen in love with the nymph Phyllis and has been rejected by her. He has now decided to ambush her and rape her. In the final scene, which follows the one presented here, after a long lament from the Satyr, still bound, the goatherd arrives to free him. Casting aside the matters of Cupid, the two give themselves up to the pleasures of Bacchus and Ceres.

233

Satiro:	Vedi come mi beffa? or s'io m'adiro!	25
Filli:	Io giuro per le tue robuste braccia	
	e per la vaga tua cornuta fronte	
	ch'io non ti beffo, né beffar ti voglio.	
Satiro:	Dunque, Fillide, m'ami e dar mi vuoi	
	del mio fido servir premio condegno?	30
Filli:	Io t'amo certo, e qual ninfa ti vide	
	giamai che non ardesse? tu sei tale	
	che chi ti mira e poi non t'ama, credo	
	che sia composto di Caucasea pietra.	
Satiro:	E perché, pazzerella,	35
	taciuto hai questo e mi li sei mostrata,	
	spiacevole e crudele?	
Filli:	Questo feci	
	per far prova di te, dolce mia vita....	
Satiro:	Per questa prima volta	40
	finger mi voglio assai modesto amante	
	e d'un sol bacio pago	
	se ben d'altro son vago.	
	Da le dolci parole alme e gradite	
	assicurato, in libertà ti rendo,	45
	luce di queste luci, e per certezza	
	di quel che tu m'hai detto un bacio chieggio	
	da quella vermigliuzza e bella bocca...	

Satyr: See how she mocks me? Now I am really getting
                  angry!   25
Phyllis: I swear by your strong arms
              and by your lovely horned forehead
              that I am not mocking you, nor do I wish to mock
                  you.
Satyr (*falling for it*):
              So, Phyllis, you love me and you want to give me
              that worthy prize for my faithful wooing?   30
Phyllis: Certainly I love you; which nymph could ever
                  behold you
              without burning for you? You are such
              that she who can behold you and not love you,
                  I believe,
              must be made of Caucasian stone
Satyr: And so why, crazy little one,   35
              have you not told me this, and why have you shown
                  yourself
              cruel and disdainful?
Phyllis: I did this
              to test you, my sweet life....
Satyr (*aside*):
              Just this once,   40
              I will pretend to be a modest lover,
              happy with just one kiss,
              although I want much more than that.
(*To Phyllis*)
              Assured by your sweet pleasing words
              I give you back your freedom,   45
              light of my eyes, and as a pledge
              of what you have told me, I request a kiss
              from that little beautiful vermilion mouth of yours....

Filli: *Dunque beata me, poiché concesso*
           mi sarà tanto ben. Ma tu, cor mio,   50
           concedimi sol questo, ch'io ti leghi
           le braccia, perché tu da la dolcezza
           che sentirai baciandomi
           tanto non mi stringessi
           che contro la tua voglia   55
           io di te, tu di me restassi privo.

Satiro: *Tu m'hai legato il core, e puoi ben anco*
           legarmi queste braccia: io mi contento.

Filli: *Volgile al tergo. O felice legame,*
           poiché t'è dato in sorte   60
           di legar sì robuste e belle braccia.
           E tu, fronzuta pianta,
           ben ti puoi dir felice
           poiché fermo terrai colui che tiene
           l'anima mia legata a sì bel nodo.   65

Satiro: *Non stringer così forte.*

Filli: *Datti pace.*
           e soffri un poco:
           poiché quanto più stretto
           ti lego, tanto più sicuramente   70
           ti bacierò dipoi.

Satiro: *Orsù, fa' presto.*

Filli: *Ecco ch'io ho finito.*

Satiro: *Adunque Filli,*
           non differir le contentezze mie   75
           più lungamente, e tue....

Filli: *Tu sai ch'il timore*
           è proprio degli amanti e non vorrei
           invece d'acquistarmi
           la grazia tua, privarmene per sempre.   80

Satiro: *Ah non temer di quello*
           di che temer non dei.

Phyllis: Lucky me, therefore, because so much good fortune
   is granted me. But you, my heart,   50
   grant me only this wish, that I may tie
   your arms so that, from the sweetness
   you will feel kissing me,
   you do not clasp me so tightly
   that against your desire   55
   I would remain deprived of you and you of me.
Satyr: Since you have tied my heart, you may as well
   tie these arms also: I consent.
Phyllis: Put your arms behind your back. Oh happy twine,
   since it is your fate   60
   to tie such beautiful strong arms!
   And you, leafy plant,
   you can call yourself happy
   because you will hold the one who holds
   my soul tied with such a beautiful love-knot.   65
Satyr: Don't bind me so tightly!
Phyllis: Be quiet!
   And suffer a little more:
   because the tighter I tie you,
   the more firmly   70
   I will kiss you later.
Satyr: Come, be quick!
Phyllis: Here, I have finished.
Satyr: So, Phyllis,
   don't put off your happiness   75
   and mine any longer....
Phyllis: You know that fear is common to lovers.
   I wouldn't want,
   instead of acquiring
   your grace, to deprive myself of it forever.   80
Satyr: Oh do not be afraid of
   what you must not fear.

Filli: *Di questo mi rallegro; ma, cor mio,*
        tu sei sì grande ch'io non posso aggiungere
        al ben desiderato ed è bisogno   85
        che con ambe le man m'appigli un tratto
        a la tua bella barba:
        in questo modo, china bene il capo.

Satiro: *Ohimé, fa' piano, che ti pensi fare?*
        Tu mi strappi la barba: ferma, ferma!   90

Filli: *Eccomi ferma: ma tu non ti muovere,*
        acciò ch'io possa darti mille baci.
        O corna mie, voi mi feristi il core!

Satiro: *Ohimé, non far sì forte! Non mi torcere*
        il collo, ohimé, daver che mi fai male!   95

Filli: *Perdonami, cor mio, ch'io non credeva*
        di farti male. Oh, che mammelle morbide!

Satiro: *Non pizzicar sì forte, ohimé, non fare!*

Filli: *Infine non mi posso contenere*
        d'accarezzarti.   100

Satiro: *Oh che belle carezze!*

Filli: *Almen non ti sdegnar, vita mia cara....*

Satiro: *Non dar sì forte! Or che insania è questa,*
        che mi fai sempre male?

Filli: *Ah, discortese,*   105
        dimmi ond'avvien ch'ogni cosa t'offende
        di quel ch'io fo? e pur n'è testimonio il Ciel
        che tutto vien da troppo amore.

Satiro: *Ti so dir ch'io l'ho concia!*

Filli: *Oh che balordo!*   110

Phyllis: Of this I am happy: but, my heart,
         you are so big that there is nothing I can add
         to the good I desire: and I suddenly I feel
            the need   85
         to grab your beautiful beard
         with both hands:
         like this, lower your head.

Satyr: Hey, slowly, what do you think you are doing?
         You are pulling off my beard! Stop, stop!   90

Phyllis: I am not moving, but you also must not stir,
         so that I can give you a thousand kisses.
         Oh horns of mine, you have wounded my heart!

Satyr: Ouch, don't pull so hard! Don't twist
         my neck! You are really hurting me!   95

Phyllis: Forgive me, my heart. I didn't realize
         I was hurting you. Oh, what soft breasts!

(*Pinching him*)

Satyr: Don't pinch me so hard! Ouch, don't!

Phyllis: Well, I can't stop myself
         from caressing you.   100

Satyr (*ironically*):
         Oh what beautiful caresses!

Phyllis: Well do not get angry, my sweet life....

(*Proceeds to torment him in other places*)

Satyr: Don't handle me so harshly! What madness is this,
         that you are always hurting me?

Phyllis: Oh, you are so discourteous!   105
         Tell me, how come everything I do
         offends you? And yet, heaven is my witness
         that everything I do comes from excessive love.

Satyr (*to himself*):
         Well I tell you, I've really got her!

Phyllis: (*aside*) Oh what an idiot!   110

Satiro: *Ella piange in disparte,*
        per quanto posso immaginarmi.

Filli: *Voglio*
        mostrar d'essere afflitta. Ohimé, dolente,
        a che son io ridotta: l'idol mio   *115*
        si sdegna perché troppo l'accarezzo,
        che deggio dunque far? che far poss'io?

Satiro: *S'io non soccorro questa meschinella*
        di dolor certo finirà sua vita.
        Filli, non t'attristar, facciam la pace   *120*
        e per segno di quella vieni omai
        a baciare il tuo bene e la tua vita.
        Non pianger più, che tu sola sarai
        la mia vezzosa. Vieni dunque a baciarmi.

Filli: *Ohimé, par che lo spirto si rinfranchi*   *125*
        alla dolce armonia de le tue voci,
        e poiché mi rintegni
        nella tua grazia e vuoi
        ch'io baci quella cara e dolce bocca,
        voglio prima mangiare   *130*
        un poco di serpillo e voglio ancora
        che ti degni mangiarne un ramoscello,
        acciò che i nostri fiati
        sieno più delicati.
        Orsù, lo piglio ed ecco ch'io son prima   *135*
        a farne il saggio, piglia il rimanente!

Satiro: *Dammelo, io son contento.*

Filli: *Che te ne pare?*

Satiro: *Ohimé, che cosa è questa?*
        cotanto amara? Temo che mi beffi   *140*
        e mi vadi schernendo; che serpillo
        è questo che m'hai dato'?

Satyr: She cries aside,
           from what I can see.
Phyllis (*aside*):
           I want
           to appear to be sad. Alas, wretched me!
           This is what I am reduced to: my idol   115
           is angry because I caress him too much.
           What should I do then? What can I do?
Satyr (*aside*):
           If I don't assist this poor little wretch
           she will surely end her life in grief.
(*To Phyllis*)
           Do not grieve, let's make peace,   120
           and as a token of this, come now
           to kiss your love and your life.
           Stop crying, you will be my only
           love. Come then to kiss me.
Phyllis: Ah, it seems that my spirit is reassured   125
           by the sweet harmony of your voice,
           and since you maintain me
           in your favor, and wish
           that I kiss your dear and sweet mouth,
           I want first to eat   130
           a little bit of thyme, and I also ask you
           to be so kind as to eat a little twig of this
           to make our breath more delicate.
           Come, I am taking it, and I am the first
           to taste it. Take the rest!   135
Satyr: Give it to me. I am willing.
Phyllis: What do you think?
Satyr (*spitting it out*):
           Hey, what is this?
           What is this bitter stuff? I fear you are mocking me
           and making a fool of me; what kind of thyme   140
           is this you gave me?

Filli: *Malaccorto,*
or hai pur finalmente conosciuto
ch'io mi beffai di te. Qual donna mai   *145*
benché diforme e vile si compiacque
d'amar sì mostruoso orrido aspetto?
Or vedi ch'io ti colsi, resta pure
schernito, come merti ch'io ti lascio….

Satiro: *Filli, Filli, ove vai? fermati, ascolta,*   *150*
slegami almeno, acciò ch'io non diventi
de l'altre come te spietate ninfe
scherzo, favola e gioco.
Ohimé, che non può fare
femina risoluta d'ingannare?   *155*
Con quai lusinghe, ohimé, con quai parole
m'ha ridotto costei,
a lasciarmi legar l'anima e 'l core
da le sciolte sue chiome.

Phyllis: You fool,
      you have finally realized
      that I have been mocking you. What woman,
      even if deformed and vile, could ever love   145
      a monstrous and horrid countenance such as yours?
      Now you see, I caught you! Stay there,
      tricked, as you deserve to be left by me.

(*Phyllis goes away*)...

Satyr: Phyllis, where are you going? Stop, don't leave!
      Untie me at least, so that I won't become   150
      a joke, a tale and a sport
      for other pitiless nymphs like you.
      What can a woman not do
      when she is determined to deceive?
      With what blandishments, alas, with what words,   155
      has she reduced me
      to let her tie my heart and soul
      with her long flowing hair![1]

1. A dramatic reading of this scene was enacted by actors Louise Wright and Stephen Spano, following Laura Stortoni's lecture, "Isabella Andreini, Poet, Actress, Playwright," during the Humanities West Conference entitled "Renaissance Women: Courtly Power and Influence," on May 18, 1996, at the Herbst Theatre in San Francisco.

SONETTO 1

S'alcun fia mai che i versi miei negletti
legga, non creda a questi finti ardori:
ché, ne le scene imaginati amori
usa a trattar con non leali affetti,
   con bugiardi non men che finti detti   5
de le Muse spiegai gli alti furori,
talor piangendo i falsi miei dolori,
talor cantando i falsi miei diletti.
   E come ne' teatri or donne, ed ora
uom fei rappresentando in vario stile   10
quanto volle insegnar Natura ed Arte,
   così la stella mia seguendo ancora,
di fuggitiva età nel verde aprile,
vergai con vario stil ben mille carte.

SONETTO 4

Qual ruscello veggiam d'acque sovente
Povero scaturir d'alpestre vena,
Sì che temprar pon le sue stille a pena
Di stanco peregrin la sete ardente;
   Ricco di pioggia poi farsi repente   5
Superbo sì, che nulla il corso affrena
Di lui, che imperioso il tutto mena,
Ampio tributo a l'ocean possente;
   Tal da principio avea debil possanza
A danno mio questo tiranno amore,   10
E chiese in van de' miei pensier' la palma.
   Ora sovra il cor mio tanto s'avanza,
Che rapida ne porta il suo furore
A morte il senso e la ragione e l'alma.

SONNET 1

If anyone should read my trifling verses,
Let him not trust in these pretended ardors,
For, in the theater, I am accustomed
To deal with loves unfaithful and untrue.
With lying, even, or invented speeches   5
The Muses teach me to depict high passions,
Weeping at times for my fictitious sorrows,
At times rejoicing in my false delights.
And, just as on the stage I may portray
A man or woman in a different style   10
As Nature teaches, or the art of acting,
So, following my star through all my ages
From the great April of swift-passing years,
I've ruled with varied pen a thousand pages.

SONNET 4

As we may often see a little brook
Arise out of a lofty Alpine spring —
So tiny that its drops scarcely suffice
To quench a weary pilgrim's burning thirst —
Suddenly, rich with unexpected rain   5
Become so proud that nothing stops its course
From bearing everything along with it
As ample tribute to the mighty ocean,
So, in its first beginning, little power
Was in this tyrannous love to do me harm   10
Or steal the palm from all my other thoughts.
Now it advances fiercely on my heart,
And carries it along with such a fury
It kills my senses, reason, and my soul.

Scherzo 1. Invocazione ad Apollo e alle Muse

Ecco l'alba rugiadosa
come rosa,
sen di neve, piè d'argento,
che la chioma inanellata
d'or fregiata,   5
vezzosetta sparge al vento.

I ligustri e i gelsomini
da' bei crini
e dal petto alabastrino
van cadendo; e la dolce aura   10
ne ristaura
con l'odor grato divino.

Febo anch'ei la chioma bionda
fuor dell'onda
a gran passo ne discopre;   15
e sferzando i suoi destrieri,
i pensieri
desta in noi de l'usate opre.

Parte il Sonno, fugge l'ombra,
che disgombra   20
Delio già col chiaro lume
la caligine dintorno:
ecco il giorno,
ond'io anch'io lascio le piume.

E infiammar mi sento il petto   25
dal diletto
che in me spiran le tue Muse,
cui seguir bramo; e s'io caggio
nel viaggio,
bel desir teco mi scuse.   30

Stortoni & Lillie

SCHERZO I. INVOCATION TO APOLLO AND TO THE MUSES

See how dewy morning glows,
    Fresh as the rose
With silver feet and breast of snow;
She shakes her curling golden hair
    With charming air,   5
As the dawn breezes blow.

Sweet-scented privet, jasmin bloom,
    She scatters from
Her alabaster shoulders fine,
And with a breath of dawning cool   10
    Revives the soul
With fragrance lovely and divine.

And Phoebus, brighter gold than she,
    Leaps from the sea;
With rapid stride his light arises,   15
And, whipping up his noble horses,
    He wakes our forces
From our accustomed enterprises.

Sleep must leave, shadow depart
    At Phoebus' art;   20
And when his brilliant light is shed
He drives the dark of night away.
    Behold the day!
Now I must leave my feather-bed.

Within my breast I feel alight   25
    A new delight,
Because I hear the summons of the Muse,
And I must follow; if I fall
    (Heeding her call)
My eagerness must be my excuse!   30

Ma s'avvien ch'opra gentile
dal mio stile
l'alma Clio giammai risuone,
si dirà: — Sì nobil vanto
dèesi al canto   35
del ligustico Anfione. —

SONETTO 25

Già vidi, occhi leggiadri, occhi ond'Amore
m'incende, in voi bella pietà scolpita,
che dolce lusingando, al mio dolore,
al mio fido servir promise aita.
    Or veggio, lassa, il troppo folle errore   5
d'ingannato pensier, d'alma tradita:
veggio che discacciata, ohimè, dal core
la pietade negli occhi era fuggita.
    O sospirati in van dolci riposi,
quali avranno i miei giorni ore tranquille?   10
qual guiderdone i miei martiri ascosi?
    Deh potessero almeno in voi le stille
de l'amaro mio pianto, occhi amorosi,
quel che possono in me vostre faville.

But if, perchance, some lovely note
   Springs from my throat,
That Clio,[1] later, may rehearse,
It will be said, so fine a song
   Surely has sprung   35
From the Ligurian Amphion's[2] verse.

SONNET 25

O lovely eyes, from which Love lit my flame,
I once saw pity shine there like a signet,
Which, flattering my burdened heart so sweetly,
Seemed to bring succor to my faithful love.
But now, alas, I see the foolish error   5
Of my deluded thoughts, my soul betrayed:
I see that pity, fleeing from your spirit,
Has taken refuge only in your eyes.
O rest and quiet, both so vainly sighed for,
What tranquil hours will come to grace my days,   10
What recompense for all my hidden sorrows?
Ah, if the drops wrung from my bitter weeping
Could but produce in you the same effect
As the bright sparks from your love-kindling eyes!

1. The muse of history. 2. In Greek mythology, Amphion was said to have raised the walls of Thebes with his singing; who the "Ligurian" poet was, we do not know.

HISTORICAL NOTE

To make clear the context in which the talented women we present were writing, we will say a few words about the political and social situation in Italy from the fourteenth to the sixteenth century.

While in the Middle Ages the Italian *comuni* (city-states) had enjoyed some degree of democratic government, in the fourteenth and fifteenth centuries the cities and the small states fell under the government of *signori*, or absolute rulers. In the fifteenth century, the main Italian states (Venice, Lombardy, Florence, the Papal States, and Naples), enjoyed a certain amount of balance and peace, mostly owing to the diplomatic skills and efforts of Lorenzo "il Magnifico" de' Medici. His death in 1492 shattered the precarious balance among Italian states, who began to fight amongst one another, especially the duchy of Milan and the kingdom of Naples.

The High Renaissance in Italy was a time of immense artistic and intellectual activity, during which Italy was the teacher of Europe, establishing an intellectual supremacy over the rest of the continent. However, it was also a time of decline, when Italy lost political autonomy. The descent of Charles VIII of France into Italy in 1494 (caused by the quarrel between Milan and Naples) began a long period of foreign invasions, in which Italian states continued to seek foreign intervention as a way to settle disputes and to gain political hegemony. After the first French descent into Italy, more than sixty years of Italian history were marred by the conflict between the French and the Spanish, taking place on Italian soil, with Italy itself as the prize.

At the beginning of the sixteenth century, the Italian states united under the leadership of Pope Julius II and his Holy League (1511) to fight back against Charles V. The major engagement was the French victory at the battle of Ravenna (1512). By 1513 the French had been temporarily driven out of Italy, but the pope's success had also been achieved with foreign aid. Charles V wanted the kingdom of Naples (including Sicily and Sardinia), since it was his inheritance from his grandfather, and French power in Italy challenged his hold over Naples. After the battle of Pavia (1525), in which Francis I was defeated and made prisoner, most of the Italian peninsula fell into the sphere of Spanish influence.

In 1527, when Pope Clement VII (de' Medici) turned against the Emperor Charles V, 20,000 German and Spanish troops marched on Rome. The sack of the city by these ferocious mercenaries irreparably destroyed works of art and antiquities, leaving the face of the city changed and ending the period of the Rome of the humanist popes. After the Sack of Rome, for a while Charles V lost ground to the French and their allies. Further wars ensued between the two powers, until 1559, the year when a final settlement was reached at the Treaty of Câteau-Cambrésis.

This treaty, marking the victory of Spain and the tightening of the Spanish grip on Italy, was followed by a hundred and fifty years (1559-1713) of Spanish domination, during which Italy was ravaged by heavy taxation and inept government. This was the time of the Inquisition, of the Index, of the power of the Jesuit Order, and of serious restrictions on freedom of thought.

Duchy
of Savoy

Duchy
of Milan

2

1

R. of
Genoa

D. of
Parma

4

D. of
Modena

Mantua

Ferrara

P. of
Trento

Venetian Republic

Hungary

Duchy
of
Florence

States
of
the
Church

5

3

3

3

Kingdom
of
Sardinia

Kingdom
of
Naples

Kingdom
of Sicily

Marquisate of Saluzzo............ 1
Marquisate of Monferrat..... 2
Stato dei Presidi 3
Republic of Lucca 4
Duchy of Urbino.................... 5
Venetian Republic...............
Spanish Possessions..............

Italy About 1559

253

GENERAL BIBLIOGRAPHY

Anthologies and Reference Books

Antologia della poesia italiana. Ed. Giacinto Spagnoletti. Parma: Guanda, 1954.

Antologia delle scrittrici italiane dalle origini al 1800. Ed. Jolanda De Blasi. Florence: Nemi, 1930.

Componimenti delle più illustri rimatrici di ogni secolo. Ed. Luisa Bergalli. Venice: Morra, 1726.

Cortigiane del secolo XVI. Lettere, curiosità, notizie. Bologna: Forni, 1967.

Dizionario biografico degli italiani. Rome: Istituto della Enciclopedia Italiana Treccani, 1960-.

Dizionario enciclopedico della letteratura italiana. Ed. G. Petronio. Palermo: Laterza-UNEDI, 1966-1970. Vols. 1-6.

Duby, Georges, and Michelle Perrot, eds. *A History of Women.* London and Cambridge, Massachusetts: The Belknap Press of Harvard University Press, 1992. Vols. 2&3.

Enciclopedia biografica e bibliografica "italiana," ser. 6, *Poetesse e scrittrici.* Ed. Maria Bandini Buti. 2 vols. Rome: Istituto Editoriale Italiano, B.C. Tosi, 1941-42.

Fr. Maurizio di Gregorio. *Rosario delle stampa di tutti i poeti e poetesse antichi e moderni.* Naples: n.p., 1614.

Gaspara Stampa e altre poetesse del '500. Ed. Francesco Flora. Milan: Nuova Accademia Editrice, 1962.

Il Cinquecento. Ed. Giuseppe Toffanin. Milan: F. Vallardi, 1954.

Il fiore della lirica veneziana dal Duecento al Cinquecento. Ed. Manlio Dazzi. Vol.1. Venice: Neri Pozza, 1956.

Le glorie immortali de' trionfi, ed eroiche imprese di ottocento quarantacinque donne illustri antiche e moderne. Ed. Pietro Ribera Valenziano. Vol. 14. Venice: n.p., 1609.

La letteratura italiana: storia e testi. Ed. C. Muscetta. Bari: Laterza, 1970-76. Vols 1-9.

Le più belle pagine di Gaspara Stampa, Vittoria Colonna, Veronica Gambara, Isabella di Morra. Ed. Giuseppe Toffanin. Milan: Treves, 1935.

Le stanze ritrovate: Antologia di scrittrici venete dal Quattrocento al Novecento. Ed. A. Arslan, A. Chemello and G. Pizzamiglio. Milan and Venice: Eidos, 1991.

Lettere del Cinquecento. Ed. Giuseppe Guido Ferrero. Turin: U.T.E.T., 1967.

Lettere di cortigiane del XVI secolo. Ed. Luigi Ferrai. Florence: Libreria Dante, 1884.

Levin, Joan. "Renaissance Literature: Italian Writers." In *Women's Studies Encyclopedia*. Vol.2: *Literature, Arts and Learning*. Ed. Helen Tierney. Westport, Connecticut: Greenwood Press, 1990.

Lirici del Cinquecento. Ed. Carlo Bo. Milan: Garzanti, 1941.

Lirici del Cinquecento. Ed. Daniele Ponchiroli. Turin: U.T.E.T., 1958.

Lirici del Cinquecento. Ed. Luigi Baldacci. Florence: Salani, 1957.

Orientamenti culturali. Letteratura italiana: i minori. Milan: Marzorati, 1961-62. Vols. 1-4.

Parnaso Italiano. Poeti italiani contemporanei maggiori e minori seguiti da un saggio di rime antiche e moderne di poetesse italiane antiche e moderne. Ed. A. Roma. Paris: Baudry, 1847.

Poesia del Quattrocento e del Cinquecento. Ed. C. Muscetta & D. Ponchiroli. Turin: Einaudi, 1959.

Poeti del Duecento. Ed. G. Contini. Milan & Naples: Ricciardi, 1960.

Rime di cinquanta illustri poetesse. Ed. Antonio Bulifon. Naples: Bulifon, 1695.

Rime di tre gentildonne del secolo XVI. Ed. Olindo Guerrini. Milan: Sonzogno, 1930.

Rime diverse d'alcune nobilissime et virtuosissime donne. Ed. Ludovico Domenichi. Lucca: Busdrago, 1559.

Russell, Rinaldina, ed. *Italian Women Writers: A Bibliographical Sourcebook*. Westport, Connecticut: Greenwood Press, 1994.

Scrittrici italiane dal XIII al XX secolo. Testi e critica. Ed. Natalia Costa-Zalessow. Ravenna: Longo, 1982.

Scrittrici mistiche italiane. Ed. Giovanni Pozzi and Claudio Leonardi. Genova: Marietti, 1988.

The Defiant Muse: Italian Feminist Poems from the Middle Ages to the Present. Ed. Beverly Allen, Muriel Kittel and Keala Jewell. New York: The Feminist Press, 1986.

Theatro delle donne letterate. Ed. Francesco Agostino Della Chiesa. Mondoví: Ghislandi & Rossi, 1620.

Wilson, Katharina, ed. *An Encyclopedia of Continental Woman Writers*. 2 vols. New York: Garland, 1991.

Works Cited and Consulted

Anderson, Bonnie and Judith Zinsser. *A History of Their Own: Women in Europe from Prehistory to the Present*. 2 vols. New York: Harper & Row, 1988.

Aretino, Pietro. *I Ragionamenti*. Rome: Frank, 1991.

Ariosto, Lodovico. *Orlando Furioso*. Transl. Barbara Reynolds. London: Penguin, 1977.

General Bibliography

Bainton, Roland. *Women of the Reformation.* Vol I, *Germany and Italy.*
　　Minneapolis: 1971.
――. *Il Petrarchismo italiano nel '500.* Padua: Liviana, 1974.
Barbiera, Raffaello. *Italiane gloriose: medaglioni.* Milan: Vallardi, 1923.
Bargellini, Pietro. *La splendida storia di Firenze.* Florence: Vallecchi, 1964.
Barnstone, Aliki and Willis Barnstone, eds. *A Book of Women Poets from
　　Antiquity to Now.* New York: Schocken Books, 1980.
Barzaghi, Antonio. *Donne o cortegiane? La prostituzione a Venezia. Docu-
　　menti di costume dal XVI al XVII secolo.* Verona: Bertani, 1980.
Bell, Susan Groag. *Women from the Greeks to the French Revolution.* Belmont:
　　Wadsworth Publishing Company, 1973.
Bellomo, Manlio. *La condizione giuridica della donna in Italia.* Turin:
　　Einaudi, 1970.
Bellonci, Maria. *Rinascimento privato.* Milan: Mondadori, 1985.
Bembo, Pietro. *Prose e rime.* Ed. Carlo Dionisotti. Turin: U.T.E.T., 1966.
Benson, Pamela. *The Invention of the Renaissance Woman: The Challenge of
　　Female Independence in the Literature & Thought of Italy and England.*
　　University Park, PA: Pennsylvania State University Press, 1992.
Benzoni, Gino. *Venezia nell'età della Controriforma.* Turin: Musia, 1973.
Bogin, Meg. *The Women Troubadours.* London: Paddington Press, 1976.
Bonora, Ettore. "Le donne poetesse." In *Critica e letteratura nel '500.* Turin:
　　Giappichelli, 1964, 91-110.
Bornstein, Diane, ed. *Distaves and Dames: Renaissance Treatises for and About
　　Women.* New York: Scholars Facsimiles and Reprints, 1978.
Boulting, William. *Women in Italy.* London: Metheuen, 1910.
Branca, Vittore. *Rinascimento europeo e Rinascimento veneziano.* Venice:
　　Sansoni, 1967.
Bridenthal, Renate and Claudia Koonz, eds. *Becoming Visible: Women in
　　European History.* Boston: Houghton Mifflin, 1977.
Burckhardt, Jakob. "The Position of Women." In *The Civilization of the
　　Renaissance in Italy.* New York: Harper and Row, 1958, 2:389-95.
Calcaterra, Carlo. "Il Petrarca e il Petrarchismo." In *Questioni e correnti di
　　storia letteraria.* Milan: Marzorati, 1949.
Canonici Fachini, Ginevra. *Prospetto biografico delle donne italiane rino-
　　mate in letteratura dal secolo decimoquarto ai giorni nostri.* Venice:
　　Alvisopoli, 1824.
Caretti, L. "Gli scritti di Olimpia Morata." In *Studi e ricerche di letteratura
　　italiana.* Florence: Nuova Italia, 1951, 37-64.
Carol, Linda. "Who's on Top?: Gender as Societal Power Configuration in
　　Italian Renaissance Painting and Drama." *Sixteenth Century Journal*
　　20 (1989): 531-58.

Casagrande di Villaviera, Rita. *Le cortegiane veneziane nel Cinquecento.* Milan: Longanesi, 1968.

Castiglione, Baldassar. *Il Libro del Cortigiano.* Venice, 1529; repr. Turin: U.T.E.T., 1964. Ed. Bruno Maier. Transl. *The Book of the Courtier* by Sir Thomas Hoby. London, 1561; repr. London: H.M. Dent, 1974.

Cesareo, Giovanni Alfredo. *La vita italiana nel Cinquecento.* Milan: Sandron, 1894.

Chemello, Adriana. "Donna di palazzo, moglie, cortigiana: ruoli e funzioni sociali della donna in alcuni trattati del Cinquecento." In *La corte e il 'Cortegiano.'* Vol. 2: *Un modello europeo.* Rome: Bulzoni, 1980, 113-32.

Chojnacki, Stanley. "Patrician Women in Early Renaissance Venice." *Studies in the Renaissance* 21 (1974): 176-203.

Clough, Cecil, ed. *Cultural Aspects of the Italian Renaissance.* Manchester: Manchester University Press, 1976.

Comba, Eugenio. *Donne illustri italiane proposte ad esempio alle giovinette.* Turin: Paravia, 1920.

Condivi, Ascanio. *Vita di Michelangelo Bonarroti.* Rome: Blado, 1553.

Crane, Thomas Frederick. *Italian Social Customs of the Sixteenth Century.* New Haven: Oxford University Press, 1920.

Croce, Benedetto. "La lirica cinquecentesca." In *Poesia popolare e poesia d'arte.* Bari: Laterza, 1967, 341-441.

———. *Poeti e scrittori del pieno e del tardo Rinascimento.* Bari: Laterza, 1952.

———. *Vite di avventura, di fede e di passione.* Bari: Laterza, 1953.

De Gubernatis, Angelo. *Poetesse italiane del secolo decimosesto.* Florence: Ademollo, 1883.

Delany, Sheila. *Writing Women: Women Writers and Women in Literature-Medieval to Modern.* New York: Schocken Books, 1983.

Del Grosso, Maria. *Donna nel Cinquecento. Tra letteratura e realtà.* Salerno: Edisud, 1989.

De Maio, Romeo. *Donna e Rinascimento.* Milan: Il Saggiatore, 1987.

Del Lungo, Isidoro. *La donna fiorentina del buon tempo antico.* Florence: Bemporad, 1906.

Di Villaviera, Rita Casagrande. *Le cortegiane veneziane del Cinquecento.* Milan: Longanesi, 1968.

Dunn, Catherine. "The Changing Image of Women in Renaissance Society and Literature." In *What Manner of Women: Essays on English and American Life and Literature.* Ed. Marlene Springer. New York: 1977, 15-38.

Eckenstein, L. *Woman under Monasticism.* Cambridge: Cambridge University Press, 1896.

General Bibliography

Effinger, John R. "Women of the Romance Countries." In *Women in All Ages and in All Countries*. Vol. 6. Philadelphia: The Rittenhouse Press, 1907.

Einstein, A. *The Italian Madrigal*. Princeton: Princeton University Press, 1971.

Ezell, Margaret. *Writing Women's Literary History*. Baltimore: John Hopkins University Press, 1993.

Fahy, Conor. "Three Early Renaissance Treatises on Women." *Italian Studies* 12 (1965): 330-55.

Ferguson, Margaret, Maureen Quilligan and Nancy Vickers, eds. *Rewriting the Renaissance: The Discourses of Sexual Difference in Early Modern Europe*. Chicago: Chicago University Press, 1986.

Ferroni, Giulio. "Il sistema poetico cinquecentesco e il petrarchismo." In *Poesia italiana del Cinquecento*. Milan: Garzanti, 1978.

Firenzuola, Agnolo. *Dialogo delle bellezze delle donne* and *Epistola in lode delle donne*. In *Opere scelte*. Ed. Giuseppe Fatini. Turin: U.T.E.T., 1966.

Frati, Ludovico. *La donna italiana*. Turin: Bocca, 1928.

Gamba, Bartolomeo. *Alcuni ritratti di donne illustri delle provincie veneziane*. Venice: Alvisopoli, 1826.

——. *Lettere di donne italiane del secolo decimosesto*. Venice: Alvisopoli, 1832.

Giglio, V. *Donne celebri*. Milan: Società editrice libraria, 1950.

Gilbert, Sandra and Susan Gubar. "Sexual Linguistics: Gender, Language, Sexuality." *New Literary History* 16 (1985): 515-43.

Gould Davis, Elizabeth. *The First Sex*. New York: Putnam & Sons, 1971.

Graf, Arturo. *Attraverso il Cinquecento*. Turin: Chiantore, 1888.

——. "Petrarchismo ed antipetrarchismo." In *Attraverso il Cinquecento*. Turin: Loescher, 1926, 3-70.

Grantham Turner, James, ed. *Sexuality and Gender in Modern Europe*. Cambridge: Cambridge University Press, 1993.

Green, Monica. "Women's Medical Care in Medieval Europe." *Signs: Journal of Women in Culture and Society* 14 (1989): 434-73.

Greer, Germaine. *The Obstacle Race: The Fortunes of Women Painters and Their Work*. New York: Farrar, Strauss, Giroux, 1979.

Grendler, Paul. *The Roman Inquisition and the Venetian Press, 1540-1605*. Princeton, N.J.: Princeton University Press, 1977.

——. *Schooling in Renaissance Italy: Literacy and Learning, 1300-1600*. Baltimore and London: John Hopkins University Press, 1989.

Hare, Christopher. *The Most Illustrious Ladies of the Italian Renaissance*. Williamstown: Corner House Publishers, 1972.

Hirshfield, Jane, ed. *Women in Praise of the Sacred*. New York: Harper Collins, 1994.

Jardine, Alice. *Gynesis: Configurations of Woman and Modernity*. Ithaca: Cornell University Press, 1985.

Jones, Ann Rosalind. "Surprising Fame: Renaissance Gender Ideologies and Women's Lyric." In *The Poetics of Gender*. Ed. Nancy K. Miller. New York: Columbia University Press, 1986, 74-95.

——. *The Currency of Eros. Women's Love Lyric in Europe, 1540-1620*. Bloomington & Indianapolis: Indiana University Press, 1990.

——. "Assimilation with a Difference: Renaissance Women Poets and Literary Influences." *Yale French Studies* 62 (1981): 135-53.

——. "Writing the Body: Towards an Understanding of *L'Escriture Feminisme.*" *Feminist Studies* 7 (1981): 247-63.

Joplin, Patricia Klindienst. "The Voice of the Shuttle is Ours." *Stanford Literature Review* I, I (Spring 1984): 25-53.

Jordan, Constance. *Renaissance Feminism: Literary Texts & Political Models*. Ithaca & New York: Cornell University Press, 1990.

Kaufmann, Linda S. *Discourses of Desire, Gender, Genre, and Epistolary Fictions*. Ithaca & London: Cornell University Press, 1986.

Kelly, Joan. "Notes on Women in the Renaissance and Renaissance Historiography." In *Conceptual Frameworks for Studying Women's History*. Ed. M. Arthur et al. Bronxville: 1975, 444-46.

——. *Women, History and Theory: The Essays of Joan Kelly*. Chicago and London: The University of Chicago Press, 1984.

Kelso, Ruth. *Doctrine for the Lady of the Renaissance*. Urbana and Chicago: University of Illinois Press, 1956, 1978.

King, Margaret L. and Albert Rabil Jr. *Her Immaculate Hand*. Binghamton: Center for Medieval and Early Renaissance Studies, 1983.

King, Margaret L. *Venetian Humanism in an Age of Patrician Dominance*. Princeton, New Jersey: Princeton University Press, 1986.

——. *Women of the Renaissance*. Chicago: Chicago University Press, 1991.

——. "Thwarted Ambitions: Six Learned Women of the Italian Renaissance." *Soundings* 59 (1976): 280-304.

Klapisch-Zuber, Christiane. *Women, Family and Ritual in Renaissance Italy*. Transl. L. Cochrane. Chicago: Chicago University Pres, 1985.

Kuehn, Thomas. *Law, Family and Women: Toward a Legal Anthropology of Renaissance Italy*. Chicago and London: University of Chicago Press, 1991.

Labalme, Patricia. *Beyond Their Sex: Learned Women of the European Past*. New York: New York University Press, 1984.

——. "Venetian Women on Women: Three Early Modern Feminists." *Archivio veneto* 5, 117 (1981): 81-109.

Larivaille, Paul. *La vie quotidienne des courtisanes en Italie au temps de la renaissance.* Paris: Hachette, 1975.

Lawner, Lynn. *Lives of the Courtesans.* New York: Rizzoli, 1987.

Lenzi, Maria L. *Donne e madonne: L'educazione femminile nel primo rinascimento italiano.* Turin: Loescher, 1982.

Lipking, Lawrence. *Abandoned Women and Poetic Tradition.* Chicago: University of Chicago Press, 1988.

Logan, Oliver. *Culture and Society in Venice, 1470-1790.* New York: Scribner's, 1972.

Luciano. *Dialoghi di dei e di cortigiane.* Milan: Rizzoli, 1986.

Macchia, Giovanni. "Quattro poetesse del Cinquecento." *Rivista Rosminiana di filosofia e cultura* 31 (1937): 152-57.

Maclean, Ian. *The Renaissance Notion of Woman. A Study in the Fortunes of Scholasticism and Medical Science in European Intellectual Life.* Cambridge: Cambridge University Press, 1980.

Magliani, E. *Storia letteraria delle donne italiane.* Naples: Morano, 1885.

Manacorda, Giuseppe. "La storia della scuola in Italia nel Medio Evo." In *Scritti di critica letteraria.* Florence: Sansoni, 1930, 68-89.

Maraini, Dacia. *Veronica, meretrice e scrittora.* Milan: Bompiani, 1992.

Marchesi, Battista G. "Le polemiche sul sesso femminile." *Giornale storico della letteratura italiana* 25 (1895): 362-369.

Marchini, Nella Elena Vanzan. "L'altra faccia dell'amore ovvero i rischi dell'esercizio del piacere." In *Il gioco dell'amore. Le cortigiane di Venezia dal Trecento al Settecento.* Milan: Berenice, 1990, 47-56.

Maschietto, F.L. *Elena Lucrezia Cornaro Piscopia (1646-1684): prima donna laureata nel mondo.* Padua: Editrice Antenore, 1978.

Masi, E. *La vita italiana nel Rinascimento.* Milan: Treves, 1893.

Masson, Georgina. *Courtesans of the Italian Renaissance.* New York: Saint Martin's, 1976.

Matter, E.A., and J. Coakley, eds. *Creative Women in Medieval and Early Modern Italy.* Philadelphia: University of Pennsylvania Press, 1994.

Migiel, Marilyn. "Gender Studies and the Italian Renaissance." In *Interpreting the Italian Renaissance: Literary Perspectives.* Ed. Antonio Toscano. Stony Brook, New York: *Forum Italicum,* 1991, 29-41.

Migiel, Marilyn and Juliana Schiesari, eds. *Refiguring Woman: Perspectives on Gender and the Italian Renaissance.* Ithaca and London: Cornell University Press, 1991.

Miller, J. Hillis: "Ariadne's Thread: Repetition and the Narrative Line." In *Interpretation of Narrative.* Ed. Mario J. Valdes and Owen J. Miller. Toronto, Buffalo, London: University of Toronto Press, 1976, 48-66.

Miller, Nancy K, ed. *The Poetics of Gender.* New York: Columbia University Press, 1986.

Molmenti, Pompeo. *La storia di Venezia nella vita privata.* 3 vols. Trieste: Lint, 1973.

———. *Curiosità di storia veneziana.* Bologna: Zanichelli, 1921.

Mondino, A. "Alcune poetesse ipotetiche dei secoli XIII e XIV." In *Gazzetta Letteraria.* Turin: Accademia delle scienze, 1869.

Muir, Edward. *Civic Ritual in Renaissance Venice.* Princeton, N.J.: Princeton University Press, 1981.

Muir, Edward, and Guido Ruggiero, eds. *Sex and Gender in Historical Perspective: Selections from Quaderni Storici.* Baltimore: Johns Hopkins University Press, 1991.

Musatti, Eugenio. *La donna in Venezia.* Padua: Forni, 1992.

Mustacchi, Marianna & Paul Archambault. *A Renaissance Woman.* Syracuse: Syracuse University Press, 1986.

Mutinelli, Fabio. *Del costume veneziano al secolo XVII.* Venice: Tip. di commercio, 1831.

Niero, Antonio. "Riforma cattolica e concilio di Trento." In *Cultura e società nel Rinascimento tra Riforma e Manierismo.* Ed. V. Branca and C. Ossola. Florence: Olschki, 1984.

O'Faolain, Julia and Lauro Martines, eds. *Not in God's Image: Women in History from the Greeks to the Victorians.* New York, San Francisco & London: 1973.

Padoan, Giorgio. "Il mondo delle cortigiane nella letteratura rinascimentale." In *Il gioco dell'amore. Le cortigiane di Venezia dal Trecento al Settecento.* Milan: Berenice, 1990, 63-71.

Paladino, G. *Opuscoli e lettere di riformatori italiani del Cinquecento.* Bari: Laterza, 1927.

Pentolini, Fr. Clodoveo. *Le donne illustri.* Livorno: Falorni, 1776-1777.

Perlingieri, Ilya S. *Sofonisba Anguissola, The First Great Woman Artist of the Renaissance.* New York: Rizzoli, 1992.

Pernoud, Régine. *La donna al tempo delle cattedrali.* Milan: Rizzoli, 1982.

Piettre, Monique. *La condition féminine à travers les ages.* Paris: France Empire, 1974.

Plumb, J.H. *The Italian Renaissance.* New York: Harper and Row, 1965.

Pomeroy, Sarah. *Goddesses, Whores, Wives, and Slaves in Classical Antiquity.* New York: Schocken Books, 1975.

Portigliotti, Giuseppe. *Donne nel Rinascimento.* Milan: Treves, 1927.

Power, Eileen. *Medieval Woman.* Ed. M.M. Postan. Cambridge: Cambridge University Press, 1975.

Pozzi, Mario. *Trattati d'Amore del Cinquecento.* Rome & Bari: Laterza, 1975.

Pullan, Brian. *Rich and Poor in Renaissance Venice: The Social Institutions of a Catholic State.* Oxford: Basil Blackwell, and Cambridge, MA: Harvard University Press, 1971.

Putnam, Emily James. *The Lady of the Renaissance*. New York & London: Putnam & Sons, 1910.

Rabil Jr., A. *Laura Cereta, Quattrocento Humanist*. Binghamton, NY: Center for Medieval and Early Renaissance Studies, 1981.

Rose, Mary Beth, ed. *Women in the Middle Ages and in the Renaissance*. Syracuse: Syracuse University Press, 1986.

Rosenthal, Margaret. "Venetian Women Writers and Their Discontents." In *Sexuality and Gender in Early Modern Europe: Institutions, Texts, Images*. Ed. James Grantham Turner. Cambridge: Cambridge University Press, 1992.

——. *Woman in Culture & Society*. Chicago & London: University of Chicago Press, 1992.

Rosi, Michele. *Saggio sui trattati d'amore del Cinquecento*. Recanati: Simboli, 1889.

Rossiaud, Jacques. *Medieval Prostitution*. Oxford: Basil Blackwell, 1988.

Ruggiero, Guido. *The Boundaries of Eros: Sex, Crime and Sexuality in Renaissance Venice*. Oxford: Oxford University Press, 1985.

——. *Binding Passions: Tales of Magic, Marriage, and Power at the End of the Renaissance*. New York & Oxford: Oxford University Press, 1993.

——. "Più che la vita caro: Onore, matrimonio, e reputazione femminile nel tardo Rinascimento." *Quaderni Storici* 66 (1987): 753-75.

——. "Re-Reading the Renaissance: Civic Morality and the World of Marriage, Love and Sex." In *Sexuality and Gender in Early Modern Europe: Institutions, Texts, Images,* Ed. James Turner. Cambridge and New York: Cambridge University Press, 1993.

Russo, Luigi. *Il petrarchismo italiano nel Cinquecento*. Pisa: Libreria Goliardica, 1958.

Scarabello, Giovanni. "Le 'signore' della repubblica." In *Il gioco dell'amore. Le cortigiane di Venezia dal Trecento al Settecento*. Milan: Berenice, 1990, 11-35.

Schiesari, Juliana. *The Gendering of Melancholia. Feminism, Psychoanalysis, and the Symbolics of Loss in Renaissance Literature*. Ithaca & London: Cornell University Press, 1992.

Servadio, Gaia. *La donna nel Rinascimento*. Milan: Garzanti, 1986.

Spiller, Michael E.G. *The Development of the Sonnet: an Introduction*. London and New York: Routledge, 1992.

Spitz, Lewis W. *The Renaissance and Reformation Movements*. Vol. 1: *The Renaissance*. Chicago: Rand McNally & Co., 1972.

Taddeo, Edoardo. *Il Manierismo letterario ed i lirici veneziani del Cinquecento*. Rome: Bulzoni, 1974.

Tafuri, Manfredo. *Venezia ed il Rinascimento*. Turin: Einaudi, 1985.

Tassini, Giuseppe. *Cenni storici e leggi circa il libertinaggio in Venezia dal secolo decimoquarto alla caduta della repubblica.* Venice: Fontana, 1886; published anonymously.

——. *Divertimenti e piaceri degli antichi veneziani.* Venice: Fontana, 1891.

Tasso, Torquato. *Discorso della virtù femminile, e donnesca.* Venice: Giunti, 1582.

Testaferri, Ada, ed. *Donna, Women in Italian Literature.* Ottawa: Dovehouse, 1989.

Thee, Rosemary, ed. *The Role of Woman in the Middle Ages.* Morewedge, Albany: SUNY University Press, 1975.

Todd, Janet M. *Women in Literature.* Vol. 7. New York: Holmes and Meier, 1989.

Toffanin, Giuseppe. *Le donne poetesse e Michelangelo.* Milan: Vallardi, 1927-65.

——. "Petrarchiste del Cinquecento." *Rinascita* 3 (1938): 76-93.

Trattati d'amore del Cinquecento. Ed. Giuseppe Zonta. Bari: Laterza, 1968.

Trattati del Cinquecento sulla Donna. Ed. Giuseppe Zonta. Bari: Laterza, 1913.

Trotto, Bernardo. *Dialoghi del matrimonio e vita vedovile.* Turin: Francesco Dolce, 1578.

Vecellio, Cesare. *Habiti antichi et moderni di tutto il mondo.* 2 vols. Venice: Sessa, 1598.

Ventura, Angelo. *Nobiltà e popolo nella società veneta del '400 e '500.* Bari: G. Laterza, 1964.

Villani, C. *Stelle femminili.* Naples: Albrighi, 1915.

Vives. *The Renaissance Education of Women.* Ed. Foster Watson. New York: Longmans, Green & Co., and London: Edward Arnold, 1912.

Vocino, Michele. *Storia del costume in Italia.* Rome: Istituto poligrafico dello stato, 1962.

Weisner, Merry. *Women in the Sixteenth Century: A Bibliography.* Sixteenth Century Bibliography 23. St. Louis: 1983.

——. *Women and Gender in Early Modern Europe.* Cambridge: Cambridge University Press, 1993.

West, Rebecca and Dino Cervigni, eds. *Annali d'Italianistica: Women's Voices in Italian Literature.* Vol. 7 (1989).

Wilson, Katharina, ed. *Women Writers of the Renaissance and Reformation.* Athens: University of Georgia Press, 1989.

Zernitz, A. *Le rimatrici e le letterate italiane del '500.* Capodistria: Priora, 1885-1886.

INDEX OF FIRST-LINES OF ITALIAN POEMS

First-Line Index

This Book Was Completed on March 14, 1997 at
Italica Press, New York, New York & Was
Set in Garamond. It Was Printed
On 60 lb Natural Paper
by BookSurge,
U. S. A./
E. U.
* *
*

Made in the USA
Lexington, KY
26 December 2012